Nietzsche's *On the Genealogy of Morality*

OXFORD GUIDES TO PHILOSOPHY

Oxford Guides to Philosophy presents concise introductions to the most important primary texts in the history of philosophy. Written by top scholars, the volumes in the series are designed to present up-to-date scholarship in an accessible manner, in order to guide readers through these challenging texts.

Anscombe's *Intention*: A Guide
John Schwenkler

Kant's *Doctrine of Virtue*: A Guide
Mark C. Timmons

Sidgwick's *The Methods of Ethics*: A Guide
David Phillips

Spinoza's *Ethics*: A Guide
Michael LeBuffe

Bentham's *Introduction to the Principles of Morals and Legislation*: A Guide
Steven Sverdlik

Mary Shepherd: A Guide
Deborah Boyle

Candrakīrti's *Introduction to the Middle Way*: A Guide
Jan Westerhoff

Vātsyāyana's *Commentary on the Nyāya-sūtra*: A Guide
Matthew R. Dasti

Hegel's *Phenomenology of Spirit*: A Guide
Terry Pinkard

Nietzsche's *On the Genealogy of Morality*: A Guide
Rex Welshon

Nietzsche's *On the Genealogy of Morality*

A Guide

REX WELSHON

OXFORD
UNIVERSITY PRESS

Oxford University Press is a department of the University of Oxford. It furthers the University's objective of excellence in research, scholarship, and education by publishing worldwide. Oxford is a registered trade mark of Oxford University Press in the UK and certain other countries.

Published in the United States of America by Oxford University Press
198 Madison Avenue, New York, NY 10016, United States of America.

CIP data is on file at the Library of Congress

ISBN 978–0–19–761182–1 (pbk.)
ISBN 978–0–19–761181–4 (hbk.)

DOI: 10.1093/oso/9780197611814.001.0001

Contents

Preface and Acknowledgments

In this book, I introduce the main arguments contained in Friedrich Nietzsche's *On the Genealogy of Morality*. I do not present a radically new interpretation of *Genealogy*'s arguments or develop a set of deep criticisms of these arguments. Nor do I try to resolve the many contemporary scholarly debates about these arguments or introduce all aspects of Nietzsche's multifaceted philosophy. I do try, to the best of my abilities, to steer you through all of *Genealogy* and expand on those of its facets that are the most important, intricate, and perplexing. In this undertaking, I will regularly refer to insights and arguments developed by other Nietzsche scholars.

My hope is that having read this guide you will be better prepared to appreciate *Genealogy*'s merits, identify some of its gaps and shortcomings, and be eager to explore the critical scholarship about the claims Nietzsche makes in it. More than that, I hope you come away eager to read more Nietzsche, for he is a challenging philosopher. Walter Kaufmann, who did more than anyone to rehabilitate Nietzsche's reputation after World War II, once said that his books are "easier to read but harder to understand than those of almost any other thinker."[1] There are many reasons why this assessment is true, but one is surely that Nietzsche combines an admirably clear, direct, and energetic writing voice with a relentlessly inquisitive and adventurous mind that rarely rests. His intellectual delight with ideas and concepts jumps off the pages of his books in ways that few other philosophers come close to achieving. Moreover, all of his books are full of philosophical and psychological intelligence, and because his mind is so fertile, each rereading reveals something new.

[1] Kaufmann 1974, vii.

Yet precisely because he is always testing out new thoughts, Nietzsche is sometimes wrong, unclear, befuddling, or a blinkered product of his time. Furthermore, he is frequently contemptuous, self-important, and hyperbolic. We will ignore most of these faults because they pale in comparison to his philosophical virtues. What matters most are his impassioned philosophical imagination, fearsome intelligence, impressive erudition, unimpeachable style, and eagerness to unleash all of them on an enormously diverse array of issues. As befits a philosopher, he is willing to experiment with disparate and sometimes contradictory thoughts, even if doing so threatens the consistency of some claims with others. Finally, his penetrating claims regarding the human condition, while routinely disquieting, express a deep love of our humanity, good humor about our weaknesses, and intense sorrow regarding our willful shortcomings and stupidities.

Nietzsche wrote *Genealogy* in about a month as a preamble to a contemplated but never completed book. As a result, it glosses over numerous complications he planned to address in that other book, and it presents something of a cross section of his mature thinking about a range of topics. These include some of his most far-reaching and notorious views, such as power and willing power, the rejection of free will, perspectivism, the slave revolt in morality, the role of ressentiment in morality, bad conscience and guilt, the sovereign individual, noble values, determinism, decadence, the ascetic ideal, nihilism, and the will to nothingness. However, in some cases, he drops an assertion about one of these matters into an argument abruptly and only as needed in that specific context, without backing it up or even acknowledging that it is as electrifying or controversial as it actually is. Luckily, he discusses most of these issues in greater detail in other books and in his unpublished notes, and we will sometimes use what he says elsewhere to fill out what remains undeveloped in *Genealogy*. As a result, this guide directly introduces you to the main arguments in *Genealogy*, while indirectly introducing you to arguments from his other books as well.

It is also pertinent to note that in *Genealogy* certain famous elements of Nietzsche's thought are not developed at all. These include his views and claims about *amor fati*, the eternal recurrence, tragedy, the ontology of power, fatalism, the Apollonian/Dionysian distinction, the

Übermensch, the last man, and his scattered thoughts about political matters. While interesting, these elements are not, I think, needed to understand anything that he introduces, discusses, or analyzes in *Genealogy*. So, where I do mention them, it will only be in passing. Some will disagree with my judgment that these elements are not needed to understand *Genealogy*. I would be happy to be shown that I am mistaken.

Other scholars who have authored books on *Genealogy* have responded in a variety of ways to all of the philosophy, psychology, religion, history, anthropology, biology, and even physiology lurking beneath the surface of *Genealogy*'s text. Brian Leiter, in his *Nietzsche on Morality* (2002), prefaces his reading of *Genealogy*'s individual essays with six chapters detailing the numerous facets of Nietzsche's critical revaluation of morality. David Owen's *Nietzsche's "Genealogy of Morality"* (2007) similarly devotes four introductory chapters to describing Nietzsche's revaluation project before examining its Preface and three essays. In *Beyond Selflessness: Reading Nietzsche's "Genealogy"* (2007). Christopher Janaway takes a topical approach, organizing chapters around select subjects. Randall Havas adopts a related method in *Nietzsche's "Genealogy": Nihilism and the Will to Knowledge* (1995), as does Lawrence Hatab in *Nietzsche's "On the Genealogy of Morality": An Introduction* (2008). The present book's approach is closest to Daniel Conway's *Nietzsche's "On the Genealogy of Morals": A Reader's Guide* (2008). Both Conway's book and this one opt for introducing the reader to *Genealogy*'s arguments as they arise in it. The chief benefit of this approach is that it follows Nietzsche's bumpy argumentative arc; the chief drawback is that it must additionally explain what lies behind *Genealogy*'s undeveloped arguments and show how arguments introduced in one section of one essay are buttressed by arguments found in other sections of other essays.

I first became interested in Nietzsche in graduate school when I was assigned to assist Professor Martha Nussbaum in a course. I was immediately persuaded that his was a philosophical voice that needed to be listened to closely and I started then to read and learn more about his work. Over the last twenty-five years, I have written about various aspects of his views in a variety of contexts. I started this particular book near the end of a two-year shift as interim dean of the College of Letters, Arts, and Sciences, a posting that started before and lasted through Covid's first year of devastation. The challenges posed by reconfiguring the college's operations on the fly hampered early progress on the book. After we hired a more permanent dean, I returned to the less hectic and friendlier world of the Department of Philosophy. Thanks largely to my chair, Professor Jeffrey Scholes, I have been able to devote the time and energy needed to see this project through to its conclusion.

In addition to Jeff Scholes, I would like to thank the other members of my department at the University of Colorado at Colorado Springs—Professors Raphael Sassower, Mary Ann Cutter, Dorothea Olkowski, Sonja Tanner, and Jennifer Kling, Senior Instructors Lorraine Arangno, Patrick Yarnell, Erik Hansen, Jennifer Jensen, and Joseph Kuzma, and Instructors Colin Lewis, Patrick D'Silva, and Karen deVries—for their collegiality and forbearance over many years. I would like to thank Christopher Shields for inviting me to contribute this volume to the Oxford Guides series and the editorial and production staff at Oxford University Press for guiding the manuscript to publication. I would also like to thank Ken Baynes, Michael Greenker, Perrin Cunningham, and Zachary Lucia for their many suggestions that have improved the book.

Citation Style and Abbreviations

It is standard practice in Nietzsche scholarship to cite quoted passages from Nietzsche's published books by abbreviated book title, first; chapter or book number, in Roman numerals or essay title, second; and aphorism or section number, in Arabic numbers, third. Thus, a quotation from *On the Genealogy of Morality*, Essay II, Section 12 goes over as *GM* II 12; one from *Twilight of the Idols*, " 'Improving' Humanity," Section 2 becomes *TI* " 'Improving' Humanity" 2; one from *Beyond Good and Evil*, Section 261 becomes *BGE* 261; one from *The Gay Science*, Book I, Section 3 becomes *GS* I 3. Nietzsche wrote all of his thoughts down in notebooks. These notebooks form the *Nachlass*. Citations to the *Nachlass* are to the *Kritische Studienausgabe* by volume number, notebook number, note number. I use Cambridge University Press English translations of Nietzsche's German texts wherever possible; where not possible (a few *Nachlass* notes), I use Stanford University Press translations from *Complete Works of Friedrich Nietzsche*. I adopt standard book title abbreviations for titles from which quotations are drawn, as follows:

A — *The Anti-Christ: A Curse on Christianity*. 2005. Ed. Aaron Ridley and Judith Norman, trans. Judith Norman. New York: Cambridge University Press.

BGE — *Beyond Good and Evil: Prelude to a Philosophy of the Future*. 2002. Ed. Rolf-Peter Horstmann and Judith Norman, trans. Judith Norman. New York: Cambridge University Press.

CW — *The Case of Wagner: A Musician's Problem*. In *The Anti-Christ, Ecce Homo, Twilight of the Idols and Other Writings*. 2005. Ed. Aaron Ridley and Judith Norman, trans. Judith Norman. New York: Cambridge University Press.

CWFN — *The Complete Works of Friedrich Nietzsche*. 1995–2022. 19 vols. Ed. Ernst Behler, Bernd Magnus, Alan Schrift,

Duncan Large, and Adrian Del Caro. Stanford: Stanford University Press.

D *Daybreak: Thoughts on the Presumptions of Morality*. 1997. Ed. Maudemarie Clark and Brian Leiter, trans. R. J. Hollingdale. New York: Cambridge University Press.

EH *Ecce Homo: How to Become What You Are*. In *The Anti-Christ, Ecce Homo, Twilight of the Idols and Other Writings*. 2005. Ed. Aaron Ridley and Judith Norman, trans. Judith Norman. New York: Cambridge University Press.

GM *On the Genealogy of Morality: A Polemic*. 1994. Ed. Keith Ansell Pearson, trans. Carol Diethe. New York: Cambridge University Press.

GS *The Gay Science: With a Prelude in German Rhymes and an Appendix of Songs*. 2001. Ed. Bernard Williams, trans. Josefine Nauckhoff. New York: Cambridge University Press.

HH *Human, All Too Human*. 1996. Trans. R. J. Hollingdale with an introduction by Richard Schacht. New York: Cambridge University Press.

KSA *Kritische Studienausgabe*. 1988. Ed. Giorgio Colli and Mazzino Montinari. 15 vols. New York: Walter de Gruyter.

TI *Twilight of the Idols, or How to Philosophize with a Hammer*. In *The Anti-Christ, Ecce Homo, Twilight of the Idols and Other Writings*. 2005. Ed. Aaron Ridley and Judith Norman, trans. Judith Norman. New York: Cambridge University Press.

WLN *Nietzsche: Writings from the Late Notebooks*. 2003. Ed. Rüdiger Bittner, trans. Kate Sturge. New York: Cambridge University Press.

Introduction

Genealogy and the Revaluation of Values

On the Genealogy of Morality (*GM* hereafter) analyzes an enormous range of topics. Its pacing is erratic, shifting instantaneously from patient strolls through arcane scholarly topics to breathless gallops through large intellectual districts at such high speed that attending to any one topic is nearly impossible. It refers to obscure eighteenth- and nineteenth-century intellectuals most twenty-first-century readers have never heard of, along with figures from the ancient world many readers will only have heard of in other contexts, and even some figures many of us are likely to think should not be mentioned in a book of philosophy. Despite these challenges and difficulties, *GM* is expansive, enlightening, entertaining, probing, and devastating.

Anyone who has read some philosophy will be taken aback both by much of what Nietzsche says in *GM* and by how he says it. There will be ample opportunity to consider what he says in what follows, but his overall approach to writing philosophy deserves comment. Most philosophers write in a formal, disengaged way, devoid of emotion. Nietzsche does not do that. It is true that he offers plenty of arguments and that those arguments often revolve around standard philosophical issues. In *GM*, for example, he discusses issues about the epistemological, semantic, etymological, moral psychological, and metaphysical assumptions and implications of morality, and he provides a history of moral evaluative practices. So too, his diagnoses of others' arguments often employ philosophical techniques, and his own proposals are sometimes congruent with those made by other philosophers. Yet he rarely uses technical terms and his writing voice is energetic, chatty, and unreserved to the point of intimacy. This style is dictated by his

Nietzsche's On the Genealogy of Morality. Rex Welshon, Oxford University Press.
 DOI: 10.1093/oso/9780197611814.003.0001

belief that "it makes the most telling difference whether a thinker has a personal relationship to his problems and finds in them his destiny, his distress, and his greatest happiness, or an 'impersonal' one, meaning he is only able to touch and grasp them with the antennae of cold, curious thought" (*GS* 345). In *GM*, he assumes that moral evaluation and moral psychology as they have been handed down are problems to be solved, not simply phenomena to be studied. Morality is something that must engage our "distress, torment, voluptuousness, and passion" (*GS* 345).

Most of Nietzsche's books from *HH* onward are collections of numbered passages rather than sequences of chapters. Some passages run to four pages, and within a passage, arguments are often developed carefully. However, he never explains why the passages are ordered as they are, so moving from one to the next can be disorienting. He often gets in and out of topics quickly, and the reader who follows him will often discover that he is already on to the next thought before fully explicating previous ones. This structure is intentional, for it forces a kind of reading that follows Nietzsche through diverse intellectual topographies, compelling and cultivating reflection—or, as he prefers, 'rumination' (*GM* Preface 8)—on the knotted contours and varied perspectives that open before the reader. He wants his reader to be a "monster of courage and curiosity, as well as something pliable, crafty, cautious, a born adventurer and discoverer" (*EH* "Good Books" 3).
A partial exception is *GM*, whose three essays address distinct topics and answer questions that Nietzsche poses about morality and moral psychology in the Preface. Even here, in a book whose structure is of a familiar kind, he throws curves. *GM*'s three essays are, according to his summary of them in *Ecce Homo*, deliberately misleading.

> Each of them has a beginning that *should* be deceptive: cool, scientific, even ironic. . . . Gradually increasing unrest; scattered moments of sheet lightning, the muffled roar of very unpleasant truths becoming increasingly audible in the distance—until finally a *tempo feroce* is reached where everything presses forward with tremendous tension. In each case, an ending with absolutely terrible detonations, a *new* truth visible between thick clouds. (*EH* "Good Books" *GM*)

This structure is one reason reading *GM* is challenging. Each of its three essays starts soberly, takes unexpected turns in the middle sections, and, by the final sections, moves so quickly that we are likely to miss something essential unless we are paying full attention. Even if we are vigilant, its arguments can be so dense, even messy, that fully understanding them upon first meeting is not guaranteed.

Nietzsche presents *GM* as a project that describes the impact of ressentiment on Christian moral evaluation (Essay I), the moral psychology of conscience and guilt (Essay II), and the meaning of the ascetic ideal and its spread through European society (Essay III). Since he advertises *GM* as a descriptive project, we might expect him to conduct himself as a scientist would, dispassionately laying out accrued evidence that supports his hypotheses. As just noted, he has no intention to engage us this way: he is going to start each essay by being cool and scientific, but he will then reveal unpleasant truth after unpleasant truth, at first in a muted way, then louder and with greater insistence, until they reach a deafening roar. As difficult as that may make it for us, we should not lose sight of what he claims to be doing. *GM* is primarily a set of studies that describe a group of biological, psychological, social, cultural/ethnographic, religious, and moral phenomena from a distinctive evaluative perspective. As such, its job is not to determine how the values it describes are to be valued. That was to have been a topic for *Will to Power*, a book he never completed.

We remark on the place of *GM* in this larger revaluation project here because as we read *GM*, we may think it is that revaluation of values. Nietzsche warns that this temptation conflates description with critique. We may, he notes,

> uncover and criticize the possibly foolish opinions of a people about their morality, or of humanity about all human morality—opinions about its origin, its religious sanction, the myth of the free will and such things—and then think [we] have criticized the morality itself. But the value of the injunction "Thou Shalt" is still fundamentally different from and independent of such opinions about it and the weeds of error that may have overgrown it. . . . A morality could even have grown *out of* an error, and the realization of this fact would not as much as touch the problem of its value. Thus no one until now has

> examined the *value* of that most famous of all medicines called morality; and for that, one must begin by *questioning* it for once. Well then! Precisely that is our task. (*GS* 345)

The revaluation project is, thus, the critical questioning of the value of a morality, and the standards he proposes to use to measure the value of a morality are whether it has "hindered or furthered human prosperity" and whether it is "a sign of distress, of impoverishment, of the degeneration of life or . . . [of] the plenitude, force, and will of life, its courage, certainty, future" (*GM* Preface 3).

Nietzsche assumes these evaluative standards and uses them to scaffold his investigations into the history—the genealogy—of our inherited Christian European morality and its attendant moral psychology. Exposing how our inherited morality grew and diagnosing its errors are *GM*'s primary tasks. However, while *GM* is framed by these evaluative standards, he rarely identifies them and never works them up in any detail in *GM*. Nor does he describe his own preferred evaluative rankings that flow from these evaluative standards. Both these evaluative standards and this alternative evaluative ranking lurk mostly in the shadows until the last sections of each of the first two essays, where they intermittently and incompletely surface. They then emerge more dramatically throughout the third essay. We will, in due course, show how these evaluative standards clarify *GM*'s efforts and glimpse facets of that alternative evaluative ranking. Until then, we keep them at bay as much as possible to better appreciate *GM*'s descriptive riches.

I.1 Overview of *Genealogy* and This Book

Chapter 1: Biography, Intellectual Development, and Legacy

It may come as a surprise that Nietzsche's life was not particularly eventful. His stature was certainly less prominent while he was alive than his reputation became after he died. He was often plagued by debilitating illness and spent the final ten years of his productive career as an intellectual vagabond, surviving on a pension and moving with the seasons from Italian seaside towns in the winter and early spring to Alpine villages in the summer and autumn. In early 1889, he went insane. Thereafter, he lingered on, incapacitated, until he died in 1900.

Nietzsche was influenced in his twenties and early thirties by the thought of Arthur Schopenhauer and the music of Richard Wagner. Indeed, the first ten years of his professional career trace their impacts on Nietzsche and his subsequent disenchantment with, and eventual disavowal of, both of them. As he moved away from their gravitational fields, he read about many of the numerous scientific advances then occurring in evolutionary biology, psychophysics, physiology, chemistry, and psychology, keeping Friedrich Albert Lange's *A History of Materialism* close at hand as a guide to the philosophical underpinnings of science and as a source of criticism of some of those assumptions. Nietzsche hit his stride thereafter, and for the next decade he wrote one extraordinary book after another.

In the final section of Chapter 1, we assess Nietzsche's legacy, which is complicated. For much of the twentieth century, his work was scorned by most philosophers and intellectuals because the Nazis appropriated Nietzsche for themselves, thereby staining everything he said. Happily, this stain has faded, thanks to the work performed by many Nietzsche scholars who have shown that he was neither a proto-fascist nor an antisemite. Nietzsche's influence on contemporary European and Anglo-American culture and philosophy is otherwise widespread and diffuse. We canvas, from a high altitude, some of these influences.

Chapter 2: *Genealogy* Preface

GM's Preface opens with the provocative sentences: "We are unknown to ourselves, we knowers: and this for a good reason. We have never sought ourselves—how could it happen that we would some day *find* ourselves?" This is not how most philosophical books about ethical and metaethical issues would begin, but it is an example, and a measured one at that, of Nietzsche's unique way of discussing philosophical issues. He intentionally uses all kinds of devices to pull the reader into what are for him intensely personal investigations, investigations that have stimulated in him an "extraordinary number of inner states" (*EH* "Good Books" 4). Trying to recreate this diversity of inward states in his readers requires effort on his part. The results are found in his books, which combine provocation, self-congratulation, poetry, scholarship, intimidation, frenzy, amusement, agony, mischief, insight, seduction, erudition, argument, self-reflection, speculation, belligerence, and intrigue.

After the provocative first section, the next two sections of *GM*'s Preface recount Nietzsche's interest in the history of morality and introduce his genealogical method for understanding that history. His genealogical method is, he warns us, polemical and combative. He is not a disinterested intellectual replaying morality's past but instead shows that modern European moral evaluation is strange and even damaging to those about whom it makes pronouncements. In Sections 4–6, Nietzsche acknowledges his intellectual debts to some precursors, chief among them Paul Rée and Arthur Schopenhauer. Having acknowledged their importance, he immediately criticizes them, Rée in particular, whom he attacks again in Section 7. Section 8 concludes the Preface with warnings that what follows in the three subsequent essays may be difficult to grasp and even more difficult to accept. That, in Nietzsche's judgment, is less a shortcoming of what he has to say than of what we as readers bring to our encounter with him.

In Chapter 2's discussion section, we consider four preliminary matters. First, we describe what genealogy is in greater detail so that we are familiar with it as a method of acquiring knowledge about our moral evaluative practices and their presuppositions. Second, we introduce Nietzsche's commitment to philosophical naturalism, a crucial and in his time somewhat unusual element for thinking about moral evaluation, moral psychology, and other philosophical topics. Third, we identify mistakes that other philosophers, theologians, and religious advocates make about moral psychology. Finally, we describe what Nietzsche thinks morality and moral evaluation are.

Chapter 3: *Genealogy* Essay I

In *Ecce Homo*, Nietzsche provides introductions to each of the three essays comprising *GM*. There he summarizes Essay I as follows:

> The truth of the *first* essay is the psychology of Christianity: the birth of Christianity out of the spirit of *ressentiment*, *not*, as is believed, out of the 'spirit,'—a countermovement in its very essence, the great revolt against the dominance of *noble* values. (*EH* "Good Books" *GM*)

We may be forgiven for thinking that something else was to be on offer. After all, neither 'Christianity' nor 'Christian' ever appears in the Preface, which instead identifies the book's topic as the history of moral values and moral evaluation. Yet Nietzsche asserts a year after *GM*'s publication that it is Christianity, not morality, whose genealogy he will examine. Why this apparent change? The answer is straightforward: morality and Christianity overlap so much that any analysis of the origins and development of one must be an analysis of the origins and development of the other. So the investigation into the history, psychology, and etymology of the language at use in our talk about good and evil—that is, the genealogy of the morality to which modern Europeans adhere—must at the same time be an investigation into the history, psychology, and etymology of the language at use in Christianity, the dominant European religion.

In the opening sections of Essay I, Nietzsche lampoons other genealogies and reviews etymological evidence about the origins of moral evaluation that warrants a set of claims regarding the semantics of 'good,' 'bad,' and 'evil.' Before modern morality, a master caste made up of warriors, knights, and aristocrats designated themselves as good because they were vigorous, strong, healthy, lusty, rich, and powerful, and designated the activities that expressed their health and power as good things to do. All others—the oppressed, the weak, and the downtrodden—were dismissed by the masters as base, mere tools or instruments to be used as needed. The clergy, although also an elite and in some ways noble caste, differed from the warriors and aristocrats by emphasizing purity and cleanliness and using rituals to breed cognitive reflection and emotional regulation. Their desire for revenge against the master caste festered incessantly, leading them to an ingenious undertaking that valorized the oppressed as morally superior and revalued knightly-aristocratic values so that even the masters no longer considered themselves exemplars of human flourishing. Modern humans are the descendants of the priests and the revolt in evaluative practices they spearheaded.

A little more than halfway through Essay I, Nietzsche abruptly changes direction. In Section 10, he introduces the psychological phenomenon of ressentiment and starts to describe its role in the slave revolt in morality, a description he does not complete until Essay III. The old master caste of warriors, knights, and aristocrats, and the distinct but still noble priestly caste designated themselves, their psychological characteristics, and what they did as good and designated commoners and slaves as bad. Slave valuation, premised in large part on ressentiment, was instead reactive. Being reactive, it was more creative. Abetted by priests, slaves affirmed that the warriors, knights, and aristocrats and what they did were evil, while they—the oppressed, the weak, the sick, the scheming, and the cowardly—were good.

Ressentiment is a response to physiological, psychological, and social weakness. The masters' happiness was realized in acts of physical strength, war, and adventure. Feeling their flourishing in physical activity and adventure, they showed and felt respect toward even those who bettered them, and they rarely resented others. Moreover, their interior life was so uncomplicated that they rarely forgave those who insulted them, not because they fretted about whether doing so was the right thing to do or because they held a grudge, but because they did not remember offenses long enough to even think about forgiving. Instead, they kept themselves in check by custom, respect, and their love of competitions and festive displays of self-assurance. Once outside the bubble of their own group, the masters behaved like predators. In such scenarios, their feeling of distance from commoners and slaves and indifference to them licensed gruesome displays of murder, arson, rape, and torture, all untouched by the slightest trace of bad conscience or guilt.

Were the impotent and the oppressed to have tried to flourish as the masters did, the result would have been inevitable defeat and humiliation. They instead turned to indirect and delayed modalities of flourishing premised on otherworldly blessedness and achieving revenge against the masters. Their ressentiment bred a cunning that expressed itself in devaluing the old masters' active strength as wicked and reappraising their own passivity and weakness as good. Those primitive anesthetizing attempts to think of themselves as worthy paled in comparison to the more fully developed clerical strategy of undermining the masters from within, by convincing them that their strength, their power, their activity, in short, their happiness, were hallmarks of how not to flourish. With the priestly caste leading the way, the masters were infected with a belief in the subject as distinct from its actions and with values that implied that the most prominent features of a flourishing life were reflection, humility, compassion, and passivity.

By unleashing the creative possibilities inherent in ressentiment, the slave revolt inverted the masters' distinction between good and bad: what was good for the masters became evil after the slave revolt and what the masters dismissed as bad became good. While acknowledging the slave revolt's success, Nietzsche disdains slave values: they leave him longing for something worthy. Still, he realizes that the revolt has made humans psychologically interesting and that all of us have internalized and must now endure the battle between master and slave within ourselves. The current task is to prevent further rot and to reimagine how humans might flourish despite having become contaminated with slave or, as he also says, herd values.

In the discussion section of Chapter 3, we first investigate Nietzsche's confusing use of the word 'morality' in *GM* and his tactic of juxtaposing distinct kinds of morality and moral psychology. We also introduce his drive/affect moral psychology, noting its various naturalist commitments and some of its problems. Chief among them is that Nietzsche appears to attribute so many talents to drives and affects that they look for all intents and purposes to be little people—homunculi—that operate at a subpersonal level just as we operate at a personal level. We argue that this appearance is neither accidental nor debilitating. Nietzsche's naturalism entails deflating the pretensions of theological and philosophical accounts of human moral psychology, and that deflationary project in turn entails explaining personal abilities by appealing to subpersonal abilities. However, the features of drives and affects that sometimes appear to require attributing reflectively consciousness to them can be understood so as not to require that they be so.

Chapter 4: *Genealogy* Essay II

In *Ecce Homo*, Nietzsche summarizes Essay II as follows:

> The *second* essay gives the psychology of the *conscience*: conscience *is not*, as is believed, 'the voice of God in man,'—it is the instinct of cruelty that is turned inwards after it cannot discharge itself outwards anymore. Cruelty is first brought to light here as one of the oldest and most persistent underpinnings of culture. (*EH* "Good Books" *GM*)

This is notably incomplete, even as summary. Nietzsche does investigate conscience and cruelty, but he devotes the essay's first half to revealing conscience's preconditions—custom, promise-making, and responsibility—which in turn presuppose punishment, emotional regulation, predictability, memory, and forgetfulness. Moreover, the summary does not even mention what he announces as Essay II's two main topics, the genealogy of bad conscience and guilt.

Nietzsche's fondness for moving in different directions at once can make tracking this essay's core arguments difficult. To keep them in sight, we should keep the following in mind. Sections 2 and 3 introduce the morality of custom and the psychological consequences of a morality of custom: emotional regulation, attention control, and a sense of obligation to the larger collective. Prudential responsibility, accountability, predictability, and self-awareness, the primary topics in Sections 4–10, evolved through promising, contracts, obligations, and bloody regimens of punishment that burned memory into early humans. Not repaying debts and not keeping promises harmed creditors, and they resolved that harm by visiting pain on offenders. An equivalence of pain for debt held punishment in check, and since it was public and eventually codified in law, it kept creditors from inflicting arbitrary and disproportionate pain, thus making both debtors and creditors more predictable and civilized. Sections 11–15 argue that it is only with the emergence of law that we find the origin of justice. Justice is not, as others think, grounded in the prelegal experience of revenge. Nietzsche also notes a curious implication about punishment: causing others to suffer is always underdetermined by function. Woven through all of punishment's various functions, purposes, and meanings is the thread of its display and the festivity of cruelty. Over the last two thousand years, delight in the spectacle of cruelty has tapered as the rule of law has become entrenched. As humans have become tamer, more predictable, more responsible, more refined, and more spiritualized, the need for flaunting pain has become less salient. Eventually, the sublimation of cruelty culminates in overcoming punishment through regimes of mercy, in which the powerful let those who cause them harm go unpunished.

Custom, ritual, promise-making, and contracts are practical or prudential social mechanisms, and the responsibility and accountability they cultivate are similarly practical or prudential. Debtors knew that if they did not repay their debt, a likely consequence was forfeiture of a body part, a spouse, or a life; community members knew that the whole sometimes demanded sacrifice and that noncompliance could result in banishment. Yet religious and moral responsibility are self-imposed states of mind. So Sections 16–22 explain how augmentations to prudential responsibility yielded spiritual and moral responsibility and bad conscience / guilt. Nietzsche abstracts from observable acts of cruelty to uncover active and aggressive drives that impose form and express will to power. With those in tow, he argues that the emergence of bad conscience / guilt can be explained by the psychological revolution attending enculturation, in which outwardly directed drives to impose form turned inward.

Sections 16–18 argue that during the early stages of enculturation, primitive humans lost outward vents for aggressive instincts, drives, and affects. So the drives to give form to and have mastery over other things and other humans turned inward on the self in campaigns of self-directed cruelty. Over millennia of customs, exchange relations, and punishment, humans gained the psychological wherewithal to take the self as raw material and stamp it with direction, structure, discipline, and control. While initially sick and self-mutilating, these campaigns made possible new forms of superimposition, reconfiguration, sublimation, and self-overcoming. This instinct for freedom (Sections 17 and 18) was the psychological crucible of bad conscience. Bad conscience does not reduce to the instinct for freedom, but all of the variants of bad conscience grew out of it. In principle, numerous developments of the primordial form of bad conscience are possible. Nietzsche focuses on two. The first, active bad conscience (Section 18), is the soil from which everything beautiful and worthwhile grows. The second is the more familiar form that through Christianity and other religions became ubiquitous, religious and moral bad conscience, also known as guilt.

Sections 19–23 describe how religious guilt developed in primitive peoples as a feeling of indebtedness to their ancestors, which continuously grew as the power of the community increased, until eventually they transformed ancestors into heroes and gods to whom all community members owed debts and in whose name punishment was allocated. Since the gods transcended the community's citizens, the debts owed to them became increasingly difficult to repay, and with the Christian God the sense of debt became maximal and religious guilt congealed into a widespread psychological condition. The Christian God exemplified nothing but perfect and perfectly antianimal and antihuman characteristics, and that perfection warranted the denunciations of human animality that pervade Christianity. When Christians came to believe that they had fallen so far from God that they could never redeem their debt, human sin became original, infinite in scope, and eternal. This overheated environment congealed religious guilt into moral guilt.

In Chapter 4's discussion section, we investigate the genealogies of subjectivity and agency. Essay II's textual surface belies Nietzsche's ambitions for it. Among the many issues he takes up, he describes how humanity's developmental path diverged from its last common ancestors so that it included becoming prudentially responsible and accountable subjects of reflective thought and agents of action. We then show how moralities of custom, exchange relations, and promising are elements for the emergence of self-aware subjectivity, prudential responsibility, accountability, and agency. We also scrutinize the doctrine of free will as Nietzsche inherited it from previous philosophers, theologians, and religious advocates, the reasons he offers for rejecting free will, and his own analysis of willing in the absence of free will. Finally, we dissect Nietzsche's concept of power, note how he thinks power and life are related, and unpack what he says about willing power.

Chapter 5: *Genealogy* Essay III

Nietzsche's *Ecce Homo* summary of Essay III is as follows:

> The *third* essay gives the answer to the question of how the ascetic ideal, the priestly ideal, acquired such incredible *power* despite the fact that it is the *detrimental* ideal *par excellence*, a will to the end, a decadence ideal. Answer: *not* because God is at work behind priests, as is believed, but instead *aute de mieux*,—because it has been the only ideal so far, because it has not had any competition. 'Because people would rather will nothingness than not will' . . . Above all, there was no *counter-ideal—until Zarathustra*. —I have been understood. (*EH* "Good Books" *GM*)

This summary also undersells what is achieved in Essay III. True, Nietzsche analyzes the ascetic ideal and shows how the ascetic ideal helps form the moral outlook that results from the slave revolt. Yet he also argues that ascetic values can be necessary conditions for all sorts of creative individuals. It appears, then, that ascetic values are both against life and also elements of some of the highest forms of life. In addition, Essay III finally answers two questions left dangling from earlier chapters. First, while Essay I described the slave revolt in morality, it did not explain why it succeeded. Second, while Essay II described the development of punishment, responsibility, and guilt, it did not explain how Christian morality capitalized on them and became the preeminent mode of moral evaluation. It is up to Essay III's scrutiny of the ascetic ideal, ascetic values, and ascetic priests to fill in these gaps.

Sections 1–10 consider ascetic values as expressed in artists and philosophers. In the first five sections, Nietzsche criticizes Wagner's fear of sensuality, lampoons *Parsifal*'s flimsy construction and concessions to Christianity, and suggests that the great composer eventually lost control of his art. Sections 5–10 discuss philosophers' more compelling use of ascetic values. Philosophers have for centuries used ascetic values as camouflage and to cultivate independence from themselves. Cultivating ascetic values prudentially, philosophers have gained a maximal feeling of power by overcoming who they have been. Indeed, not only philosophers but all fruitful and inventive spirits may cultivate ascetic values prudentially. These individuals do not condemn those who reject ascetic values; instead, they recognize that their life is one of a number of distinct kinds of flourishing lives and that the values that structure their kinds need not be those that structure others.

Unlike philosophers, moral ascetics make a blanket judgment against all of life and demand that the rest of us accept that negative evaluation. The consequences of this blanket judgment are discussed in Sections 11–22, the heart of Essay III. Ascetics in general and Christian priests in particular display their self-abnegation, insisting that it can apply to everyone as an ideal. They hoist their ascetic ideal as a showpiece, attracting others to the parade and providing everyone the chance to participate in guilt for not being better. The ascetic ideal fastens onto moral guilt and sucks the life-enhancing drives out, leaving the hosts withered shells of who they once were or might have become.

The ascetic ideal enhances kinds of life that are already so debased that only denying the conditions that in general make life possible make these particular kinds of life endurable. It is only a sick and declining life shot through with guilt and self-loathing that finds the prospect of rejecting drives and affects altogether a prescription for health. Although all humans seek to be powerful—strong, healthy, intelligent, creative, disciplined, rich in contradictions—such a life is difficult and few ever achieve it. The rest are failures and miserable. Hating themselves and those who are better, they grasp for any evaluation scheme according to which they too are exemplars, especially if doing also entails laying low the powerful. Ascetic priests are only too prepared to offer an evaluative system that explains suffering, identifies its causes, and prescribes a cure. They argue that the sources of suffering are not unrealized drives and resentment of the powerful; rather, it is being power-driven creatures at all that causes suffering. In brief, humans are morally responsible for their own suffering.

The priest's cure for human suffering first instills the belief that divine punishment for sin is justified and then prescribes extirpating passion and the drives and giving ourselves over to the church so that the inevitable suffering that attends them will cease. Herd animals thus become their best selves by trying to unwind the conditions that make life possible. The genius of ascetic morality is revealed as an evaluative system that permits life's failures to succeed at something, even if what they succeed at is confounding the conditions of a healthy life. Christian ascetic morality inverts the order of values and provides a reason for life's failures to strive after something, but accomplishing this inversion requires disguising perspectivity. Christian ascetic morality must dissemble about the perspectivity of ascetic values and must deny that they serve the interests only of particular types.

If Christianity is exposed as an enslaving tyrant that pretends to be something it is not, might science liberate humanity from and provide an alternative to ascetic values? Nietzsche thinks not, and in Sections 23–28, he presents his case. The great hope of the Enlightenment was to replace the superstition and myth of folk religion with the clarity and reason of scientific method and scientific truth. Nietzsche is willing to allow that science exposes Christianity's absurdities, but he also thinks that science is a secularized expression of what it criticizes. Science may be stripped of metaphysical and moral excess, but it relies on truth and an objective world beyond interpretation and it encourages abstraction from life in order to view the world objectively, both of which are twisted expressions of the ascetic's adherence to chastity. So science is, after all, asceticism's ally. Nietzsche demands that we subject truth to a critique that, like the analysis of the ascetic ideal he has been engaged in, poses risks. Still, faced as we now are with the imminent collapse of the ascetic ideal and its attendant morality, we can review our own past. We will discover that the ascetic ideal has, among other things, provided huge swaths of humanity with a meaning for their suffering. This meaning is, of course, nihilistic, but nihilistic and meaningful suffering allows humans to stave off nihilistic and meaningless suffering. The ascetic ideal has saved humanity by providing suffering with meaning, thus proving that people "would rather will *nothingness* than *not* will" (*GM* III 28).

In Chapter 5's discussion section, we focus on three sets of issues. The first set revolves around Nietzsche's claims that sensory perception and interoception, and so knowledge and truth as well, are perspectival. Each claim is extraordinary, so we discuss them individually. Second, we mention the relativist threat posed by perspectival knowledge and truth and examine the paradoxicality of perspectival truth. Finally, we add to Chapter 4's descriptive analysis of will to power its evaluative dimension, which warrants Nietzsche's arguments regarding asceticism and decadence and what he has to say about the meaninglessness of life and nihilism.

Further Reading

For more on the revaluation project and *GM*'s place in it, see Guay 2006; Havas 1995; Hussain 2007, 2013; Janaway 2007; Leiter 2002; May 1999; Owen 2007; Reginster 2006; Richardson 2020; Ridley 2006; Robertson 2020; Schacht 1983, 2013b.

1
Biography, Intellectual Development, and Legacy

1.1 Introduction

In this chapter, we fulfill three preliminary tasks. First, a biographical sketch allows us to get a glimpse of Friedrich Nietzsche's life. Although he experienced early personal losses, Nietzsche enjoyed childhood and school. After graduating from university, he was named professor at the University of Basel, a post he kept until ill health forced an early resignation. Thereafter, he followed the seasons, renting rooms in various villages, towns, and cities in Italy, Germany, Austria, and Switzerland. In early 1889, his mental health collapsed and he was placed under his mother's care. For a decade, he remained under her care, and, after her death, his sister's. He died in 1900. Second, we summarize Nietzsche's intellectual development, focusing on his two most significant early philosophical influences, Arthur Schopenhauer and Friedrich Albert Lange, and some of his later scientific influences, Roger Boscovich, Maximilian Drossbach, Wilhelm Roux, and William Henry Rolph. Nietzsche eventually soured on Schopenhauer's pessimism but remained impressed by his intellectual abilities. Nietzsche's reaction to Lange was until much later less ambivalent: he admired Lange's *History of Materialism* and read it a number of times. Boscovich, Drossbach, Roux, and Rolph proved influential on more localized regions of Nietzsche's thinking. Finally, we briefly discuss Nietzsche's tortured legacy.

Nietzsche's On the Genealogy of Morality. Rex Welshon, Oxford University Press.
 DOI: 10.1093/oso/9780197611814.003.0002

1.2 Biography

Childhood

Nietzsche was born in the village of Röcken, Prussia, on October 15, 1844. His father, Karl Ludwig (1813–1849), was well educated, cultured, antidogmatic, skilled at the piano, and pastor of the local Lutheran church. His mother, Franziska (1826–1897), was pious, kind, poorly educated, and conservative, and ran the household with Karl Ludwig's mother, Erdmuthe, and two stepsisters, Auguste and Rosalie. Franziska was eighteen when she gave birth to Friedrich; in 1846, she gave birth to Elisabeth (1846–1935), and two years later to Joseph. Sadly, Karl Ludwig fell ill in the fall of 1848, suffering convulsions and depression. The illness progressed rapidly, causing blindness and condemning him to bed until, on July 27, 1849, he died at age thirty-six. An autopsy revealed that a quarter of his brain was atrophied at the time of death. A year later, Joseph died, not yet two years old. Since the village needed a new parson, the remaining members of the Nietzsche household had to leave the vicarage. They all moved to Naumburg, about twenty miles away, where Augusta died in 1855 and Erdmuthe a year later. Thereafter, Nietzsche lived with his mother Franziska, stepsister Rosalie, and sister Elisabeth until he went away to school.

Nietzsche attended school in Naumburg from 1854 until 1858 and, from 1858 until 1864, at the Pforta boarding school, four miles outside of Naumburg. The Pforta school was and still is a highly selective private preparatory school. Daily life followed a strict routine: students were washed, dressed, and ready for prayers at 5:20 a.m., classes started at 6:00 a.m., and bedtime came at 8:30 p.m. While at Pforta, he started to experience the headaches that would plague him throughout his life. No one at the time diagnosed their cause, but his shortsightedness was probably a contributing factor. Despite the headaches and other ailments that sporadically required bed rest, the teenage Nietzsche was engaged in his studies at Pforta. He appreciated ancient cultures and convinced himself that music supplied a portal to a transcendent domain. He also started to question his faith and to display both his skill at the piano and, sometimes to the bewilderment of his teachers, his daunting intellect. In his last year, he started a friendship with Paul Deussen (1845–1919) that would, despite various difficulties, continue until 1887. Deussen later became a leading European Sanskrit and Hindu scholar.

Upon graduating from Pforta in 1864 after sixth form, Nietzsche enrolled at the University of Bonn, in part because the classical philologists Otto Jahn (1813–1869) and Friedrich Ritschl (1806–1876) taught there, in part because Deussen had decided to attend there as well. Nietzsche joined a fraternity, drank too much, and visited a brothel. Although he expected to follow his father into the clergy, he soon tired of theology and switched to philology, a decision that disappointed Franziska and threw Elisabeth into a crisis of faith. A rift formed then between Nietzsche and his mother and sister that never completely healed.

Nietzsche's favorite professors at Bonn, Ritschl and Jahn, had been embroiled in an academic feud for years, so when Ritschl accepted a position at the University of Leipzig, Nietzsche, dissatisfied with his own intellectual development at Bonn and eager to live somewhere closer to home, transferred as well. Nietzsche admired Ritschl enormously, calling him "the only brilliant scholar I have ever come across" (*EH* "Why I Am So Clever" 9). He delighted in Ritschl's expertise, self-organization, generosity, unedited appraisals of himself, and eccentricities, such as putting money in books and gleefully finding it there later. About a month after arriving in Leipzig in the fall of 1865, Nietzsche stumbled across a copy of *The World as Will and Representation* (*Die Welt als Wille und Vorstellung*) by Arthur Schopenhauer (1788–1860) in his landlord's bookshop; nine months later, he read *History of Materialism and Critique of Its Significance for the Present* (*Geschichte des Materialismus und Kritik seiner Bedeutung in der Gegenwart*) by Friedrich Albert Lange (1828–1875) for the first time. Both books had a significant impact on his thinking, and together they triggered his interest in philosophy. He also befriended Erwin Rohde (1845–1898), a fellow classicist and Ritschl student. Rohde became a leading classical scholar, with a specialty on Greek cults. Their friendship suffered over time.

In 1866–1867, while still working on his degree, Nietzsche served briefly in the Prussian army and achieved lance corporal status before a riding accident cut short his military ambitions. When he returned to Leipzig, he became a music critic for the *Deutsche Allgemeine Zeitung* and started to listen closely to the music of Richard Wagner (1813–1883), meeting him for the first time in November 1868 and becoming an instant convert. Shortly thereafter, Nietzsche learned that Ritschl had recommended him for the recently vacated chair of philology at the University of Basel in Switzerland. In February 1869, at the age of twenty-four and before even obtaining his doctorate, he was appointed to the position. The degree followed in March.

The Basel Years

Nietzsche's Basel years from 1869 to 1879 mixed success, illness, frustration, and friendship. He was promoted to the rank of full professor within a year of arriving, an achievement virtually unheard of in German university life. He was, by all accounts, a good teacher. Of his talents, Nietzsche claimed later that he belonged "among those involuntary educators who neither need nor possess pedagogical principles" (*KSA* 13 24[1]), no doubt a slap in the face to administrators even then. He also befriended Franz Overbeck (1837–1905), a historian who studied Christianity despite not believing himself, and he tried to befriend Jakob Burckhardt (1818–1897), a historian of the Renaissance and classical Greece. He and Burckhardt respected each other, but Nietzsche never broke through Burckhardt's social distance and melancholy. Overbeck, on the other hand, became Nietzsche's best friend. The two of them remained close until the end; indeed, it was Overbeck who rescued him from Turin and returned him to Germany after he collapsed in early 1889.

Of equal significance was Nietzsche's growing friendship with Richard Wagner and his soon-to-be-wife, Cosima von Bülow (1837–1930). Between 1869 and 1872, Nietzsche visited the Wagner house at Tribschen, overlooking Lake Lucerne, more than twenty times (he would later call Tribschen "a distant island of blissfulness" [*EH* "Good Books" *HH* 2]). Wagner was a magnetically attractive model of the flourishing, cultured, creative, and significant life that Nietzsche most desired for himself and would later champion in his work. Wagner was a musical talent of the highest order, and Nietzsche, a composer of middling talent, admired it. Moreover, Wagner was a brilliant and witty conversationalist, a cultural impresario, and someone who shared Nietzsche's fascination with Schopenhauer. Additionally, Cosima supplied another model for Nietzsche, that of an intellectual comrade, friend, and ideal of femininity. He would try in vain to replicate her, and, indeed, the entire nonconformist Tribschen milieu, in his own life. When the Wagners moved to Bayreuth, where their music festival was taking shape, Nietzsche continued to take part in plans for it and even offered to take leave from his university post to help bring it to life.

The Franco-Prussian War erupted in July of 1870 and lasted until January 1871. Although the war was over in only six months, a staggering 180,000 French and Prussian soldiers were killed during that time, another 200,000 were injured, and as many as 250,000 civilians died from disease, primarily smallpox spread by soldiers. Nietzsche was granted leave from the university to serve as a medical orderly for the Germans, which he did for August and part of September, but he contracted dysentery and diphtheria taking care of the injured and sick and was bedridden until his condition improved enough to return to Naumburg, and then, in mid-October, to Basel. Unfortunately, he continued to suffer stomach ailments, insomnia, exhaustion, and depression so severe that he ended up taking sick leave for the spring term of 1871.

In 1872, Nietzsche's first book, *The Birth of Tragedy from the Spirit of Music* (*Die Geburt die Tragödie aus dem Geiste der Musik*), was published. The Wagners eagerly praised it and Rohde wrote a positive review, but Ritschl was evasive and defensive and other reviews were scathing. One consequence was that Nietzsche suffered low enrollments in his courses for more than a year. Still, his social life in Basel was active, and he continued to support the Bayreuth endeavor and went out of his way to flatter Wagner in letters even as his visits declined. In 1873, while writing the first of the essays that would be published over the next three years as *Untimely Meditations*, his eyesight worsened to the point that he could no longer read and had to wear sunglasses when outside. Luckily, his eyesight improved after a month in the Swiss Alps without books.

If Nietzsche's eyesight improved, his mood did not. Through the winter of 1873 and spring of 1874, he was so depressed that Wagner heard about it and suggested in crass terms that what he needed most was to marry. Nietzsche was amused but unpersuaded. Still, he recognized that the daily toil of being a professor was wearing him down. He had since he started at Basel taught not only at the university but also at the high school affiliated with it, and in 1874 he added stress by becoming an administrator. As a result, he was worn out and started thinking about resigning his position. Later that year, his incipient restlessness with life in Wagner's shadow became plain when, during an August visit to Bayreuth, he dared to suggest that a composition by Brahms had value. Wagner came completely unglued; Nietzsche said nothing in response and just stared back. This was, as Wagner himself recognized, the moment the spell broke: he and Nietzsche were never to be as close again, and Nietzsche never spent another night under Wagner's roof.

The next year, 1875, began with more headaches, more intestinal trouble, and a critical review of the first three *Untimely Meditations* (*Unzeitgemässe Betrachtungen*) in the *Westminster Review*, an academic journal started by the British utilitarian philosophers and social activists John Stuart Mill and Jeremy Bentham. Nietzsche was delighted for the notice outside of Germany, even if he was annoyed with the reviewer's doubts about his dedication to Schopenhauer. That summer, he traveled to Steinebad to try a dietary cure for his health troubles. It was a failure: he returned to Basel exhausted and moved into an apartment with Elisabeth. Throughout 1875–1876, he routinely suffered headaches so debilitating that he was bedridden regularly. Eventually, in January 1876, his poor health forced him to abandon all of his high school teaching and to cancel some meetings of his university courses.

Despite his misery, Nietzsche managed to propose marriage to Mathilde Trampedach, who turned him down flatly. They had spent no more than a few hours in each other's company when his proposal arrived, and, more importantly, she loved the man whom Nietzsche had asked to deliver his proposal. Nietzsche also began in 1876 a friendship that was to prove significant. Paul Rée (1849–1901), a lapsed Schopenhauerian, wrote *Psychological Observations* (*Psycholigische*

Beobachntungen) in 1875 while working on his doctorate. Nietzsche informed him by letter that he had enjoyed the book and invited him to form a friendship premised on mutual interests. Thus began a close relationship that lasted six years, until it unraveled in 1882.

In the summer of 1876, the first Bayreuth festival finally came to fruition. Nietzsche attended and was appalled by its ostentatious commercialism, nationalism, and banality, and he finally realized he could no longer tolerate the toadies that hovered about Wagner's inner circle. After two weeks, he fled the spectacle to the mountains and began work on what would become *Human, All-Too-Human: A Book for Free Spirits* (*Menschliches, Allzumenschliches: Ein Buch für freie Geister*). Strengthened again by mountain air, he returned to Bayreuth and stayed almost to the end, viewing its proceedings now with jaundiced detachment.

Nietzsche took medical leave from Basel during the academic year 1876–1877, and he spent it in Sorrento, Italy, at the invitation of Malwida von Meysenbug (1816–1903), a member of the German aristocracy and twenty years his senior. Meysenbug was a feminist, democrat, and socialist; her autobiography, *Memoirs of an Idealist* (*Memorien einer Idealistin*), was recently published and well known. At the villa rented for the season, she, Nietzsche, and Rée spent the days hiking and sightseeing and the evenings discussing poetry, literature, music, and other topics of high culture. The Wagners were staying at the Grand Hotel Excelsior Vittoria a few minutes away. Nietzsche spent a number of evenings with them there in October and November, after which they left for a series of concerts in London. He would never meet with the Wagners again.

Nietzsche's conversations with Rée, who was at the time writing *The Origins of Moral Sensations* (*Der Ursprung der moralischen Empfindungen*), fundamentally changed the direction of his thinking. Predictably, he also suffered various ailments in the early months of 1877, and the doctor he consulted in Naples recommended regular sexual activity. He complied by visiting brothels. He and Meysenbug also talked frankly about finding a rich wife so he could resign from his professorship. Several candidates were named, but nothing ever came of their scheming. Instead, he left Sorrento in May and took up residence for the balance of his leave in the mountain village of

Rosenlauibad, Switzerland, near the Eiger and Reichenbach Falls (made famous by Conan Doyle's fictional detective Sherlock Holmes).

Returning to Basel in October, Nietzsche met with Dr. Otto Eiser and Dr. Gustav Krüger. Eiser ruled out the progressive brain disease from which his father had died as the cause of Nietzsche's headaches. Instead, he and Krüger diagnosed damage to the cornea, the cure for which was to stop reading and writing. Nietzsche wrote to Cosima Wagner about the diagnosis and prescription, with which, he dryly noted, he was unlikely to comply, and she reported the news to her husband. Despite not being a doctor, Wagner wrote Eiser suggesting his own diagnosis, that Nietzsche was a pervert and an onanist whose unnatural deeds were causing him to go blind. Somehow, the Wagner-Eiser letters became public after they were written, and Nietzsche learned of them some time after that (we do not know exactly when, but it was certainly no later than 1882, when their contents were the talk of the second Bayreuth festival). Understandably, he was horrified that the letters existed, furious with Wagner's effrontery, and humiliated that they had become public. Already distrustful of Wagner's egomaniacal abusiveness and disdainful of his vulgarity and antisemitism, this personal betrayal helped cement Nietzsche's antagonism and started to feed a loathing that later found expression in *The Case of Wagner* (*Der Fall Wagner*).

The Peripatetic Years

HH was published in May 1878, again to mixed reviews. Burckhardt admired it; in particular, he welcomed its distance from Wagner. On the other hand, the Wagners and their disciples detested the book, specifically condemning Rée's influence on Nietzsche's thinking. Worse, their opinions were peppered with antisemitic tropes. Nietzsche's health continued its downward trend. By the end of 1878, he was again barely able to read, and he was nauseated so often that he canceled lectures and classes on a regular basis. In May 1879, shortly after *Assorted Opinions and Maxims* (*Vermischte Meinungen und Sprüche*) was published, he resigned his professorship from the

University of Basel. The university offered him a pension for the next six years, supplemented by a second pension from the Basel Voluntary Academic Association. Together, the two equaled about two-thirds of his professor's salary. Thereafter, and until insanity descended ten years later, Nietzsche did not have a permanent home, moving from rented rooms in French and Italian seaside towns and cities during the winter to rented rooms in the Swiss Alps during the summer. Late in December, *The Wanderer and His Shadow* (*Der Wanderer und sein Schatten*) was published. None of the three books sold well. In 1886, he combined and published them as a set of two volumes, the first being the original *HH*, the second incorporating *Assorted Opinions* and *The Wanderer*.

Nietzsche's health reached its nadir in the winter of 1879–1880, when he was thirty-six, the same age his father had been when he died. Nietzsche wrote to Eiser that he suffered nausea so severe that he vomited for days on end and could speak only with difficulty, that he could neither read nor write regularly, and, worst of all, that he could not listen to music. He self-diagnosed migraines as the cause, and modern scholarship has tended to agree with him. Matters became so bad that, in January 1880, he predicted impending death in a letter to Meysenbug. Fortunately, his self-knowledge turned out to be faulty and his prediction a false alarm. Instead of dying, he accepted an invitation from a former student and friend, Heinrich Köselitz (1854–1918)—better known by the name that Nietzsche assigned him, 'Peter Gast'—to visit Venice. There he began work on what would become *Daybreak: Thoughts on the Presumptions of Morality* (*Morgenröte: Gedanken über die moralischen Vorurtheile*), the book that he later credited as being the start of his "campaign against morality" (*EH* "Good Books" *D* 1). Nietzsche enjoyed Venice so much that he stayed until July, driving Gast batty with his incessant and eccentric requests. Then he was on the move again, first to Marienbad, then to Naumburg, and finally, in November, to Genoa, where he remained until May 1881. Genoa was a haven; he loved the city and his isolation in it. He wandered around the palace-lined streets and down to the Mediterranean, where he sat quietly on the rocks pinning down his thoughts, trying to fix "things that slip by without a sound" (*EH* "Good Books" *D* 1).

Nietzsche sent the manuscript of *D* to the publishers in March 1881 and left for the Alps in May, where, after a sequence of missteps, he assumed summer residence in a house in the village of Sils-Maria, found in the Engadine Valley between Lake Sils and Lake Silverplana. Here, by his own account, his best thinking occurred, and he would return repeatedly to the house for the summer months. His room in the back of the house was paneled in pine, unheated, and shady. When the weather allowed, he took morning walks through the shaded forests surrounding the house until lunch, then more walking, thinking, and writing things down in a notebook again until supper. Since the house had no electricity and he had only a single lamp in his room, he was in bed and asleep shortly after dark. It was on one of his daily walks during his first summer in Sils-Maria that the eternal return first occurred to him: "The thought of eternal return . . . belongs to August of the year 1881: it was thrown onto paper with the title '6,000 feet beyond people and time'. . . I stopped near Surlei by a huge, pyramidal boulder. That is where this thought came to me" (*EH* "Good Books" *Z* 1). The rock is now adorned with a plaque, commemorating the episode.

The eternal return featured in *The Gay Science* (*Die fröhliche Wissenschaft*), Nietzsche's next book, which he started in Sils-Maria and continued to work on through the winter of 1881–1882 while in Genoa. Again, he relished the warm weather and anonymity of the Italian coast. He swam in the Mediterranean in January, walked around in a linen suit, and enthused in letters about the blossoming peach trees. Rée visited in February. They traveled together to Monte Carlo, where Nietzsche read Copernicus, Boscovich, and Spinoza and Rée lost so much gambling that Nietzsche had to front him return train fare. *GS* was published in August 1882.

The spring and summer of 1882 were significant for another reason. Nietzsche fell in love with, and was rejected and humiliated by, Lou Salomé (1861–1937). This pathetic chapter started when Rée met Salomé in Rome at Meysenbug's rented home. Salomé, the daughter of a Russian general, had been sent south from St. Petersburg to recover her health. She was twenty-one, philosophically astute, dialectically clever, and determined to live independently. Rée fell in love with her, as did others. Rée and Salomé suggested that the three of them recreate the Sorrento interlude from a few years earlier by living together and starting a retreat for free spirits. Within days of meeting her, Nietzsche, misreading the situation, proposed marriage. Uninterested at that time in sex or its prerequisite marriage, Salomé refused at once. Nonetheless, over the next four months, Nietzsche fell deeply in love, and he and Rée each vied for her romantic feelings. Although she was deeply impressed with Nietzsche's daring intellect, Salomé was never interested in a romance with him, thinking him too old. Unfortunately, she and Rée misled Nietzsche by not disclosing to him their romantic feelings for each other, and Nietzsche again proposed marriage and was again rebuffed.

In late May 1882, the three of them visited a photography studio in Lucerne, where they staged a picture of Salomé sitting in a tiny cart, whip in hand, Rée and Nietzsche acting as draft horses. Later that summer, when she visited the Wagners in Bayreuth with Meysenbug and Elisabeth for the first performance of *Parsifal*, Salomé showed the picture to a number of people in Wagner's inner circle, mocking Nietzsche as she did so. Elisabeth witnessed some of these antics and was so outraged on her brother's behalf that she abruptly left, returned to Naumburg, and told her mother what had happened. Franziska announced that Salomé would never again be allowed in her house and that Nietzsche's recklessness had disgraced the family. Nietzsche, who was visiting, moved out and rented rooms in Leipzig, where he remained until November. Astonishingly, even after Elisabeth told him about Salomé's malice, he still harbored hopes of living together with her and Rée as an intellectual threesome. It was only when Rée and Salomé visited him in Leipzig that he realized that neither of them had any intention of following through on the idea.

Nietzsche sulked off to Rapallo, east of Genoa, to lick his wounds and indulge himself in the kind of bitter recrimination against Salomé and Rée that only frustrated lust seems to cause. Despite feeling forlorn, a long spell of mild weather in January 1883 lifted his spirits enough to start work on *Thus Spoke Zarathustra* (*Also Sprach Zarathustra*). Over the next year and a bit, he wrote all of its parts, some in Rapallo, some in Genoa, some in Sils-Maria, and some in Nice, where he moved in December 1883 after concluding that he had exhausted Genoa's hiking trails. During the year, he reached a more balanced judgment about Salomé, acknowledging that his respect for her intellectual powers remained undiminished and hoping that his sister's desire for revenge would ease. It never did: Elisabeth continued to nourish an intemperate hostility toward her. Meanwhile, Elisabeth was pursuing Bernard Förster (1843–1889), an antisemite who was planning an experimental Teutonic colony called 'Nueva Germania' in South America. In part because of her love for Förster, in part because he realized that she had poisoned his judgment about Salomé, Nietzsche and his sister came to a distrustful deadlock.

From 1884 through to his collapse in January 1889, Nietzsche kept to his peripatetic ways, determined to find places where average daily temperatures hovered between 50° and 60° Fahrenheit. He wintered in Nice from late November or early December until May, moved from Nice to a transitional town or city until the snow melted in the Alps, spent the summer months until late September or early October in Sils-Maria, and traveled again to a transitional town or city until Nice cooled down enough in late November or early December for his return. During these five years, Nietzsche's health vacillated from decent to dreadful. He continued to experiment with his diet, usually with detrimental results, and, as a consequence, he also continued to self-medicate with chloral hydrate, opium, cocaine, and perhaps hashish. As much as was consistent with his bouts of depression, irritable digestive tract, vomiting attacks, nausea, and headaches, Nietzsche kept to the same routine: up, washed, and fed by seven; walking and transcribing or polishing thoughts through the morning until noonish; lunch break; more working, walking, and writing through the afternoon; supper in the early evening; and more work until bedtime.

Regardless of location, Nietzsche was rarely without visitors, some of them welcome, others irritating. A number of his callers came courtesy of Meysenbug, who arranged several visits between Nietzsche and free-thinkers and feminists eager to talk with him. Perhaps the most significant of these was Meta von Salis (1855–1929), the first Swiss woman to receive a doctorate, for a dissertation on Agnes of Pitou, empress and regent of the Holy Roman Empire in the eleventh century. Salis and Nietzsche remained close, and he looked forward to her annual visit to Sils-Maria. He also tried, without success, to smooth things over with his sister and mother. Despite his objections, Elisabeth married Förster in May 1885; Nietzsche refused to attend the ceremony. Finally, in October and just before the Försters departed to South America, he met with Elisabeth in Naumburg for the last time before he went insane. She sailed for Paraguay in February 1886 and remained there until well after Förster committed suicide and the colony went bankrupt.

Nietzsche continued to visit regularly with Gast, who served as part-time secretary and helped prepare manuscripts for publication, and more irregularly with Overbeck. In 1886, he met again with Rohde, but it was heartbreaking for both: they realized they no longer had much to say to one another and parted knowing their friendship was done. Then, in 1887, he met for the last time with Deussen, who had just published his translation of and commentary on the *Sutras of the Vedanta*. Nietzsche admired the book for its philosophical subtlety and deep scholarship, and each of them was eager for the visit. However, Deussen was distressed by Nietzsche's spartan life, diminished physical bearing, and philosophical alienation. When Deussen departed for Greece after two days, Nietzsche wept.

Despite, or perhaps because of, his increasing solitude, these five years were Nietzsche's most productive period. *Beyond Good and Evil: Prelude to a Philosophy of the Future* (*Jenseits von Gut und Böse: Vorspiel einer Philosophie der Zukunft*); *On the Genealogy of Morality: A Polemic* (*Zur Genealogie der Moral: Eine Streitschrift*); *Twilight of the Idols, or, How to Philosophize with a Hammer* (*Götzen Dämmerung, oder, Wie man mit dem Hammer philosophiert*); *The Anti-Christ: Curse on Christianity* (*Der Antichrist: Fluch auf das Christentum*); *The Case of Wagner* (*Der Fall Wagner*); *Ecce Homo*; and Book V of *The Gay Science* were all written between 1884 and 1888.

Nietzsche published the individual parts of *Z* through 1884 and into early 1885. After ditching his antisemitic publisher, Schmeitzner, in 1885, he published *BGE* with a new publisher in August 1886. During the winter of 1886–1887, Nietzsche produced revised editions of his already published works, complete with new prefaces and, in the case of *Gay Science*, its fifth book. Preparatory work complete, Nietzsche started in 1887 to get serious about what had been percolating for at least two years as his great project. Numerous plans for this magnum opus—initially called *The Will to Power* and later *Revaluation of All Values*—had been sketched out since 1885, but the spring of 1887 saw him committing himself almost full-time to the project. During a three-week burst in July at Sils-Maria, he wrote most of what he considered a preparatory study for the project, *On the Genealogy of Morality*, published with Naumann in November 1887. While in Nice again for the winter, he received a letter from Georg Brandes (1842–1927), a Danish social and literary critic who had just discovered Nietzsche's works and admired what he called their "aristocratic radicalism." Nietzsche was pleased and humbled that someone of Brandes's cultural stature understood his philosophy, and the two began corresponding.

Collapse, Incapacitation, and Death

Nietzsche traveled to Turin in the late spring of 1888 to continue work on his revaluation-of-values project. His health improved dramatically while he was there, even if the growing arrogance and machismo of the German monarchy, which he feared would lead to hostilities even more deadly than the Franco-Prussian War, distracted him. The death, from cancer, of the young German emperor, Friedrich III, in June 1888 after only a few months in power sealed his gloom about the political future of Europe. Friedrich III was cultured, opposed to war, and progressive. His successor, Wilhelm II, was his polar opposite: bellicose, xenophobic, antisemitic, and imperialistic. Indeed, his terrible judgment was a contributing cause of World War I.

In a markedly anti-German mood following Friedrich III's death, Nietzsche diverted himself briefly during his summer in Sils-Maria with a decisive statement on Wagner, published in September 1888 as *The Case of Wagner*. Unfortunately, various frustrations and visits from friends and acquaintances (including Salis and Julius Kaftan, a theology professor at Berlin, neither of whom noted any signs of incipient madness) made that final alpine summer less productive than he had hoped. In the autumn, he returned to Turin, determined to complete the revaluation-of-values project. Until October, his letters to Overbeck and his mother suggest that work was continuing. He shaped some already written material from the project into two manuscripts, *Twilight of the Idols* and *The Anti-Christ*, published in

1889 and 1894, respectively. And he composed *Ecce Homo*, his smart, self-aware, and extraordinarily flamboyant autobiography, beginning it on his birthday, October 15, and completing it less than a month later, in early November.

Alas, by December, his psychological grip was loosening. He started to sign letters with various noms de plume, usually "Dionysus" or "The Crucified," and his friends noticed that his handwriting was deteriorating and that the content of his letters was becoming ever more histrionic. Nietzsche recorded in some of those letters that he occasionally dissociated from his body and that he increasingly lacked control over his facial expressions. In a letter to Brandes from December, he reported that he had become "the most terrible dynamite there is" and that his next book, *A*, would have to be published in all European languages, a million copies in each language. In another, to Salis, he announced that he was throwing the pope in jail and having all antisemites shot. Just before Christmas, he asked his landlords to prepare the house for an imminent visit from the king and queen of Italy, and then, between Christmas and New Year's Day, he played Wagner incessantly and loudly on the house piano and danced—naked, singing, and shouting—around his room for three straight nights before finally recapturing himself. On January 3, 1889, the final, irreversible break came. As was his custom, he left his lodgings for a midmorning walk. An account published in a Turin newspaper some years later reported that he happened upon a tradesman beating a horse and tried to intercede. After creating a disturbance and collapsing on the ground, police officers helped him back to his room, where he was tranquilized.

Meanwhile, Burckhardt and Overbeck had each received unhinged letters by early January. They met and agreed that Overbeck would travel to Turin at once. Arriving by train on January 7, he found Nietzsche in his room holding the page proofs for *Nietzsche contra Wagner*, a collection of earlier writings about Wagner peppered with some new observations. Together with a local doctor, Overbeck escorted Nietzsche to the train by persuading him that a gala reception awaited him in Germany. Instead, they transported him to the Basel asylum. Overbeck wrote to Gast that he had just left "the rubble of what only a friend would recognize. . . . He suffers from delusions of infinite grandeur, but also from much else—it's hopeless. I have never seen such a horrific picture of destruction" (as quoted by Julian Young [2010], p. 550). A week later, Overbeck watched Nietzsche board another train, this time bound for Germany and another asylum, at Jena.

At the Jena asylum, Nietzsche was diagnosed with a progressive brain disorder and placed in the care of the psychiatric clinic, where he remained for a year. He made no improvement. Although he continued to play piano beautifully for a few months, he also put his fist through a window, kicked patients, erupted into terrifying explosions of rage that ended as inexplicably as they had begun, and engaged in various other antisocial behaviors. After stripping naked and swimming in a lake one day in March 1890, he was transferred to his mother's care. Franziska and Nietzsche returned to the family house in Naumburg, where Elisabeth joined them from Paraguay in 1893. Following Franziska's death in 1897, Elisabeth moved Nietzsche from Naumburg to Weimar, where she had set up the Nietzsche archive. By the mid-1890s, his celebrity was increasing and visitors came to pay their respects. What they found was a shell, uncaring, incompetent, and silent. After a pair of strokes in 1898 and 1899, he died on August 25, 1900.

No autopsy was performed, so the cause of Nietzsche's insanity has never been confirmed, and speculation, some informed, some not, has flourished. Various physiological hypotheses compete for explaining his collapse. His own doctors at Basel and Jena claimed that he suffered from syphilis and that his collapse was the result of tertiary symptoms of the disease, but recent scholarship suggests that this diagnosis was improperly made at the time and that it was inconsistent with the symptoms he displayed. Some claim that he had a brain tumor from early in his life and that it progressively worsened over time until eventually causing cognitive collapse. Others maintain that his use of chloral hydrate over many years led to a compromised nervous system. Still others suggest that he had CADASIL, a genetic disorder of cranial blood vessels that causes migraine, strokes, and progressive cognitive impairment. A distinct, psychological hypothesis proposes that he suffered from bipolar disorder that eventually deteriorated into psychosis. With the exception of the syphilis hypothesis, all of the others can with certain liberties be made consistent with Nietzsche's symptoms throughout his life and, at the end, his rapid cycling between euphoria and rage. We will probably never know which, if any, of them is correct.

1.3 Intellectual Development

Philology studies the nature, structure, and historical development of language. Nietzsche was trained as a philologist of the classical period of Greece and Rome, not as a philosopher. Yet this explains virtually nothing about Nietzsche's skill, or lack thereof, as a philosopher. His training at Leipzig centered around ancient Greek philosophy, general history of philosophy, archaeology, and grammar. Among other things, he read the pre-Socratic philosopher Democritus and the third-century historian of philosophy Diogenes Laertius, and he published an essay on the latter. While studying for his doctorate, he also read voraciously and widely on topics not assigned for coursework; we have already remarked that Schopenhauer's *The World as Will and Representation* and Lange's *History of Materialism* were particularly important. He also read Kant's *Critique of Judgment,* numerous Kant interpreters, and some of the single and multivolume histories of philosophy then available. He planned his dissertation on the concept of the organic since Kant, even though, as noted, he was appointed professor at Basel before receiving his doctorate, thus making the dissertation moot. At Basel, Nietzsche taught courses on Diogenes Laertius, the pre-Socratic philosophers, Plato, Cicero, and aesthetics. He also delivered public lectures on topics as diverse as the future of German education, Hesiod, Aeschylus, Theognis of Megara, Plato, Greek and Roman literature, Greek religious culture, and rhetoric. While he prepared the manuscript of *Birth of Tragedy*, he read Aristotle's views on aesthetics and tragedy.

Nietzsche was an insatiable reader, despite what he sometimes claimed: "I did not read anything else for years—the *greatest* blessing I ever conferred on myself!" (*EH* "Good Books" *HH* 4). In one way, this claim is uninterestingly true: between 1875 and 1880, his eyesight was so bad so regularly that he often had others read books to him. Otherwise, the claim is false: from an early age through his last year of sanity, Nietzsche read consistently, widely, and sometimes deeply. True enough, he was never wealthy and did not own a large library, at least if the more than one thousand volumes that Elisabeth eventually corralled from various lodgings and storage facilities for the Nietzsche archive in Weimar are thought not to be substantial. When he could not afford books, he borrowed them from friends or libraries. Indeed, he chose to live in Nice, Leipzig, and Venice in part because their libraries were of high quality.

Nietzsche's curiosity led him to consume books on an impressive motley of topics, including philology, history, biography, philosophy, poetry, Greek tragedy, physics, chemistry, biology, physiology, psychology, and diet. He read and reread five philosophers repeatedly: Ralph Waldo Emerson, Arthur Schopenhauer, Plato, Friedrich Lange, and Immanuel Kant. At various times, other philosophers impressed him in one way or another. Pre-nineteenth-century philosophers who did so include Democritus, Baruch Spinoza, Michel de Montaigne, Voltaire, David Hume, Friedrich Schiller, Roger Joseph Boscovich, and John Locke; nineteenth-century philosophers include David Strauss, Herbert Spencer, Eduard von Hartmann, John Stuart Mill, Afrikan Spir, Eugen Dühring, Maximilian Drossbach, and Richard Avenarius. In addition, Nietzsche read the works of numerous contemporary scientists, including William Henry Rolph, Wilhelm Roux, Ernst Haeckel, and Hermann von Helmholtz. He also became familiar with the work of Charles Darwin through Lange's *History of Materialism*.

It is customary to distinguish three periods or stages of Nietzsche's philosophical thought. 1869 to 1874 is the early Nietzsche and is represented by *BT* (1872) and *UM* (1873–1876). The middle stage covers his output between 1875 and 1882. Here are included *HH* (1878–1879), *D* (1881), and, with some qualification, *GS*, Books I–IV (1882). The late Nietzsche covers the rest of his output, from 1883 to 1889. Most of his most famous books come from this time. They include *Z* (1883–1885); *BGE* (1886); *GM* (1887); *GS*, Book V (1887); *CW* (1888); *TI* (1889); *NCW* (1889); *A* (written in 1888, published in 1894); and *EH* (written in 1888, published in 1908).

The early Nietzsche read Emerson, Plato, and Schopenhauer more than any others. He read German translations of Emerson while still at

Pforta and continued to dip in and out of *The Conduct of Life*, *Essays*, and *New Essays* until his collapse. It has been suggested that many of Nietzsche's philosophical themes—perspectivism, the Übermensch, eternal return, and will to power, among them—were inspired by similar Emersonian ideas.[1] Some influence cannot be denied. Nietzsche also read Plato's dialogues over and over during his graduate school days and after becoming a professor at Basel, in no small part because he lectured on Plato four times during his career there. He remained ambivalent about Plato to the end. While recognizing the ingenuity of his philosophical systematizing, Nietzsche thought that Plato was a coward in the face of reality and that his system was mistaken from the ground up and ideal down.

Schopenhauer

For almost ten years, Schopenhauer's was the single most important philosophical voice for Nietzsche. His early philosophical views cannot be understood without acknowledging his indebtedness to the views of this "great teacher" (*GM* Preface 5), even if he soon rejected some and later most of them. Although he owned numerous titles, the two works that he read most, *The World as Will and Representation* (1819), the systematic statement of Schopenhauer's philosophical views, and *Parerga and Paralipomena* (1851), a collection of essays designed by Schopenhauer as augmentations to those views, made lasting impacts.

Schopenhauer wrote in the considerable wake of Kant. Like Kant, Schopenhauer argued that the world presented to our sensory apparatus disguises another world, the real or true world. The distinction between the apparent or phenomenal world and the real or noumenal world, central to Kant's transcendental idealism, led him to infer that we can know nothing of the noumenal world or its denizens, things as they are in themselves independent of our sensory perception. Contrary to Kant, Schopenhauer affirmed the knowability of the noumenal world. Nietzsche's views about the phenomenal and noumenal

[1] See Stack 1992.

worlds evolved, from initially agreeing that both existed to eventually claiming that the noumenal world was superfluous and that its redundancy was sufficient refutation of its existence. Having repudiated the noumenal world, Nietzsche inferred the emptiness of any distinction between it and the phenomenal world. There are not two worlds, one apparent and one real; instead, there is only one world, the world as presented to the senses. As he put it, "The 'true world' and the 'world of appearances'—in plain language, the *made-up* world and reality" (*EH* Preface 2).

Further discussion of these epistemological and metaphysical debates can be deferred for the time being. Of immediate relevance is that Schopenhauer affirmed, contrary to Kant, not only that can we know the real world's nature, but, further, that we can know that this nature is willing. To the extent that it can be made clear, Schopenhauer's view seems to have been that we live in a world whose organic and nonorganic citizens are presented to our sensory apparatus as distinct individuals and that an inner nature to all things, living and nonliving alike, can be described as undifferentiated striving or willing. Schopenhauer invoked human suffering as evidence for the truth of this remarkable claim. Ever-present in human life, suffering is the direct consequence of willing. We suffer when we do not have what we desire, so we strive, that is, we will, to get what we lack. Yet, even if we transiently relieve our will when it is satisfied, we soon enough return to suffering again, remembering our momentary satisfaction and desiring it again. Hence, the cycle reboots and continues to do so until we die or liberate ourselves from it.

Schopenhauer thought we can release ourselves from the incessant cycle of suffering by recognizing its omnipresence, understanding that its causes lie in willing itself, and then detaching ourselves from willing. By renouncing our own acts of willing and becoming a disembodied, will-free subject, we free ourselves from the suffering that embodied willing inevitably entails. Nietzsche argued that this "cure" overheated by more than a few degrees: even if suffering characterizes life and willing causes it, Schopenhauer's proposed cure for it was inane. Late in 1888, he dryly remarked that this kind of cognitive "therapy" deserves about as much respect as dentists "who *pluck out* people's teeth just to get rid of the pain" (*TI* "Morality as Anti-nature"

1). For Schopenhauer, annihilating the will and abandoning embodiment, a state of liberated selflessness that is as much metaphysical as it is moral, stood out as an ideal. Nietzsche countered that this metaphysical/moral state is "the *great* danger to mankind" (*GM* Preface 5) and that obliterating the will and forsaking embodiment is nothing less than to will against life itself. In making this state an ideal to strive after and a goal to organize around, Schopenhauer revealed his nihilistic willingness to undermine life in order to ward off its unavoidable suffering.

Since Schopenhauer thought selfless renunciation of desire is an ideal, his emphasis on *Mitleid* (literally, 'suffering with'; we shall translate it as 'compassion' rather than, as some do, 'pity') as the fundamental moral response toward others should be unsurprising. After all, if our own highest state is one in which individual distinctness merges with the undifferentiated whole, and if willing is repudiated, we liberated and desire-free subjects understand, sympathize with, and feel compassion for the suffering that desire causes in others. Yet, for Nietzsche, compassion is symptomatic of all that makes morality wrongheaded:

> What was especially at stake was the value of the "unegoistic," the instincts of compassion, self-abnegation, self-sacrifice, which Schopenhauer had gilded, deified, and projected into a beyond for so long that at last they became for him "values-in-themselves," on the basis of which he *said No* to life and to himself. But it was precisely *these* instincts that there spoke from me an ever more fundamental mistrust, an ever more corrosive skepticism! (*GM* Preface 5)

As will be seen, Nietzsche's opposition to Schopenhauer on these matters is important for understanding his criticism of morality.

Schopenhauer's influence on Nietzsche can be seen especially in *The Birth of Tragedy*, which responds to a standard question posed by Schopenhauer: Is life worth living? Whereas Schopenhauer thought not, Nietzsche gives a positive answer by distinguishing between two forces, the Apollonian (logic, reason, and civility) and the Dionysian (amoral energy). Nietzsche interpreted Greek tragedy as a combination of the Apollonian poet's contemplation of images and forms imposed on the world and Dionysian music. This combination produces a unique synthesis that shows that while life has no happy conclusion, we can nevertheless affirm it by aesthetic intoxication with the unity of the noumenal world. Given this possibility, music can even now underwrite an aesthetic justification of existence. So, instead of seeing in ancient Greece a culture of nobility and rationality, Nietzsche saw an amoral and energetic Dionysian force that was actively suppressed by Apollonian forces. To our detriment, the Apollonian forces have won out.

Lange, Boscovich, and Drossbach

A second important influence on Nietzsche's early philosophical development was Friedrich Lange, whose *History of Materialism* (1866) opened Nietzsche's eyes to the riches and limitations of this philosophical school, which traces its origins back to Leucippus and Democritus. *History of Materialism* is a monumental book. Originally published as a single volume, it expanded during Nietzsche's life to two volumes, each more than five hundred pages long.

Materialism asserts that everything that exists is physical matter or can be reduced to something that is physical matter. Physical matter is thus the substance of what exists. Materialism typically ascribes to matter a restricted class of properties, including extension, hardness, impenetrability (or indivisibility), mobility, and inertia. Materialistic atomism conjoins materialism with the claim that matter reaches a minimum extension in microscopic bits that are impenetrable, indivisible, changeless, and without structure. So, materialistic atomism is the view that material atoms, aggregations of material atoms, and their extension, hardness, impenetrability, mobility, and inertia exhaust existence. To materialism and materialistic atomism may be added the methodological claim that the behavior of atoms and aggregations of them can best be explained mechanistically, where a mechanistic explanation is a mathematical analysis that reduces physical behavior to predictable law-abiding events of matter in motion. Conjoining the ontological claim of materialism and materialistic atomism with the restrictions of mechanism yields mechanistic materialism, the view that matter and aggregations of matter exhaust what exists, and that the behavior of matter and its aggregations is exhaustively explicable as law-abiding events of matter in motion.

Building on and expanding from Isaac Newton's mechanistic physics, significant advances during the nineteenth century in human physiology, chemistry, and physics re-energized mechanistic materialism in Germany. Lange wrote *History of Materialism* in this heated intellectual environment. Nietzsche read and reread it repeatedly for more than ten years, equipping himself to battle mechanistic materialism. Lange both laid out the history of materialism from atomism to mechanistic physics and criticized its many variants from a neo-Kantian perspective. Lange's neo-Kantianism comprised three claims: (1) the phenomenal world as presented in sensory experience is a product of our own cognitive organizational capacities; (2) our sensory organs and our sensory processes of vision, audition, olfaction, taste, and touch are part of the phenomenal world; and (3) our self in and of itself is as unknown to us as are things in themselves.[2] With these claims in tow, Nietzsche argued, with Lange, that materialism, mechanistic physics, mechanistic chemistry, and mechanistic physiology were all mistaken.

Nietzsche objected to both the mathematization of mechanical explanations and the assumption that enduring material objects make up their domain. He thought to the contrary that mechanistic descriptions of physical, chemical, biological, and physiological processes and events employ concepts that inaccurately describe those processes and events. One source of the mismatch was, he thought, that mechanistic concepts are simply a mathematical calculus applied to dynamic processes. Even if such concepts are useful to us as we try to gain knowledge about dynamic processes, they presuppose entities, such as enduring material objects and mathematical features, that are fictions. He put this point as follows in *Gay Science*: mechanistic physics "permits counting, calculating, weighing, seeing, and grasping, and nothing else" (*GS* 373), a set of limitations that flows from the scientist's decision to "operate only with things that do not exist—with lines, surfaces, bodies, atoms, divisible times, divisible

[2] See Brobjer 2008; Green 2002; Hill 2003; Stack 1983.

spaces" (*GS* 112). Since mechanistic concepts misdescribe dynamic processes and events from the start, mechanistic descriptions do not accurately describe what they are invoked to describe, and mechanistic explanations that presuppose those mistaken descriptions do not explain what they are thought to explain.

Nietzsche, following Lange, insisted on the unknowability of any realm beyond the sensory realm and on the falsity of mechanistic descriptions and explanations of what was presented to the senses. Instead, he experimented with views of force that were distinct from Newton's, created proposals about dynamically coupled physical and biological systems, and stressed the importance of evolution in human cognitive development. In these efforts, Nietzsche augmented Lange's neo-Kantian criticisms of materialism and atomism with arguments first developed by Roger Boscovich (1711–1787). Boscovich criticized materialistic atomism and proposed a rival dynamicist account of what matter is if not material. Nietzsche agreed with these proposals. In *BGE* 12, he claims that Boscovich "taught us to renounce belief in the last bit of earth that *did* 'stand still,' the belief in 'matter,' in the 'material,' in the residual piece of earth and clump of an atom." Boscovich argued that materialist atomism made atoms nothing more than submicroscopic ball bearings. Since such corpuscular atoms occupy the base level of explanation in physics, and since all other physical properties and relations reduce to them or aggregations of them, their behavior must be explicable entirely in terms of extension, hardness, impenetrability, mobility, and inertia. As a replacement, Boscovich offered an account of matter that conceives of atoms as nonextended inertial points surrounded by repulsive forces. Such dynamic atoms are centers of forces surrounded by a field of other such centers of forces.

During his mature period, Nietzsche also experimented with different accounts of causation, some more plausible than others. His proposals were influenced both by Boscovich and by Maximilian Drossbach, whose *Über scheinbaren und wirklichen Ursachen des Geschehens in der Welt* (*On Apparent and Real Causes of What Happens in the World*) from 1884 argues among other things that causes and effects make up a continuum of dynamic and constantly interacting forces. Most of Nietzsche's related experiments with causation remained unpublished *Nachlass* notes, but at least once, at *BGE* 36, a version bubbles up into print. Unsurprisingly, *BGE* 36 remains contentious in the scholarly community. Most interpret the passage as advocating a general methodological hypothesis about the reducibility of all forms of causation into drives and will to power, while some offer interpretations that avoid such reduction. We return to these issues in Chapter 4's discussion of will to power. It suffices to note that between 1883 and 1888, Nietzsche was, even if circumspect, not averse to testing ontological, methodological, and epistemological hypotheses that would supply a completely general philosophical backstop for his naturalism.

Roux and Rolph

During the late 1870s and early 1880s, Nietzsche absorbed so many scientific advances that by 1885 he was more than passingly familiar with significant stretches of physics, physiology, experimental biology, and evolution. When he wrote *GM* in 1887, he was already convinced that the experimental biological sciences were well on their way to replacing religious, metaphysical, and philosophical speculation about organisms, their properties, the events, states, processes that occurred within them, and the systems that made them function. He was also fascinated with evolutionary science's discoveries about organisms' origins and their ontogenetic and phylogenetic development. With some qualifications (to be discussed in Chapter 5), he supported many different branches of scientific knowledge and the methods used to gain it. While ambivalent and skeptical about some empirical scientists' pretensions and their widespread commitment to mechanism, he continued to believe that the methods and findings of experimental science sufficed to overturn the wild conjectures about the organic and the psychological domains offered up by religious salespeople, theologians, metaphysical philosophers, and pseudoscientists. One of the components of his naturalism was debunking metaphysical and religious accounts of human agency that start from the presumption that humans are different in kind from the rest of earth's citizens and must, as a consequence, have a distinct transcendental origin from them. He affirmed to the contrary that humans are earthly organisms rather than unearthly beings and that our origins are continuous with and as worldly as those of all natural organisms.

As will be discussed in Chapters 2 and 3, Nietzsche's developmental approach to the origins and spread of moral values and moral evaluative practices paralleled evolutionary investigations into the origins and spread of genetically coded adaptations. Nineteenth-century evolutionary theorists and scientists influenced his rejection of designs, purposes, and logical progression. The work of two contemporary evolutionary physiologists, Wilhelm Roux (1850–1924) and William Henry Rolph (1847–1883), helped jumpstart his thoughts about the nature of organic life. Both emphasized the functional characterization of bodily organs and systems, the ever-changing interplay between parts of an organism, and the dynamic structure of a functioning body. More significantly, both argued that relations between organism and surrounding environment are highly dynamic and complex. Nietzsche took their work as support for his drive/affect psychology and will to power hypotheses. Indeed, it is possible, although unlikely, that he developed the will-to-power hypothesis as a result of reading them (unlikely because Boscovich and Drossbach also discussed force and power at length). It is more likely that all of them helped sharpen his thinking about the ways that drives and power work in human biology, physiology, and psychology.

Roux, a student of Ernst Haeckel and the founder of embryology, published *The Battle of the Parts of the Organism* in 1881. Here he argued that physiology studies self-organizing and dynamic systems whose components, from molecules to cells to tissues to organs, process stimuli and struggle for sustenance in the organism. Components that enhance the organism's adaptation to the external environment tend to survive the intraorganismic battle, while those that do not atrophy and disappear. Since each component has a particular function partially determined by the overall functioning of the organism, transitory equilibria between components develop and dissolve in service of those organismic functions. And since the organism is embedded in a constantly changing environment, whatever internal equilibria emerge are continuously subjected to ongoing external disruption, thus eventuating in the emergence of organismic self-regulation and self-governance.

Nietzsche closely examined Roux's dynamicist physiology and developed some of its implications in the *Nachlass* notes from 1883 onward. Nietzsche agreed with Roux that organisms are dynamic and self-organizing complexes, that these self-organizing systems are internally structured in a hierarchical manner so that some components command while others obey, that these hierarchically structured self-organizing systems are self-regulating and engage in self-originating motion and behavior, and that command-and-obedience hierarchies provide the self-organization necessary for suborganismic and organismic self-regulation. As will be seen, self-regulation and self-governance are the basis of Nietzsche's understanding of what allows social organisms such as human beings to survive. The body comprising a person is a battleground of causally coupled self-regulating systems, tissues, and organs, each playing a role in satisfying physiological functions that themselves self-regulate and compete with other such functions. Even cognitive abilities such as rationality, logic, and consciousness are components of this dynamic self-regulative regime, and they work together to enhance life.

Indeed, thinking of consciousness as a dynamic self-regulative regime in the service of enhancing life was so compelling that Nietzsche suggested that we rehabilitate the term 'soul' in its terms. We can, he claimed, think of the soul as "subjective multiplicity" or "as social structure of the drives and affects" (*BGE* 12). Given this new understanding, the word 'soul' can refer to something natural rather than something abstract and transcendental. Of course, understanding this newly naturalized soul is intimidating, for it entails a full account of our human form of life and the role of consciousness in it:

> By putting an end to the superstition that until now has grown around the idea of the soul with an almost tropical luxuriance, the new psychologist clearly thrusts himself into a new wasteland and a new suspicion. The old psychologists might have found things easier and more enjoyable—: but, in the end, the new psychologist knows by this very token that he is condemned to invention—and, who knows? perhaps to discovery. (*BGE* 12)

In short, we now have to reinvent our conception of ourselves, the nature of our subjectivity, our agency, and our unity or identity over time. We return to these issues in Chapter 4's discussion of subjectivity and agency.

Rolph published *Biologische Probleme* in 1882. Contrary to then-popular interpretations of Darwin, Rolph argued that the struggle for existence is not the primary mechanism for evolutionary development and that the instinct for self-preservation does not exist. He countered that all organisms seek to expand themselves and their influence on the world by assimilating and appropriating whatever they find and giving new form to it, even if it jeopardizes their own existence. Nietzsche read Rolph's book in 1884, and thereafter his *Nachlass* notes are peppered with similar concepts and arguments. For example, he agreed with Rolph that assimilation, appropriation, and reshaping are paramount drives, and he frequently couched his own developing concept of will to power as the expansion of influence on the environment by accumulating and discharging force through appropriation, assimilation, and form-giving.

During this period, he also reflected on Rolph's claim that self-preservation is not found in every organism. Nietzsche frequently rejected Rolph's categorical claim that there is no drive for self-preservation, preferring instead to claim that such a drive is found only in suffering organisms whose other drives are degraded. A passage from *GS* states his alternative view clearly:

> To wish to preserve oneself is a sign of distress, of a limitation of the truly basic life-instinct, which aims at *the expansion of power* and in so doing often enough risks and sacrifices self-preservation . . . in nature, it is not distress which *rules,* but rather abundance, squandering—even to the point of absurdity. The struggle for survival is only an *exception,* a temporary restriction of the will to life; the great and small struggle revolves everywhere around preponderance, around growth and expansion, around power and in accordance with the will to power, which is simply the will to life. (*GS* 349)

Here the drive to self-preservation is a symptom of distress and weakness rather than health and strength. When organisms are exhausted their concerns turn to self-preservation, rest, relaxation, and peace so that they might recover. On the other hand, the healthy and the strong routinely ignore what is best for their own self-preservation because their drives are for more opponents to conquer and more opportunities for their power to be exercised. Of course, relentless assimilation, appropriation, and form-giving can risk self-destruction, for where one reaches beyond what can be done to self-organize and self-regulate what has been appropriated, disorganization ensues. In such cases, self-destruction or division are the only way forward. Hence, at every level of description of biological organisms, appropriation, assimilation, and incorporation are risky, even to the point of self-destruction. Again, we return to these matters in Chapter 4 and Chapter 5.

1.4 Legacy

Nietzsche's impact on twentieth- and twenty-first-century culture is wide, deep, varied, and troubled. Since even summarizing its many aspects in a few pages is impossible, we will instead trace its general trajectory and suggest a few of its dimensions.

During the ten years that he lingered after collapsing in 1889, Nietzsche developed into the intellectual "*force majeure*" (*EH* "Why I Am a Destiny" 8) he had expected to become. As noted above, Georg Brandes served as his European herald. Between 1889 and World War I, in both Europe and the United States, Nietzsche's work was discussed and dissected by an entire generation of intellectuals, political radicals of both the left and right, anarchists, romantics, creative artists, theologians, philosophers, cultural historians, psychologists, and social critics. Indeed, it must sometimes have seemed during this period that most of the European and American cultural elite thought of themselves or their movement or their thought as exemplifications or applications of, or at least consistent with, some aspect of Nietzsche's thought. A partial list of those influenced by Nietzsche includes authors H. L. Mencken, D. H. Lawrence, Hermann Hesse, Franz Kafka, Joseph Conrad, Jack London, Thomas Mann, Upton Sinclair, and Kahlil Gibran, playwrights George Bernard Shaw, August Strindberg, and Eugene O'Neill, socialists Max Eastman and Hubert Harrison, philosophers George Santayana, Josiah Royce, Martin Buber, Theodor Lessing, and William James, psychologists Carl Jung and Sigmund Freud, composers Richard Strauss, Gustav Mahler, and Frederick Delius, occultists Rudolf Steiner and Aleister Crowley, the anarchist Emma Goldman, and the Zionist Theodor Herzl.

When World War I broke out, Germany's frightening militaristic ambition and ugly ethnic nationalism came into full view. So too did its regrettable willingness to exploit Nietzsche's work as ideological justification for its xenophobic aggression. German soldiers were given copies of *Z* to take with them to battle, and German propagandists raved about Nietzsche's warrior philosophy. As a result, his reputation among European and American intellectuals was by the end of World War I decidedly tarnished. Despite continued philosophical interest in his thinking during the interwar period, expressed by Karl Jaspers, Karl Löwith, George Bataille, Jean-Paul Sartre, Albert Camus, Paul Tillich, and Martin Heidegger, his standing plummeted when German Nazis and Italian fascists appealed to passages from his work—*GM* and *Z* in particular—to justify their odious brutality against Jews, Romani, sub-Saharan Africans, Slavs, gay people, and other "non-Aryans." Nietzsche's sister Elisabeth abetted the cause by encouraging antisemites in particular to worship him as a prophet, something that would have horrified him had he witnessed it.

By 1945, Nietzsche was a pariah, his philosophical work rejected or ignored by most serious intellectuals, revealing how even a tenuous connection with the loathsome can result in censure. For Nietzsche was neither a proto-Nazi nor a proto-fascist. As others have shown, he ridiculed nineteenth-century antisemites, thought of himself as an anti-antisemite, and was contemptuous of the militaristic nationalism fermenting in Germany. He mocked antisemites who "roll their Christian-Aryan-Philistine eyes and try to stir up the bovine elements in the population through a misuse . . . of the cheapest means of agitating, the moralistic attitude" (*GM* III 26), and he loathed Germans and Germany, stating that one of his ambitions was to be the "despiser of Germans *par excellence*" (*EH* "Good Books" *CW* 4). The rallying cry "*Deutschland, Deutschland, über alles*" was, he thought, symptomatic of a national neurosis, and he condemned Germans as being solely responsible for "*all the great crimes of the past four hundred years*" and for cheating all of Europe out of "the harvest, the meaning, of the last *great* age, the age of the Renaissance" (*EH* "Good Books" *CW* 2; see also *GM* III 26). Finally, he asserted that Germans themselves "have no idea how vulgar they are; . . . they are not even *ashamed* of being merely Germans" (*EH* "Good Books" *CW* 4). Hence, forty years before the emergence of Nazism, Nietzsche had already denounced Germany and its citizens for antisemitism, cultural arrogance, nationalism, and Teutonic pride. However, it was exactly these fixations that Adolf Hitler and other Nazis such as Alfred Rosenberg and Alfred Baeumler would later glorify and organize German National Socialism around. A parallel argument applies to Benito Mussolini's glorification of Nietzsche in fascist Italy.

Nietzsche occasionally offers up stereotypes of ancient Jewish religious leaders. So, if stereotyping ancient Jewish religious leaders is sufficient for being antisemitic, then Nietzsche was an antisemite. Of course, he stereotypes many other groups as well—Christians, Germans, English, the old masters, aristocrats, priests, warriors, slaves, the herd (the list goes on for quite some time)—so his stereotyping tendencies are multidimensional. However, even if stereotyping is intellectually lazy and supplies targets for bigotry, more than stereotyping is needed for bigotry. Nietzsche never infers, as antisemites do, that modern Jews are dangerous to other groups. Nor does he ever suggest that vengeful actions against Jews are justified. Indeed, contrary to nineteenth-century antisemitism, he argues against shutting down Jewish immigration into Germany. As he notes, Jews "thirst for some place where they can be settled, permitted, respected at last and where can put an end to the nomadic life; . . . and this urge and impulse . . . should be carefully noted and accommodated—in which case it might be practical and appropriate to throw the anti-Semitic hooligans out of the country" (*BGE* 251). Instead, he defends keeping Germany open to Jewish immigrants because they are "without a doubt the strongest, most tenacious and purest race now living Europe," and he is convinced that "Jews, if they wanted (or if they were forced, as the antisemite seem to want) *could* already be dominant or indeed could quite literally have control over present-day Europe" (*BGE* 251). Similarly, he notes that "Europe owes the Jews no small thanks for making its people more logical, for *cleanlier* intellectual habits. . . . Wherever Jews have gained influence, they have taught people to make finer distinctions, draw more rigorous conclusions, and to write more clearly and cleanly" (*GS* 348). Although notions of Jews running the world continue to cause harm to this day, Nietzsche's hospitable embrace of Jewish immigrants in Germany and his praise of their strength, tenacity, and intellectual health are utterly at odds with antisemitism.

Between 1950 and 1980, Nietzsche's reputation slowly re-formed, and philosophers, literary critics, sociologists, and cultural critics once again took up his work. Given the fecundity of his thought, it was predictable that this rehabilitation was multifaceted. In Japan, Nishitani Keiji studied Nietzsche extensively and was especially impressed with Nietzsche's analyses of nihilism. In Europe, German critical theorists Max Horkheimer, Theodor Adorno, and Herbert Marcuse, along with social psychologists Erich Fromm and Rollo May, relied on Nietzsche's bleak assessments of modern society to help understand the failure of the Enlightenment and science to prevent the horrors of fascism and, more generally, to clarify some of the deep pathologies of twentieth-century civilization. Nietzsche's suspicious distrust of scientifically accepted views of complex psychosocial matters influenced Paul Ricœur's hermeneutic philosophical anthropology, Michel Foucault's detailed archaeologies of social power and genealogies of punishment, and Gilles Deleuze's and Félix Guattari's work on memory and the formation of social collectives. So too, Nietzsche's rejection of the myths we tell ourselves about the grand projects of history, culture, and philosophy, his rejection of absolute truth, knowledge, and determinate semantic meaning, and his insistence that we investigate the genealogical details of the formation of human subjectivity and the incremental development of social organization helped undergird deconstructionist and postmodern directions in European thought in the 1970s and early 1980s, as exemplified in the work of Jacques Derrida, Paul de Man, Sarah Kofman, Jean-François Lyotard, and Maurice Blanchot.

During this same period in the United States, Nietzsche's influence on philosophy and culture was significant, but not as pronounced as in Europe. Walter Kaufmann's *Nietzsche: Philosopher, Psychologist, Anti-Christ*, originally published in 1950 and still in print, effectively defended Nietzsche against the charge of being a proto-Nazi and presented his thought as a precursor to existentialism and secular humanism, thus earning him a role in the counterculture's rejection of bourgeois establishment values during the 1960s and 1970s. Kaufmann's book also reopened the door for academic philosophers to read Nietzsche without embarrassment, and a small cohort—Arthur Danto, Robert Solomon, Philippa Foot, Ivan Soll, Richard Schacht, and John Wilcox, among them—began digging through his arguments more carefully during the 1960s, 1970s, and early 1980s. As in Europe, other intellectuals found elements of Nietzsche's thinking to be a springboard for their own. Thomas J. J. Altizer used Nietzsche's *GM* analyses of Christianity and asceticism to warrant the death-of-God movement; Richard Rubenstein adopted some of Nietzsche's reflections about modern Judaism to better understand his own faith; and Huey P. Newton applied Nietzsche's understanding of power, slave morality, ressentiment, and fluid semantic meaning to the Black Panthers' analysis of oppression of African Americans and the call for Black Power and liberation from racist social and legal structures.

Matters became more intellectually combustible in the 1980s and 1990s when deconstructionist and postmodernist uses of certain themes in Nietzsche's philosophy infiltrated feminist theory, literary criticism, and American philosophy. In feminist theory, Judith Butler applied Nietzsche's rejection of essences and his criticism of philosophical concepts of subjectivity to sexual and gender identity, arguing that the former is not necessarily linked to the latter and that both are less static than typically assumed. Stripped of biological essence and freed from mythological constraints imposed on subjectivity by philosophers, gendered subjectivity and personhood are instead loci of liberation, construction, and creation. This antiessentialist conceptual framework helped usher in third-wave feminism in the United States and Europe.

Literary critics, including Paul de Man, J. Hillis Miller, and Geoffrey Hartmann, also absorbed deconstruction and postmodernism. By so doing, they exposed their indebtedness to Nietzsche's rejection of determinate semantic meaning and a unified subject. These critics used Nietzsche's claims to drive deflationary and wildly relativistic conclusions regarding the meaning of a text, the author's intentions for a text, and the audience's reception of a text. Unsurprisingly, this direction in criticism prompted a backlash from other critics. Allan Bloom named Nietzsche as a precursor of an unpalatable cultural relativism, while his student Francis Fukuyama appropriated Nietzsche's critical stance against democracy to argue against the relativism postmodernists celebrated. Nietzsche's example as a unique literary voice was also a catalyst for Harold Bloom's peevish disputes with many trends in criticism. He especially admired *GM*, which he thought was the "profoundest study available to me of the revisionary and ascetic strains in the aesthetic temperament."[3]

Unsurprisingly, Nietzsche became a lightning rod in philosophy as well, attracting postmodernists sympathetic to his rejection of essences and epistemological foundations and attracted to his perspectivist conception of truth and the relativism they inferred from it. In response, those opposed to postmodernism's stultifying consequences but sympathetic to Nietzsche tried to find ways to accept his views and reject the postmodernists' use of them. Similarly, pragmatists such as Richard Rorty and Emersonians such as Stanley Cavell appropriated certain of Nietzsche's views to infer quite extraordinary conclusions about the collapse of ontological, epistemological, alethic, and moral foundations, and even to infer that we are now adrift in a postphilosophical world without direction. Rorty played the leading role in this stream of Nietzsche interpretation and application. In *Contingency, Irony, and Solidarity* and other works, he interpreted Nietzsche's advocacy of contingent subjectivity, perspectivist truth, ironic good spirits when confronted by human pretensions to absolutes, creative self-discovery, and self-perfection as precursors to his own antifoundationalist views, even if he parted ways with what he thought was Nietzsche's pessimism regarding social progress, solidarity, and democracy.

This turbulent intellectual environment once again made it clear that Nietzsche's thoughts about a host of philosophically charged issues were subject to different, even contradictory, interpretations, and that careful assessments of his arguments about these issues were needed. It would be too much to say that without the postmodern and pragmatic

[3] Bloom 1997, 8.

appropriations of Nietzsche in the 1980s and 1990s, Nietzsche scholarship would not have flourished as it has since then. Still, disagreements with those approaches did provide a milieu in which Nietzsche's continued relevance to philosophy and culture was confirmed. That in turn has led to renewed scholarly interest in all of the many facets of his thought, and in the last twenty-five years thousands of articles and hundreds of books have been published about Nietzsche, many of them about arguments developed in *GM*. With this proliferation, academic scholarship about Nietzsche has finally achieved the level of care, rigor, and sophistication that his work has always deserved and that the work of other great philosophers has received for many decades.

Further Reading

For more on Nietzsche's life, see Hayman 1980; Hollingdale 1999; Huenemann 2013; Kaufmann 1974; Parkes 2013; Salome 1894/2001; Young 2010.

For more on Nietzsche's intellectual influences, see Brobjer 2008; Green 2002; Hill 2003; Janaway 1998, 2007; Kaufmann 1974; Moore 2002; Müller-Lauter 1971/1999; Schacht 1983; Simmel 1907/1991; Soll 2013; Stack 1983, 1992; Zavatta 2019.

For more on Nietzsche's alleged antisemitism, see Holub 2015; Kaufmann 1974; Leiter 2015; Yovel 1998, 2006. For more on various facets of Nietzsche's legacy, see Aschheim 1992; Bloom, A. 1987; Bloom, H. 1997; Gemes 2001b; Ratner-Rosenhagen 2012; Robertson and Owen 2013; Schrift 1995.

2
Genealogy Preface

2.1 Introduction

When even the first sentence of a book's preface disorients expectations, we know we are in for an unsettling read. Why would anyone start a scholarly book on morality by admitting that those of us who work to gain knowledge about morality do not know ourselves precisely because we try to know? Nietzsche uses this curiously personal question to grab our attention. His answers, some of which he does not offer until the last section of Essay III, leave us no choice but to remain vigilant to the differences between *GM* and other books we have read. As he continues, it becomes clear that the issues he discusses in *GM* are not just theoretical exercises but matters that lie at the core of how he thinks about himself, how we all think about ourselves, and how we all interact with each other and the natural environment.

In the discussion section for this chapter, we describe Nietzsche's claims on behalf of the genealogical method of knowledge acquisition and show that the method is conceptually similar to some used in evolutionary biology. We next introduce Nietzsche's philosophical naturalism, which is a set of claims about what exists, what can be known, and how knowledge is best acquired. Nietzsche is a consistent, albeit unusual, philosophical naturalist. Third, we summarize errors made by previous philosophers, theologians, and religious advocates about moral psychology. Finally, we introduce what Nietzsche thinks morality and moral evaluation are.

Nietzsche's On the Genealogy of Morality. Rex Welshon, Oxford University Press.
 DOI: 10.1093/oso/9780197611814.003.0003

2.2 The Preface by the Sections

Sections 1–3

A preface typically states a book's subject or topic, its scope, the author's aims for writing the book, and a little of the author's own history with the topic. Nietzsche does this, but only later in his Preface. Section 1 starts with the provocation, how could we knowers ever know about ourselves since we have never looked for ourselves and are, by necessity, strangers to ourselves? He supplies no direct answer here, nor, for that matter, in the rest of the Preface. Why, then, does he start the book with this loaded question? Splitting the question up into its two constituents will help us find an answer. The first question is, how could we knowers ever know about ourselves if we have never looked for ourselves? The second question is, how could we knowers ever know about ourselves if we are, by necessity, strangers to ourselves?

The first question is directed to those of us who seek knowledge and the treasure that it promises. We knowers do not have the time or, as he puts it, the "seriousness" (*GM* Preface 1), for the rest of life's experiences. In our drive to gain ever more knowledge, we knowers live in a bubble of learning, oblivious to ourselves and to our own lives. We are, as he puts it, like someone distracted by a daydream, so preoccupied that even a nearby tolling bell goes unheard until it breaks through and we ask ourselves what all the noise is about. Given our distraction, we knowledge seekers—intellectuals of all types but scientists, scholars, and philosophers in particular—are strangers to ourselves so long as we are still in thrall of our pursuit. We avoid knowing anything about ourselves or our experiences that might be inconsistent with the pursuit of knowledge, and so we end up foregoing self-knowledge. Indeed, we face a dilemma. Either we pursue knowledge and remain strangers to ourselves and our experience, or we learn about ourselves and our experience and abandon the pursuit of knowledge. So long as we continue to pursue knowledge, "[W]e *have* to misunderstand ourselves" (*GM* Preface 1).

Two other questions appear at once. First, why does Nietzsche open *GM* in this idiosyncratic manner? Second, is it true that so long as we pursue knowledge, we must misunderstand ourselves? An answer to the first question is that Nietzsche is alerting the reader that he includes himself within the scope of analysis of what is to come. *GM*'s analysis of the origins of morality, moral values, and the spread of moral evaluative practices—the genealogy of these phenomena—and all the implications that flow from that genealogy apply to those who accept it, including Nietzsche himself. However, this suggestion only skims the surface of a more interesting answer. By including himself within the scope of the upcoming study, Nietzsche acknowledges that as an exemplar of the philosophical type he too is ignorant of himself.

It can seem that Nietzsche is simply wrong that we cannot both pursue knowledge and know ourselves. After all, jointly achieving the two tasks is impossible only if something about the one entails the impossibility of doing the other. But here in the Preface, Nietzsche merely asserts that this is so; he gives no reasons for the assertion. Of course, doing both to the exclusion of the other is impossible, but that is an uninteresting semantic consequence of the word "exclusion." Short of exclusion, Nietzsche owes us an explanation of why pursuing knowledge is inconsistent with knowing ourselves. It cannot simply be that we lack the time or energy to do both. We can selectively allocate energy and time; working on knowledge of other things some of the time and getting to know ourselves better at other times is certainly possible. Nietzsche does offer an answer later, and we return to it later, in Chapter 5. For the time being, this concern and the one broached in the previous paragraph remain unresolved.

Section 2 starts to do what we typically expect from a preface. Nietzsche announces that the subject of *GM* is the origin (*Herkunft*, which can also be translated as "descent") of the prejudices (*Vorurteil*, which can also be translated as "presumption") of morality. He acknowledges that this is not an entirely new topic for him and that embryonic versions of his thoughts about it have already emerged in earlier works. Still, it was only during his sabbatical year in Sorrento that he started to commit these thoughts to paper, eventually published in *HH* (he later draws attention to *HH* I 45, 92, 96, 99, 136 and to *WS*, 22, 26, and 33). So for ten years his thoughts about the matters previously discussed in *HH*, again in *D*, *GS*, and *BGE*, and investigated in detail here in *GM*, have been consistent.

As the book's subtitle states, *GM* is a polemic, an intentionally contentious argument about a controversial topic. His target is the origin of our moral prejudices or presumptions and their subsequent historical spread, which at least as he phrases the matter are controversial topics. After all, why think that moral values and moral evaluation are prejudicial or presumptuous? And why think that moral values and moral evaluation disperse through a group and have histories? We address these questions below in the discussion section. Moreover, the method he has chosen will, he tells us, be deliberately combative. Of course, he thinks that combativeness is exactly what should be demanded from a philosopher like him, someone who, as he admits elsewhere, is fundamentally "warlike by nature" (*EH* "Why I Am So Wise" 7).

In Section 3, Nietzsche admits that he is, and has been since he was a teenager, fascinated by the origins of good (*Gut*) and evil (*Böse*). This attraction has been so strong in him that he openly wonders whether he might call it his "a priori." That is an odd thing to say, since "a priori" means a kind of knowledge that is independent of observation or experience or a kind of reasoning that proceeds by deduction, or both. So Nietzsche here suggests that his curiosity was something that, at the age of thirteen, he discovered without experiential prompting, and, moreover, that it led him to hold God responsible for the creation of evil. (Given this solution to the problem of evil—typically stated as the question, How, if God is all-powerful, all-knowing, and all-good, can there be evil?—one understands why his teachers at Pforta were sometimes astonished by Nietzsche's precocity.)

What follows this disclosure is prototypically Nietzschean: a dense, gratuitously autobiographical, and perversely elliptical sequence that leads to a substantive philosophical conclusion. He contrasts his curiosity about the worldly origins of good and evil and his explanation of them with Kant's contrary explanation that good and evil come from "*behind* the world" (*GM* Preface 3), the realm that only human souls inhabit insofar as we are rational agents. This "real" world behind the world given in sensory experience is the source of Kant's famous categorical imperative, one version of which states that we must act so that the maxim of our action can be willed as a universal law. Nietzsche counters with his own "anti-Kantian" (*GM* Preface, 3) imperative: psychology, philology, and history should be used to guide inquiries into why people believe as they do about morality; describe how linguistic and social practices about moral evaluation develop to accommodate and express our beliefs about morality; and fix the physiological, psychological, social, and cultural mechanisms by which those beliefs and practices have over the centuries been implemented.

The genealogical project is, thus, to ask,

> [U]nder what conditions did humanity invent the value judgments of good and evil? *and what value do they have themselves?* Have they so far promoted or hindered the thriving of human beings? Are they a sign of distress, impoverishment, degeneration of life? Or conversely, do they reveal the fullness, strength, and will to life, its courage, confidence in its future? (*GM* Preface 3)

Genealogy has two components. The first is to describe how we came to hold our beliefs and judgments about good and evil and to identify the mechanisms for enforcing those beliefs, and the second is to critically analyze the value that moral values have. Most of *GM* is devoted to the first task of genealogy, but it must be acknowledged that toward the end of each essay, Nietzsche's descriptions become laden with evaluative judgments about the topics he is describing. Recall too that the entirety of *GM* lies within the scope of the evaluative context fixed by the second task, that of critiquing the values whose development is described, even if that task is not its primary focus. As Sections 5 and 6 of the Preface make clear, Nietzsche never doubts that the two components are distinct: as he puts the point elsewhere, a "*history of the origins* of [moral] feelings and valuations" is quite different from a "a critique of those feelings and valuations" (*GS* 345).

The critique of moral valuations and determining the value of moral values are more interesting endeavors than providing the history of moral valuation. Finding an answer to those questions is, as already noted, the goal of Nietzsche's planned magnum opus on the revaluation of values, for which *GM* provides "three crucial preparatory works" (*EH* "Good Books" *GM*). While these preliminary studies do not state the results of that revaluation, they do rely on those results. Here in the Preface, as indeed throughout *GM* for that matter, he shows some of the cards in his hand. The standard against which the value of moral values and ideals should be measured is whether they promote or hinder human flourishing, that is, whether they are symptoms of psychological and cultural sickness and decadence or psychological and cultural flourishing health. Of course, it is up to the revaluation of values to determine and describe human flourishing, and we know that Nietzsche did not complete that project. Here it is enough to note that *GM* is a recognizable intellectual project that presents historical, psychological, philological, and philosophical evidence about the origins of our moral beliefs, our moral evaluative practices, and our moral values. And, given that morality has historically been understood as the branch of intellectual inquiry that lays down the principles of how one ought or should live, the gravity of the project is manifest. We return to these matters in Chapter 3's discussion of life, strength, and health, Chapter 4's discussion of will to power, and Chapter 5's discussion of asceticism and nihilism.

Sections 4–6

Nietzsche's thinking about moral values sharpened considerably during the six months he spent in Sorrento with Paul Rée; indeed, it might never have gone in the direction it did without having read Rée's *Psychological Observations* before Sorrento, without their daily discussions about moral psychology during their time together, and without having read Rée's *The Origin of Moral Sensations* when it appeared in 1877. The letters from this period leave no doubt that he was so impressed with Rée's insights that his own philosophical perspective fundamentally changed. Yet all that Nietzsche distills here from these transformative encounters is that he opposes virtually everything that Rée says in *The Origin of Moral Sensations*. He derides Rée as a genealogist of an English kind (which, we will see, is an insult), and he presents Rée's book as noteworthy only because it is contrary to his own earlier efforts and to what he now says in *GM*. In the last part of the section, Nietzsche mentions certain sections from *HH*, both as proof for his long-lasting interest in these topics and as comparison points with Rée's views about the same topics. Beyond that, he acknowledges nothing.

Even while writing *HH* and *D*, Nietzsche was interested in something larger than the origin of morality, namely, the value of unegoistic moral values, compassion chief among them, that Schopenhauer championed. Nietzsche acknowledges in Section 5 that understanding the origins of morality is only one way among others to come to a fuller understanding about the more important philosophical task of valuing morality. Other kinds of studies will help reveal other facets of morality and will therefore also contribute to a better knowledge of its value. He does not mention what these other studies are, but he later suggests that "*all* science must, from now on, prepare the way for the future work of the philosopher: this work being understood to mean that the philosopher has to solve the *problem of values* and that he has to decide on the *rank order of values*" (*GM* I 17). Nietzsche's claim is notable. In his mind, *GM* is a modest book that presents a description of how our moral evaluative practices have developed over the previous three millennia, but it does not critique those practices. This critique is more significant than what *GM* offers, and we know that it remained unfinished. However, we should take care not to dismiss *GM's* importance. Its instrumental value does not imply that it has no value until the value of morality is settled. Uncovering the history of moral values matters because otherwise the principal undertaking of critiquing those values will be flawed. We return to this matter in the discussion section.

Given what he has already said, Section 6 is a little repetitious, although it clearly states Nietzsche's aims for *GM*. He again uses a topographic metaphor to explain how his original doubts about the value of Schopenhauerian compassion led him to a dizzying vista where faith in the value of our inherited morality is held up to scrutiny. This extensive project is described here:

> We need a *critique* of moral values, *the value of these values themselves must first be called into question*—and for this what is needed is knowledge of the conditions and circumstances from which they grew and under which they evolved and changed (morality as consequence, as symptom, as mask, as tartuffery, as illness, as misunderstanding; but also morality as cause, as remedy, as stimulus, as

> obstacle, as poison), such knowledge as has never before existed or even been desired. (*GM* Preface 6)

The disruption that Nietzsche foresees if this critique and its attendant revaluation of moral value were to be completed is considerable, for it threatens to destabilize every moral code premised on the assumed value of useful or unegoistic actions. His critique might expose that morality endangers human flourishing, that it is a seductive narcotic and poison that undercuts future possibilities for a robust and cheerful life. If so, the subsequent revaluing of moral values might find that existing moral codes are "the danger of dangers" (*GM* Preface 6) and require an absolute veto.

Sections 7–8

In Section 7, Nietzsche again disparages Rée and others who have investigated the origins of morality. He had hoped that Rée would be a "comrade," a fellow investigator of the "hidden land of morality" (*GM* Preface 7). Indeed, he claims that he tried to warn Rée away from the "English indulgence" of random hypotheses created out of the blue. Sadly, he failed and is still looking for others who share his conviction that what we must attend to when investigating humanity's moral past is that which has actually happened. Rée strayed when he followed the English habit of cramming contemporary morality together with the explanatory viewpoint of Darwinian evolution and the utility of actions for others. As will be seen in Essay I, Nietzsche is not unequivocally hostile to Darwin or evolutionary hypotheses about morality. After all, Darwin recognized the animal in humanity and so avoided the ludicrous and antinatural explanations offered by most philosophers and all theologians. However, when Rée's Darwinian beast (*Darwin'sche Bestie*) holds hands with the modern moral wimp (*Moral-Zärtling*), the result is a forced attachment according to which the moral animal is preferable simply because it has been reproductively more successful. This moral animal who "no longer bites" (*GM* Preface 7) is so feeble and weary that it cannot even recognize that the origins and later development of morality need to be taken seriously.

Even less can Rée or the other English psychologists diagnose this moral animal as a problem. Yet, recognizing that morality is a problem is the crucial issue: "The question of the origins of moral values is a question of the *first rank* for me because it determines the future of humanity" (*EH* "Good Books" *D* 2). Few things are more important than understanding this origin and the bewildering nature of the contemporary moral animal that developed from that origin. More than any other single institution, Nietzsche holds religion in general and Christianity in particular responsible for molding the human animal into its modern moral form:

> The demand that people *believe* that everything is really in the best hands, that one book, the Bible, gives us definitive assurances of the divine control and wisdom presiding over the fate of humanity—translated back into reality, this is the will to suppress the fact that the pathetic opposite has been the case so far, that humanity has been in the *worst* hands, that it has been governed by people who are in bad shape and full of malice and revenge, the so-called "saints," these slanderers of the world and desecraters of humanity. (*EH* "Good Books" *D* 2)

At the end of Section 7, he adds that seriousness must be coupled with cheerfulness. Stripped of transcendental origins and theological trappings, morality becomes one more naturalized possibility "for the Dionysian drama of the 'destiny of the soul' " (*GM* Preface 7). Thus, morality becomes part of the comedy of that "great, ancient, eternal comic poet of our existence" (*GM* Preface 7).

Nietzsche concludes the Preface with more warnings. He suggests that if we find *GM* grating or incomprehensible, that is not his fault. Without already having read his earlier books (he mentions *Z* in particular), we will not have already been wounded and delighted by his thoughts. Most *GM* readers would probably be grateful if Nietzsche were a little less severe with us and a little more accepting of our shortcomings. But he will not patronize us or appease our deficiencies. He requires that we intellectually and emotionally engage, as he has, with a project that has never been tried by anyone whose spirit is clearer, more relentless, or more joyful.

2.3 Discussion

Among the many claims that Nietzsche makes in the Preface, his stated goal to supply genealogical descriptions of the origins of the ways we think about moral values and moral evaluation stands out. These genealogical descriptions will puncture the pretensions of otherworldly and non-natural religious, theological, and philosophical descriptions of these matters and replace them with earthly and natural ones. As a deflation and replacement project, Nietzsche's genealogy prepares the ground for the revaluation of values and evaluative practices that he never completed. However, we know that during 1887 he was working hard on that project and that its philosophical commitments are always lurking below the surface of *GM*'s text.

To be better prepared for what we will later encounter, we here describe in a little greater detail what genealogy is, introduce Nietzsche's philosophical naturalism, identify some psychological mistakes made by previous philosophers, theologians, and religious advocates, and describe what he thinks morality and moral evaluation are. In later chapters, we will unpack these general sketches in greater detail.

Genealogy as a Method

Humans, like other mammals, are ethological and etiological organisms, that is, we have certain natural characteristics that have identifiable causal histories. Genealogy is Nietzsche's etiological method for describing the causal history of select ethological characteristics. While *GM*'s genealogy focuses directly on the morality we have inherited over the last two or three thousand years, it also implicates genealogies of moral psychology, metaphysics, theology, and numerous social practices and institutions. And while genealogy supplies histories of these physiological, psychological, social, and religious phenomena, it does more than that. By describing them as historical, genealogy exposes that they are contingent, that they could have been otherwise than they are. This point cannot be overemphasized. Morality and theology have typically presented themselves as unconditional rather than contingent in origin and as unqualified rather than restricted in scope; moral psychology has typically been presented as demarcating the necessary conditions of human subjectivity and agency; and the purposes of our social institutions have typically been thought to remain constant over time. Genealogy exposes that human nature is neither transcendental nor fixed, that theology and morality are neither divinely inspired nor universal, and that social functions are neither stable nor immutable. Each is as contingent and as dependent on our place in natural and social environments as every other facet of human life. Genealogy shows how we emerged as the complicated and tortured animals we are, why we organized ourselves socially and morally, how and why we created gods and God, and how and why we came to believe the fictions we tell ourselves about ourselves and our place in the world. Deflating the pretensions about who we think we are, what we believe about moral values, and how we think about religious matters and social institutions is built into *GM*'s project. For this reason alone, *GM* is highly destructive.

At the very center of *GM*—*GM* II 12—Nietzsche describes the genealogical method in more detail than anywhere else in *GM*, or, for that matter, anywhere else in his published work. He confirms here that genealogy is a method of historical inquiry and that his specific targets are the origins and development of certain evaluative, moral, religious, social, and psychological characteristics and phenomena in human populations. The beginning of this passage states the method clearly:

> [T]he origin of the emergence of a thing and its ultimate usefulness, its practical application and incorporation into a system of ends, are *toto coelo* separate; . . . anything in existence, having somehow come about, is continually interpreted anew, requisitioned anew, transformed and redirected to a new purpose by a power superior to it; . . . everything that occurs in the organic world consists of *overpowering, dominating*, and in their turn, overpowering and dominating consist of re-interpretation, adjustment, in the process of which their former "meaning" [*Sinn*] and "purpose" must necessarily be obscured or completely obliterated. No matter how perfectly you have understood the *usefulness* of any physiological organ (or legal institution, social custom, political practice, art form or religious rite), you have not yet thereby grasped how it

> emerged: uncomfortable and unpleasant as this may sound to more elderly ears,—for people down the ages have believed that the obvious purpose of a thing, its utility, form and shape, are its reason for existence, the eye is made to see, the hand to grasp. (*GM* II 12)

As can be seen, one of the crucial elements of genealogy is its insistence that there is a distinction between understanding how an organic "thing" (that is, an organic object, property, event, state, process, or system) originally emerges in a population and how it subsequently becomes part of a "system of ends" in that population. We can neither infer anything about how an organic phenomenon originates from its purpose or function nor infer anything about an organic phenomenon's purpose or function from how it originates. We return to the issue of power and domination mentioned in this passage in Chapter 4.

The parallel between genealogy and evolutionary biology is apparent. Evolutionary biology similarly distinguishes between the origin of a genotype and the history of that genotype's subsequent distribution in a population. Genetic mutation and recombination are the sole sources of genotypic novelty. The evolutionary mechanisms of natural selection and genetic drift do not explain genotypic novelty but instead explain how a genotype then becomes distributed in a population of geographically close and interbreeding conspecifics. Genetic drift is the change in the relative frequency of genetic mutations due to random sampling, and natural selection is the change in the relative frequency of mutations due to fitness, where fitness is understood as nothing more complex than there being a future in which organisms with a particular mutation probably have more descendants than those without that mutation. As will be seen in Essay I, Nietzsche argues similarly that the origins of values and moral evaluation are distinct from the development and distribution of values and moral evaluation once in existence.

The origin of an organic thing or feature is distinct from its subsequent distribution and development. Moreover, distribution and development are processes of being incessantly "requisitioned anew, transformed and redirected to a new purpose." This methodological principle is restricted in *GM* to the organic world, but elsewhere—at, for example, *BGE* 36 and in many *Nachlass* notes—Nietzsche experiments with extensions of this view to the nonorganic physical world. These experiments were informed by Lange, Boscovich, and Drossbach, and they make up Nietzsche's will to power ontology.[1]

For the time being, we focus, as Nietzsche does, on the organic world. According to *GM* II 12, the organic world includes everything from physiological organs to organisms, legal institutions, social customs, political practices, art forms, and religious rites. Once any of them come into existence, they then disperse through a population by being requisitioned, transformed, redirected, reinterpreted, and adjusted by others. The work of other nineteenth-century genealogists is thereby undone. After all, the purposes and functions of morality they appeal to in explaining the origins of moral values and evaluative practices are nothing more than the product of their idiosyncratic requisitioning, redirection, transformation, and reinterpretation. Yet they naively think that their nineteenth-century presumptions about morality can be projected back to the origins of moral values and evaluative practices to explain their initial emergence. Such projection from the present to the past, however, entails a kind of magical backward causation whereby a contemporary function or purpose of a moral value or evaluative practice is taken to cause its original emergence thousands of years ago. That, Nietzsche thinks, is unfit for an honest genealogist or scientist.

Given that he rejects projecting contemporary functions and uses back onto a thing's origins, it should come as no surprise that Nietzsche also dismisses attributing designs, purposes, and logical elements to the development of organic entities after their emergence. Consider, for instance, this passage from later in Essay II Section 12:

> [E]very purpose and use is just a *sign* that the will to power has achieved mastery over something less powerful, and has impressed upon it its own idea [*Sinn*] of a use function; and the whole history of a "thing," an organ, a tradition can to this extent be a continuous chain of signs, continually revealing new interpretations and adaptations, the causes of which need not be connected even

[1] See Poellner 1995; Doyle 2018; Welshon 2004.

> amongst themselves, but rather sometimes just follow and replace one another at random. The "development" of a thing, a tradition, an organ is therefore certainly not its *progressus* towards a goal, still less is it a logical *progressus*, taking the shortest route with the least expenditure of energy and cost,—instead it is a succession of more or less profound, more or less mutually independent processes of subjugation exacted on the thing, added to this the resistances encountered every time, the attempted transformations for the purpose of defense and reaction, and the results, too, of successful countermeasures. (*GM* II 12)

Neither subindividual organs, tissues, or systems nor individual organisms themselves, nor supraindividual clades, populations, and species, nor even social and cultural traditions exemplify designs, purposes, or logical progression: "[*W*]*e* have invented the concept 'purpose': there *are* no purposes in reality" (*TI* "The Four Errors" 8).

Instead, a given phenomenon comes into existence and other phenomena try to subjugate it through "mutually independent processes." In response, the given phenomenon reacts to these attempts at subjugation. This incessant battle is constitutive of the development of an organic thing or feature. However, other nineteenth-century genealogists of morality mistakenly presume that development implies improvement toward an end. As Nietzsche argues in Essay I, there is no evidence that moral values or moral evaluative practices have improved since they first emerged, much less that their development converges triumphantly as modern genealogists describe.

A second similarity between genealogy and evolutionary biology may be mentioned. For both genealogy and evolutionary biology, how an organic thing or feature originates explains nothing about its current function or adaptation. Consider: "[V]ision was *not* the intention behind the creation of the eye, but that vision appeared, rather, after *chance* had put the apparatus together. A single instance of this kind—and 'purposes' fall away like scales from the eyes!" (*D* 122). Still, both genealogy and evolutionary biology claim that certain past developments found in an organism's ancestors are irreversible and so constrain the direction of future development of those ancestors' progeny. These developmental constraints may appear to direct development and can be so stringent that it may appear that organic things progress over time toward a goal. However, these constraints are contrary to back projection of current functions and goals onto the development of an organic thing. Whereas a goal must take a future feature of an organic thing as a cause of its past development and while a function can, under some interpretations of 'function,' take a current feature of an organic thing as a cause of its past development, a past constraint simply narrows the range of current and future developments. Like a bottleneck that narrows a stream of liquid, a past constraint squeezes the present and future path of development.[2] Here there is no backward causation.

Two problems may also be introduced. Look again at the quoted passage above. Something odd becomes clear. Surprisingly, in the same sentence that Nietzsche rejects intentional explanatory categories such as purposes, designs, and logical progression as superfluous when explaining organic processes and phylogenetic development, he also invokes will to power. Indeed, he reinforces the need for will to power in historical inquiry:

> To speak plainly: even the partial *reduction in usefulness*, decay and degeneration, loss of meaning [*Sinn*] and functional purpose, in short death, make up the conditions of true *progressus:* always appearing, as it does, in the form of the will and way to *greater power* and always emerging victorious at the cost of countless smaller forces. . . . —I lay stress on this major point of historical method, especially as it runs counter to just that prevailing instinct and fashion which would much rather come to terms with absolute randomness, and even the mechanistic senselessness of all events, than the theory that a *power-will* is acted out in all that happens. (*GM* II 12)

How, after rejecting purposeful and goal-driven explanations in genealogy, can Nietzsche invoke a category of explanation—will to power—that appears on all counts to be an exemplar of what he claims to reject? After all, will to power is will *to* power, which makes it look very

[2] See Emden 2014.

much like a goal-directed explanatory category. And in the next sentence, where he sketches his own genealogical description of organic processes and phylogenetic development, he appeals to struggles, subjugation, resistance, and defense, categories that look to be every bit as purposeful and goal directed as will to power. If so, he appears to reject certain purpose-driven and goal-directed descriptions of organic processes and phylogenetic development and then turn right around and use purpose-driven and goal-directed descriptions that aim at achieving a specific goal—power—in his own genealogical accounts of ontogenetic organic processes and phylogenetic development. This apparent inconsistency runs through *GM*. While it can be neutralized, doing so is not always easy. We show why this is so in greater detail in Chapter 4's and Chapter 5's discussion sections.

Second, we might turn a skeptical eye to genealogy because it may appear to us that there is no historical basis for it. If there are no historical records for the slave revolt in morality that Nietzsche identifies in Essay I, we might think we should reject his proposed genealogy. It is certainly true that we will struggle to find documents reporting insurrections that have flown under banners proclaiming death to master morality. That is because the slave revolt in morality has taken place at levels different from those verified by datable episodes and protests. Nietzsche's interest in *GM* is not to chronicle specific judgments or actions of high- or low-born individuals or responses to them. Rather, he wants to uncover the moral principles and moral ideals that lie behind such judgments and actions, to understand the development of the moral concepts that we bind ourselves to, and to disclose developments in moral psychology and agency that have shaped who we now are and how we now think about ourselves.

To understand these matters, he repeatedly juxtaposes species of moral evaluation against one another and uses those contrasts as a framework for understanding how contemporary herd morality and herd moral psychology have come to acquire the features characteristic of them. This investigation requires etymological, philosophical, psychological, and physiological detective work that uncovers conceptual transformations in other, usually older and more primitive, evaluative systems and reveals the many layers of interpretation we have offered to ourselves about who we are and why we act. The slave revolt in morality consists of these conceptual transformations and interpretive layers. That revolt's product, herd morality, is the morality we adhere to today.

Naturalism and Philosophy

Although he rarely uses the term, Nietzsche is and thinks of himself as a philosophical naturalist. In *BGE*, for instance, he announces that his task is "to translate humanity back into nature; . . . to make sure that, from now on, the human being will stand before the human being, just as he already stands before the *rest* of nature today, hardened by the discipline of science, . . . deaf to the lures of the old metaphysical bird catchers who have been whistling to him for far too long: "You are more! You are higher! You have a different origin!" (*BGE* 230). Similar passages can be found in his work from *HH* forward. Of course, describing Nietzsche's views as examples of naturalism is only as helpful as the term 'naturalism' has a clear meaning, so let us take a moment to describe it.

First, naturalism is a view about what exists: it is the ontological claim that reality is exhausted by what exists in nature, where 'nature' refers to the set of all causally efficacious phenomena (objects, properties, processes, states, events, systems) that are found in the spatiotemporal world and studied by the natural sciences (physics, earth science, space science, and chemistry), the life sciences (biochemistry, evolutionary biology, genetics, botany, physiology, zoology, and ecology), the social sciences (psychology, sociology, anthropology/archaeology, linguistics, economics, political science, and human geography), and the formal sciences (mathematics and logic). Naturalism is, second, a view about what can be known: it is the epistemological claim that we can have knowledge only of what exists in nature, as understood above. Third, naturalism is a view about how to acquire knowledge: it is the methodological claim that the cognitive tools, procedures, and routines by which we acquire knowledge of what exists in nature are continuous in some sense between philosophy and empirical science.

Since what is causally efficacious is exhausted by nature, there can be no causally efficacious non-spatiotemporal objects, properties, processes, states, events, or systems. Since knowledge is exhausted by knowledge of what exists in nature, there can be no knowledge of non-spatiotemporal objects, properties, processes, states, events, or systems other than those studied by mathematics and logic. And since philosophy and the empirical sciences work together to develop knowledge of the natural world by using their different methods—conceptual analysis, logic, mathematics, and various empirical methods and techniques—there can be no means of gaining knowledge of nature that transcend these methods.

This conjunction about what exists, what can be known, and how knowledge can be acquired is consistent with most of Nietzsche's various statements about his philosophical naturalism from *HH* and *D* onward. However, as will be seen, Nietzsche also thinks that the methods of philosophy, logic, mathematics, and empirical science as practiced by his contemporaries are sometimes mistaken, sometimes presumptuous, and sometimes misdescriptive. Throughout *GM*, he is openly critical of others who advertise themselves as naturalists, and in Essay III he expresses skepticism about the reach of science and some of its methods. It suffices to note here that he is hostile to all non-naturalistically minded philosophers, theologians, and religious advocates, and hostile to many, but not all, philosophers and scientists who present themselves as naturalists or who present their work and methods as examples of naturalism.

Nietzsche is determined to show that moral beliefs, moral values, and moral evaluation are proper subjects of naturalist examination. If he succeeds, all descriptions of them that posit non-spatiotemporal phenomena, or that presuppose knowledge of a "real" or "true" world beyond the world presented to the senses, or that employ knowledge acquisition methods other than those found in naturalized philosophy and science will turn out to be worthless. Any description of moral values and moral evaluation that presupposes entities such as souls, the unified subject or 'I,' atoms, substances, things-in-themselves, or a "real" or "true" world will be ruled out. Any account that presupposes the existence of faculties and abilities such as free will or pure reason will be ruled out. Any account that presupposes the existence of kinds of causal forces such as purposes, final causes, motives, acts of a willing faculty, or even some forms of conscious thought will be ruled out.

Finally, any account that presupposes knowledge of such nonexistent entities, faculties, and kinds of causal forces is ruled out, and any account that uses methods such as faith, rational intuition, insight, or pure reason will be ruled out. In brief, naturalistic restrictions on what exists, what can be known, and how we gain knowledge will rule out all religious and theological, all metaphysical, and even most philosophical and scientific descriptions of the origins of moral values and moral evaluation and their subsequent history and development.

Philosophical and Theological Psychology

Nowhere is the prevalence of magical thinking, confused causal attributions, and explanatory presumptions more entrenched than in the psychological speculations of philosophers, theologians, and other religious advocates, most of whom revel in attributing fictitious psychological structures to us and deriving from them fictitious cognitive capacities and causal powers. Nietzsche dismantles this entire psychological superstructure, leveling one criticism after another against philosophical and theological/religious psychological inventions. In their place, he offers a description of the human psyche that takes it to be a collection of causally potent drives, desires, emotions, and affects and causally impotent conscious motives and free will.

The general contours of Nietzsche's criticisms of philosophical and theological psychologies can be introduced with a useful summary presented in *TI*, one of the last manuscripts he prepared for publication before collapsing. *TI*'s summary states four errors common to philosophers, theologians, and other religious advocates. These errors are, first, to confuse cause and consequence, second, to posit false causes, third, to posit imaginary causes, and fourth, to posit free will. Each identified error is a core element of some theological/religious or philosophical psychology, and Nietzsche uses the four errors to outline his opposition to such psychologies, thereby clearing the decks for his alternative view.

When philosophers and religious advocates confuse cause and consequence, they identify some event or state as causing another event or state when in fact the latter causes the former. For instance, they might recommend a low-consumption diet as a recipe for long life. Nietzsche counters that it is instead an "exceptionally slow metabolism and a minimal level of consumption" that causes a "meagre diet" (*TI* "The Four Great Errors" 1). More dangerously, religion and morality, to the extent that they are distinct, are also guilty of this error. While they both argue that virtue has happiness as its consequence, Nietzsche counters that happiness has virtue as its consequence. As he puts it, "leading a long life, having many descendants, these are not the rewards of virtue; rather, virtue is itself a deceleration of the metabolism that brings about (among other things) a long life with many descendants" (*TI* "The Four Great Errors" 2).

Second, philosophers and religious advocates routinely posit false causes. They identify some event or state as causing another event or state when in fact the former does not cause the latter. Nietzsche identifies three such false causes: willing, conscious thoughts, and the subject (that is, the I). We think that the subject of conscious thought—the I—causes conscious thoughts, that conscious thoughts cause acts of a willing faculty, and that acts of a willing faculty cause various events inside and outside of us. Of the three, the single most convincing phenomenon for us is the supposed causation of the will. The other two causes, consciousness and the subject, were, Nietzsche thinks, "latecomers that appeared once causality of the will was established as given, as *empirical*" (*TI* "The Four Great Errors" 3). Contrary to this philosophical/theological psychology, Nietzsche asserts, "the will does not do anything any more, and so it does not explain anything any more either—it just accompanies processes" (*TI* "The Four Great Errors" 3). Finally, the subject of these conscious thoughts and motives has likewise "become a fairy tale, a fiction a play on words: it has stopped thinking, feeling, and willing altogether!" (*TI* "The Four Great Errors" 3). Nietzsche does not shy away from inferring the disturbing conclusion that cutting these false causes implies: "there are no mental causes whatsoever! All the would-be empirical evidence for this goes to hell!" (*TI* "The Four Great Errors" 3).

Third, philosophers and religious advocates have a penchant for introducing imaginary causes. They identify some event or state as causing another event or state when in fact the identified event or state is fictional. Human beings are experts at manufacturing explanations, and theologians and philosophers actively participate in this practice. Nietzsche thinks that we are all prone to a familiar pattern of thinking. We experience something new and want to know what has caused it. To relieve the dissonance, confusion, and anxiety that attends ignorance, we try to explain the new phenomenon by fitting it into our already existing and usually crude web of beliefs and knowledge. Since we are "not too particular" about easing our anxiety, our search for explanation usually ends by latching onto something we have already encountered and registered in memory . . . The banker immediately thinks of 'business,' the Christian of 'sin' " (*TI* "The Four Great Errors" 5). Such "explanations," while sometimes serviceable for easing dissonance and confusion, ignore that what we are most familiar with and what we find most plausible are rarely good measures for fixing the actual causes of a phenomenon. Nietzsche is convinced that "the entire realm of morality and religion belongs to this concept of imaginary cause" (*TI* "The Four Great Errors" 6). We will, in due time, catalog numerous examples of Nietzsche's relentless battle against human intellectual laziness and the imaginary causes that it habitually fabricates.

Finally, philosophers and religious advocates assert the existence of free will. They identify an act produced by free will as an event or state freely chosen by a subject when in fact free will is a fiction and so cannot freely choose any act. Nietzsche's focus here is distinct from his earlier focus on the causal power of the will. His earlier point was that contrary to what we typically believe, the willing faculty is not a cause at all; here, the claim is that contrary to what we typically believe, the willing faculty is not free to choose in one way or another. The notion of will was "essentially designed with punishment in mind, . . . conditioned by the desire of its architects (the priests at the head of the ancient community) to establish their right to inflict punishment—or to assign the right to God . . ." (*TI* "The Four Great Errors" 7). As he puts it: "people were considered 'free' so that they could be judged and punished so that they could be guilty: consequently, every act had to be thought of as willed, every act had to be seen as coming from consciousness" (*TI* "The Four Great Errors" 7). This incomplete argument is spelled out in more detail in *GM* Essays I and II.

If psychologies developed by other philosophers, theologians, and religious advocates are shot through with mistakes regarding cause and consequence, if they posit the existence of false and imaginary causes, and if they require the fiction of free will, then Nietzsche's alternative psychology must reject these errors and replace them with a psychology that gets cause and consequence right, that posits true and actual causes, and that eschews free will. But how is such a psychology to be developed? After all, "by putting an end to the superstition that until now has grown around the idea of the soul with an almost tropical luxuriance, the *new* psychologist clearly thrusts himself into a new wasteland . . . and is condemned to invention" (*BGE* 12). This is precisely what Nietzsche does over the course of *HH*, *D*, *GS*, *BGE*, *GM*, *TI*, and *A*. He argues contrary to "naturalists . . . [who] barely need to touch 'the soul' to lose it," that the human psyche is to be understood instead "as subject-multiplicity" and "as a society constructed out of drives and affects" (*BGE* 12). This system of subpersonal drives, desires, emotions, and affects, many of which are unconscious and none of which are free in the sense that some philosophers and theologians think, is Nietzsche's working hypothesis about the structure of the human psyche. It is a hypothesis that is intermediate between philosophers and theologians who fantasize about nonspatial souls with imaginary causal powers, on the one hand, and on the other hand, clumsy naturalists who cannot understand that, much less explain how, humans are more interesting than frogs or worms.

Nietzsche's alternative description of the human psyche will steer a course between three errors. First, his account will avoid the mistakes of most philosophical and all theological/religious accounts that try to constitute the human psyche of supernatural elements (reason, logic, consciousness, moral values, otherworldly purposes, and holy designs) and that therefore inflate false pretensions humans have about themselves. Second, it will avoid the errors committed by any of the naturalized scientific descriptions of the human psyche that remain contaminated with such supernatural elements. And third, it will avoid the errors of other naturalized scientific descriptions that reduce the human psyche to something mechanical or chemical, which therefore discount how curious humans really are. By using the methods of knowledge acquisition found in science and naturalized philosophy and by renouncing all non-natural objects, properties, processes, events, states, or systems, he will offer a description of the human psyche that is grounded in nature and science, one that neither reduces it to something welded only to mechanistic physics and chemistry nor puffs it up into something that floats free of the natural world.

While Nietzsche assumes that humans are animals, he also acknowledges that we are peculiar animals, for we engage in activities and practices that, to date, have appeared to us so disjoint from the rest of nature that we have been unable to explain them as natural developments. Describing these phenomena and their development—in particular, phenomena such as moral values, moral beliefs, moral evaluation, and their psychological prerequisites—is *GM*'s primary focus. His project uses the methods and findings of science and naturalized philosophy to describe the development of morality and the human psyche in such a way that both blocks supernatural explanations of moral phenomena and our capacities and guards against explaining them away. This ambition helps explain why Nietzsche zeroes in on the drive (*Trieb*) and affect (*Affekt*) as the most important constituents of human psychology. He mentions other elements as well, such as instincts, powers, forces, emotions, desires, sensory perception, interoception, and conscious thoughts, but by far the most frequently mentioned are drives and affects. We describe them in greater detail in the next chapter; we describe perception, interoception, and conscious thought in Chapters 4 and 5.

Morality and Moral Evaluation

The question of the value of morality—the value of its values—mandates and justifies Nietzsche's efforts in *GM*. With this larger project of revaluing values always in mind and armed with the "new questions and as it were with new eyes" it provides, he sets off in *GM* to explore the "vast, distant and hidden land of morality—of morality as it really existed and was really lived" (*GM* Preface 7). During his trek through this territory, the revaluing project's philosophical commitments help him understand what he sees and hears (and, as he frequently says, smells), and they are rarely far from the expedition report's textual surface. These commitments fuel *GM* and make reading its descriptions of morality and moral psychology gripping, for we are aware that his descriptions of morality and moral psychology are from a specific perspective, one that will reveal why morality is not to be trusted as universally binding or even healthy, and why its presumptions about our psychology are dubious.

Throughout *GM*, his perspective's psychological, epistemological, metaphysical, and methodological elements now and again break through to the surface, sometimes unexpectedly and often without much articulation beyond what is immediately required to support a specific claim. And this feature makes reading *GM* frustrating. We are rarely, if ever, provided with a fuller account of the perspective's interlocking elements regarding naturalized psychology, the subject, agency, willing, goals and purposes, will to power, and the nature and scope of moral evaluation. We discuss all in due time. Here let us introduce moral evaluation.

Moralities are sets of beliefs, judgments, and principles about what has value and what does not, prescriptions for what has value, and proscriptions against what does not. As befits a philosopher, Nietzsche asks and answers questions regarding these core elements of morality. He asks, for instance, what valuing consists in, what kind of a thing a value is, what the logic of prescribing a value is, and what moral beliefs and moral judgments are. The initial point to make is that he thinks values do not exist in the world to be discovered as, say, unclimbed mountains might be. Values are always and only the result of valuing by an organism. He puts the point this way: "Whatever has *value* in the present world has it not in itself, according to its nature—nature is always value-less—but has rather been given, granted value, and *we* were the givers and granters" (*GS* 301).

Four consequences immediately follow. First, values result from some kind of experience that gives or grants value to some state of affairs. Hence, a state of affairs has value only because it is given or granted value by and from experience. Second, values cannot be dissociated from those valuing experiences and so cannot exist independently of them. Hence, there are no states of affairs that are valuable in themselves. Third, valuing is contingent and variable rather than necessary and fixed. Hence, a kind of experience can at one time grant value to a state of affairs while at another time not value or even disvalue it, just as a specific state of affairs valued by one kind of experience at one time can be valued by another kind of experience at another time. Fourth, values are contingent rather than necessary. Hence, there are no states of affairs that are necessarily valuable or valuable for all conceivable kinds of experience.

These four features of Nietzsche's description of values suffice to bring them out of the metaphysical clouds where philosophers, theologians, and religious advocates have claimed to find them and embed them instead in the contingent and variable experience of earthly organisms. Of course, this description is skeletal and does not contain enough information to understand how or why contingent experience grants value to certain states of affairs. Much less can it provide what is required to explain all of the twists and turns that valuing has taken over our phylogenetic history.

However, we can already infer that the distinctive features of Nietzsche's naturalized description of valuing will reject appeals to moral truths or moral facts, abjure positing transcendental domains or religious injunctions to justify the activity of valuing, and deny that moral knowledge and judgments are uniquely warranted:

> [*T*]*here are absolutely no moral facts*. What moral and religious judgments have in common is the belief in things that are not real. Morality is just an interpretation of certain phenomena or (more accurately) a *mis*interpretation. Moral judgments, like religious ones, presuppose a level of ignorance in which even the concept of reality is missing and there is no distinction between the real and the imaginary; a level where "truth" is the name for the very things that we now call "illusions." That is why moral judgments should never be taken literally: on their own, they are just absurdities. (*TI* "'Improving' Humanity" 1)

Indeed, the phenomena gathered under the concept of morality are, in Nietzsche's considered judgment, deeply perplexing. They present themselves as being about one thing when they are instead about something quite different: "[I]f you know what to look for, moral judgments reveal the most valuable realities of the cultures and interiorities that did not *know* enough to 'understand' themselves. Morality is just a sign language, just a symptomatology: you have to know *what* it means in order to take advantage of it (*TI* "'Improving' Humanity" 1). If so, then we need to know why moral judgments are illusions and absurdities, and we need to understand what morality is a sign language for and why morality is a symptomatology.

A sign language is a communicative format understood by those who cannot understand language formatted as speech, and a symptomatology is a set of physical or psychological features that indicate a medical condition. Claiming that morality is a sign language and a symptomatology implies then that morality is a set of features communicated to us in a format we understand but obscures from us the condition for which those features are symptoms. We do not recognize the condition those features indicate because their moral presentation poses a format hurdle to recognizing or diagnosing it. One of Nietzsche's tasks in *GM* and in the revaluation project of which *GM* is a part is to expose and diagnose the condition by re-interpreting and untangling its symptoms so that their moral formatting is replaced by another format that we also understand and, more importantly, that explains the symptoms better than the moral format does.

Nietzsche's preferred format is informed by a naturalized psychology that translates valuing into what was originally a phenomenon constitutive of all animal behavior (indeed, all organic experience). To presage what will be argued at length in later chapters, animals, the human animal included, have complex psychologies dominated by perceptual and interoceptive states and episodes, instincts, drives, emotions, and desires, and an array of affective states and feelings. Instincts, drives, emotions, desires, and affective states in particular are impelling psychological phenomena that either aim at particular future states of affairs or respond to particular occurrent or past states of affairs. These activating forces come loaded with what one scholar helpfully calls "affective orientations."[3] These affective orientations form the basis of valuing in general. Nietzsche puts the point as follows: "Our moral judgments and valuations are only images and fantasies upon a physiological process unknown to us" (*D* 119; see also *BGE* 187: "morality is just a *sign language of the affects*"). Thus, we now

[3] See Katsafanas 2016, 127.

have an answer to the question posed above regarding the role of contingent experience in granting value to certain states of affairs: being comprised of drives and affects entails that an animal's ongoing experience will grant value to certain states of affairs that are beneficial to it and will not grant value to other states of affairs that are not beneficial to it. Of course, we do not yet know enough to know how valuing works; much less do we know what we need to in order to explain all of the twists and turns that valuing has taken over our phylogenetic history. Those questions are answered in subsequent chapters.

Nietzsche thinks his drive/affect psychology has considerable explanatory scope. If adopted, it warrants an assessment of moral phenomena from an entirely naturalized perspective that re-configures moral valuing and moral judgments as outgrowths of what were originally basic biological drives and affects that have, over the last several thousand years, been overlain with, altered by, or redirected into, increasingly social, moral, and religious valuing. One of the tasks of *GM*'s descriptive project is to use this naturalized perspective to map the emergence of social, moral, and religious evaluations, record their features, and follow their impacts on us and who we take ourselves to be.

Among the things he records are drives that set us off from our last common ancestors. One of them is the drive or instinct that compels us to join together in groups. Once a group is formed, it spurs a set of fundamental changes inside its members, changing them from what they were once like in the wild into a vastly different kind of animal:

> For as long as there have been people, there have been herds of people as well (racial groups, communities, tribes, folk, states, churches), and a very large number of people who obey compared to relatively few who command. So, considering the fact that humanity has been the best and most long-standing breeding ground for the cultivation of obedience so far, it is reasonable to suppose that the average person has an innate need to obey as a type of *formal conscience* that commands: "Thou shalt unconditionally do something, unconditionally not do something," in short: "Thou shalt." This need tries to satisfy itself and give its form a content, so, like a crude appetite, it indiscriminately grabs hold and accepts whatever

> gets screamed into its ear by some commander or another—a parent, teacher, the law, class prejudice, public opinion—according to its strength, impatience, and tension. The oddly limited character of human development—its hesitancy and lengthiness, its frequent regressions and reversals—is due to the fact that the herd instinct of obedience is inherited the best and at the cost of the art of commanding. (*BGE* 199)

The herd instinct functions in the background as a drive to maintain the group and the authority of its commands. Since it is beneficial for the group's maintenance, the herd instinct disperses across individuals in groups in a manner similar to the way a beneficial genetic mutation spreads in a population. When the herd instinct is conjoined with other psychological characteristics, a particular kind of human animal—the human herd animal—develops. And when the herd animal comes under the tutelage of a particular kind of commander—the priest—the consequences are explosive, causing what Nietzsche calls the "slaves' revolt in morality" (*GM* I 10; *BGE* 195).

Further Reading

For more on genealogy as a method, see Blondel 1994; Conway 2008; Foucault 1977; Guay 2006; Janaway 2006; Kail 2011; Katsafanas 2011; Owen 2007; Prescott-Crouch 2015; Schacht 2013b; Williams 2000.

For more on naturalism and naturalizing philosophy, see Acampora 2006b; Cox 1999; Doyle 2018, 2019; Emden 2014; Janaway 2006; Kail 2009, 2015; Leiter 2002, 2013; Richardson 1996, 2004; Schacht 2012a, 2012b; Welshon 2014; Williams 2000.

For more on evaluation and values, see Foot 1994, 2001; Forster 2015; Gemes and Janaway 2005; Guay 2013; Hussain 2007, 2011, 2013; Katsafanas 2013a; Poellner 2007; Richardson 2020; Robertson 2020; Schacht 1983; Silk 2017.

3

Genealogy Essay I

3.1 Introduction

Essay I is probably the best known of *GM*'s three essays because it contains the most extensive descriptions of the slave revolt in morality and the first analyses of ressentiment. The slave revolt names a set of changes to evaluative practices that seeped through societies when monotheistic religions, Christianity in particular, emerged as social and cultural movements. These changes became sedimented in European morality in no small part because the ubiquity of ressentiment gave them a rich psychological medium in which to grow.

This chapter's discussion section addresses four issues. First, Nietzsche uses 'morality' in different ways and both endorses and condemns it. We show how this apparent equivocation can be eased. Second, we describe Nietzsche's argumentative tactic of juxtaposing different species of morality and moral psychology to uncover presuppositions that are difficult to acknowledge, much less describe. Third, we introduce his naturalized drive/affect moral psychology, noting its explanatory power and some of its problems. One of the most serious of these problems is that Nietzsche appears to think that human drives and affects do so much that they can replace what persons do. We show that this is indeed an implication of his moral psychology and that, properly understood, it is not as troubling as sometimes alleged.

Nietzsche's On the Genealogy of Morality. Rex Welshon, Oxford University Press.
 DOI: 10.1093/oso/9780197611814.003.0004

3.2 Essay I by the Sections

Sections 1–3

Nietzsche opens Essay I by paying English historians and psychologists of morality a backhanded compliment. Who are these English historians and psychologists? Nietzsche identifies three by name. The first, his erstwhile friend Paul Rée, was not English. Nonetheless, Nietzsche identifies Rée's *Origins of Moral Sensations* in the Preface as being the work of an English genealogist and discusses Rée's arguments in *GM* I 2. The second is Herbert Spencer (1820–1903), a biologist, sociologist, philosopher, and social Darwinist. Nietzsche read Spencer's *The Data of Ethics* and *Introduction to the Study of Sociology* and mentions him in *GM* I 3. The third is Henry Thomas Buckle (1821–1862), who wrote a colossal *History of Civilization* (11 volumes and unfinished when he died), parts of which Nietzsche read and annotated. Nietzsche mentions him in *GM* I 4. Three other unnamed English psychologists can be included. Nietzsche was familiar with the utilitarian moral philosopher John Stuart Mill (1806–1873) and read a number of titles from his *Collected Works*, and he was also familiar with David Hume (1711–1776), who proposed that moral sentiments were universal across cultures. One other lesser-known name is William Edward Hartpole Lecky (1838–1903), who wrote a two-volume *History of European Morals from Augustus to Charlemagne*.

The English psychologists are interesting because they bring shadowy and more chastening facets of our inner world into the light so that we can better understand what actually guides our actions. He uses the French *partie honteuse* here, a term that translates as 'shameful part' or 'genital.' So these English psychologists divert attention away from what our "intellectual pride" (*GM* I 1) would like to nominate as the causes of our mental states and action, redirecting instead toward more bestial, ruder causes. He admits that he finds their inquiries fascinating, in part because he cannot determine what pushes them in this direction. Perhaps it is some combination of a taste for paradox, for the grotesque, the absurd, the vulgar, the gloomy, the anti-Christian, and "a bit of a thrill and need for pepper" (*GM* I 1). Nietzsche is fully on board with the English venture, knowing that he and they will end up mired in the swamp that is the history and psychology of morality and Christianity. He also shares their drive for truth; wherever that drive directs him he will follow, even if it eventually leads him away from them.

Immediately after complimenting them for at least having a historical sense, he charges that the English psychologists betray themselves by being unhistorical. Instead of excavating the historical and archaeological record of how evaluation emerged in ancient societies, and instead of digging through the etymological evidence about the meanings attached to ancient evaluative words, the English historians short-circuit their own efforts by projecting back into the beginning of morality's descent a modern meaning of 'good.' Using a small clutch of psychological mechanisms—utility, routine, error, and forgetting—they then try to explain how that back-projected sense of 'good' came forward through history. Nietzsche criticizes this maneuver in a way familiar to anyone who has previously encountered a state-of-nature argument.[1] Such an argument risks getting out of the state of nature only what is put into it; if so, the exercise of appealing to the state of nature is either circular or false.

Nietzsche's first criticism of the English psychologists accuses them of hypothesizing a state of nature that never occurred. They assume that being morally good was originally being useful to (or having utility for) others but that, over time, being morally good changed from being useful to being unegoistic. So, in the state of nature, when one person called another person's action 'good,' what that meant was that the first found the other's action useful; we then eventually habituated ourselves to thinking that the goodness of actions consisted not in their being useful, but in their being unegoistic. However, these two

[1] In state-of-nature arguments, a hypothesis is offered about how contemporary moral practices and/or political structures originally emerged from a state of affairs where they did not exist—the state of nature. By doing so, these arguments thereby justify contemporary moral practices and/or political structures. State-of-nature arguments or variants on them are found in the work of Thomas Hobbes (1588–1679) and John Locke (1632–1704) in the seventeenth century, Jean-Jacques Rousseau (1712–1778) in the eighteenth century, Rée, Mill, Spencer, Buckle, and Lecky in the nineteenth century, and John Rawls (1921–2002) and Robert Nozick (1938–2002) in the twentieth century.

evaluative distinctions, between the useful and useless and between the unegoistic and egoistic, are modern distinctions projected back to the origin of evaluation. Neither existed at the origin of evaluation or even for a long time after that. The English psychologists thus fail in their historical analysis of the origins of moral evaluation by being bad historians.

A second, more specific, objection is that Rée's version requires a psychological absurdity to work. Suppose with Rée that the usefulness/utility of actions was what moral evaluation evolved from and was the reason why such actions were and are praised as good. If so, then we should also expect that since the usefulness/utility of actions has been reinforced continuously over thousands of years of everyday life, that criterion of moral value would remain. Yet Rée argues that we have instead forgotten that usefulness/utility for others was once thought to be the standard of goodness, meaning that we now praise unegoistic actions as intrinsically good, that is, independent of consequences and, hence, independent of usefulness or utility. This conclusion is asinine. Forgetting usefulness/utility when it is reinforced continuously by daily life amounts to trying to forget what is "*unforgettable*" (*GM* I 3). But forgetting what cannot be forgotten is a psychological nonstarter, so we must reject Rée's hypothesis. If we think that usefulness and utility have something to do with the moral good, we should side with Herbert Spencer, who straightforwardly equates the good with the useful now and then. Spencer's alternative explanation is also wrong, but it at least avoids the premise on Rée's nonsensical fantasy. Still, Nietzsche's own hypothesis on the origins of morality illuminates Spencer's mistake.

By Nietzsche's hypothesis, goodness did not originate in being useful for others but in being someone who was good, and actions were good not because they were useful for others but because they were the actions of good individuals, those who were "noble, the mighty, the high-placed and the high-minded, who saw and judged themselves and their actions as good, I mean first-rate" (*GM* I 2). These glorious individuals—the old master caste of warriors, knights, and aristocrats, whose self-worth coincided with their sociopolitical superiority—designated their actions as good solely because they performed them:

> It was from this *pathos of distance* that they first claimed the right to create values and give these values names: usefulness was none of their concern! The standpoint of usefulness is as alien and inappropriate as it can be to such a heated eruption of the highest rank-ordering and ranked defining value judgments: this is the point where feeling reaches the opposite of the low temperatures needed for any calculation of prudence or reckoning of usefulness. (*GM* I 2)

So what existed at the source of moral evaluation was a species of evaluation that spontaneously flowed from knightly and aristocratic classes reflecting on their own splendor and naively describing themselves and whatever they and others like them did as good. The contrary value, bad, was created as "an aside, an afterthought, a complementary color" (*GM* I 11) that applied to the knavish commoners, the poor rabble, the oppressed and the enslaved, and to whatever they did.

Nietzsche includes wealthy aristocrats, warriors, knights, the powerful, and the well-born in the class of masters. Otherwise, he provides little detail here about them. The masters called themselves good for a reason no more cognitively strenuous than that their lives were demonstrably better than the lives of commoners. Unlike the poor masses, the masters were healthy and cheerful (*GM* I 7), vigorous and active (*GM* I 10), powerful and rich (*GM* I 5), warlike and godlike (*GM* I 5), filled with life and passion (*GM* I 10), honest, trustful, confident, and open (*GM* I 10), and considerate, self-controlled, delicate, loyal, proud, and friendly (*GM* I 11). "The 'well-born' *felt* they were 'the happy' (*GM* I 10). They enjoyed each other's company and engaged in activities such as "war, adventure, hunting, dancing, war games and in general all that involves vigorous, free, and cheerful activity" (*GM* I 7) that preserved their privileged status.

The old warriors and aristocrats also thought of themselves as being the zenith of society, a point noted in *BGE*: the aristocracy felt "itself to be the *meaning* and highest justification (of the kingdom or community)—and, consequently, . . . it accepts in good conscience the sacrifice of countless people who have to be pushed down and shrunk into incomplete human beings, into slaves, into tools" (*BGE* 258). This glorified status in which others existed to serve the noble classes shows why Herbert Spencer is wrong to project usefulness/utility back to the origin of evaluation. The warrior and aristocratic classes had contempt for the "cowardly, apprehensive, and petty, people who thought narrowly in terms of utility" (*BGE* 260). Since they created values rather than discovered them in existing social interactions, the nobility had no use for calculating the consequences of their actions. That sort of thing was reserved for the rabble: "[S]lave morality is essentially a morality of utility" (*BGE* 260).

When evaluation originated, then, the contrast was not between what was useful and what was not, or what was egoistic and what was not, but only between who and what was noble and who and what was not. Hence, the origin of the distinction between 'good' and 'bad,' and that between 'good' and 'evil,' was "definitely not linked from the start and by necessity to 'unegoistic' actions" (*GM* I 2). Of course, if Nietzsche's alternative history is correct, then the moral praiseworthiness that now attaches to unegoistic actions and the moral blameworthiness that now attaches to egoistic actions must have emerged as a later change to these earlier evaluative practices. Nietzsche will tell us soon enough what that change is, who was responsible for it, and how it shifted the evaluative landscape.

For future reference, it is helpful to catalog here some of the characteristics of the old masters and slaves. We do not include the priests here because, while also noble, their emphasis on purity and cleanliness makes them a unique case, which we will return to presently.

Masters	Slaves
Socioeconomic dimensions	
Aristocratic/noble (*GM* I 2, 3, 5, 7, 10, 11)	Lower-class/herd/commoner (*GM* I 2, 3, 7, 10)
Knightly/warlike/warriors (*GM* I 5, 7)	Peaceful/pacifists (*GM* I 14)
Wealthy/prosperous/well-born (*GM* I 5)	Poor/unfortunate/ill-born (*GM* I 2, 3, 7, 10)
Privileged (*GM* I 5)	Deprived / beast of burden (*GM* I 10)
Dominating/oppressive (*GM* I 11, 13)	Oppressed/ill-treated (*GM* I 10, 11, 13)
Superior (*GM* I 2, 6)	Mediocre (*GM* I 11, 12)
Admirable but feared (*GM* I 11, 12)	Contemptible but harmless (*GM* I 11, 12)

Masters	Slaves
Physiological dimensions	
Healthy (*GM* I 7)	Sickly/diseased/ill (*GM* I 6, 11, III, 15, 16)
Energetic/vital (*GM* I 10)	Weary/lethargic/exhausted/leaden (*GM* I 11, III 16)
Powerful/potent/strong (*GM* I 2, 7, 10, 13)	Powerless/impotent/weak (*GM* I 7, 10, 13, 14, III 17)
Active/vigorous (*GM* I 7)	Reactive/passive (*GM* I 10, 13)
Beautiful/hulking (*GM* I 7, 10)	Ugly/stunted (*GM* I 7, 10, 11, 12)
Psychological dimensions	
Happy (*GM* I 7, 10)	Unhappy/miserable (*GM* I 10, 11, 13, 14)
Cheerful/enthusiastic/passionate (*GM* I 10)	Depressed/melancholic (*GM* III 17)
Creative/dominating (*GM* I 10)	Reactive/submissive (*GM* I 10)
Affirmative/yes-saying (*GM* I 10)	Negative/no-saying (*GM* I 10)
Adventurous/dominant (*GM* I 7)	Timid/submissive (*GM* I 13, 14)
Proud (*GM* I 6)	Humble (*GM* I 13, 14)
Brave/daring/frenzied (*GM* I 10, 11)	Cowardly/craven/serene (*GM* I 5, 13, 14)
Spontaneous/naive	Scheming/suspicious/clever (*GM* I 8, 10, 12, 13)
Indifferent to suffering (*GM* I 11)	Compassionate about suffering (*GM* Preface 5)
Cavalier/confident (*GM* I 10)	Insecure/diffident (*GM* I 10, 13)
Open/honest/truthful (*GM* I 5, 10)	Secretive/dishonest/deceitful (*GM* I 5, 10, 14, 15)
Impatient (*GM* I 11)	Patient (*GM* I 7, 13, 14)
Forgiving (*GM* I 10)	Vindictive/spiteful (*GM* I 13, 14)
Trusting (*GM* I 10)	Envious (*GM* I 10, II 1, III 15)
Happiness consists in activity (*GM* I 10)	Happiness consists in inactivity (*GM* I 10)
Ressentiment quickly discharges (*GM* I 10)	Ressentiment festers (*GM* I 10, 11, 14, III 14, 15)

In addition to these contrasts, Nietzsche also describes at various places the masters' relations with one another and with the oppressed. For example, the masters were "held in check by custom, respect, habit, gratitude and even more through spying on one another and through peer-group jealousy," and they behaved toward each other by showing "resourcefulness in consideration, self-control, delicacy, loyalty, pride, and friendship" (*GM* I 11; see also *BGE* 259 and *BGE* 260). However, outside of their peer group, they were "not much better than uncaged beasts of prey" who delighted in "murder, arson, rape, and torture" and who appeared to their victims to be "cold, cruel, lacking feeling and conscience, crushing everything and coating it with blood" (*GM* I 11). He rarely says much about the old slaves' relations with one another, although in Essay II he discusses creditor-debtor relations found across strata of ancient societies.

We will return to one or more of these contrasts often as we move through *GM*.

Sections 4–5

We might think that Nietzsche's alternative historical hypothesis accomplishes nothing more than replacing one state of nature with another and that since the former is objectionable, then his is as well. These and the following sections show why this counter fails. They provide etymological, psychological, and even physiological evidence for the hypothesis that the origin of evaluation was tied neither to an action's utility nor to its being unegoistic. Rather, it was tied to the designation by the master classes of themselves and their own actions. In Sections 4 and 5, he focuses on etymological evidence; in Sections 6–11, he focuses on psychological and physiological evidence.

Nietzsche claims to have discovered a "conceptual transformation" (*GM* I 4) in the way that terms originally used by the masters to describe their social, economic, and political superiority came to characterize what is individually noble. A similar conceptual transformation governs how descriptive terms once reserved for the lower social classes, that is, the commoners, the rabble, the herd, parallel descriptive terms for what is base and vulgar in an individual. Some will think that this etymological evidence, provided in Section 4 for certain German words and in Sections 5 and 6 for words in various ancient languages, is contentious, but Nietzsche thinks this resistance can be chalked up to corrupt historical methods, in particular to our contemporary democratic prejudice against unearthing aristocratic origins of evaluation. After all, if what was once noble has since become plebeian, honest historians of value would be obliged to explain it, but they are themselves a consequence of these democratizing forces, so the last thing they want to confront is evidence contrary to their own plebeianism. This is made clear in the "notorious case of Buckle," who flaunts the modern commitments with all of the "vulgar eloquence" of a "mud volcano" (*GM* I 4).

Section 5 is about a scholarly topic, a "*quiet* problem [that] addresses itself only selectively to a few ears" (*GM* I 5). Nietzsche's interest in "words and roots" (*GM* I 5) as evidence about the origins of evaluative practices requires him to expand beyond the German language. So he considers the conceptual transformation identified in the previous section as it is found in ancient Sanskrit, ancient Greek, and Latin. For example, the ancient Sanskrit word *arya*, from about 1000 BCE, refers both to wealthy ownership and well-born classes and to the character trait of being noble and privileged. *Arya* is, of course, also the root for 'Aryan,' a term that served as a self-designating endonym for people living then in what is now northwestern India, Pakistan, Afghanistan, and Iran. (It is also the basis of 'Iran' and 'Iranian.') Similar etymological evidence for a cluster of Greek and Latin terms warrants a surprising generalization: in all three ancient languages, the primordial evaluative terms were self-reflexive designations by members of a master class of aristocrats and warriors that subsequently underwent a conceptual transformation to become self-reflective descriptions of their individual character traits.

We pause here long enough to redeem a promise made in Chapter 1. Nietzsche is done a disservice by assuming that because he uses 'Aryan' and because the Nazis use 'Aryan,' what he and they refer to is the same. This assumption is one reason some have assimilated Nietzsche into Nazism. However, the assumption is mistaken. For a philologist trained during the middle to late nineteenth century, the term 'Aryan' referred neutrally to a set of ancient languages and to the people who used them. These ancient populations used languages that belonged to what was then called the 'Indo-Aryan' or 'Aryan' family of languages, from which many European languages subsequently diverged and developed (unsurprisingly, since World War II, 'Indo-European' has largely supplanted 'Indo-Aryan'). Those who spoke one of these ancient Aryan languages were, then, Aryans. Among the old Aryans were those who spoke Sanskrit, Indo-Iranian, Hellenic Greek, Celtic, Latin, Balto-Slavic, and proto-German.

Nietzsche's observations about Aryans in Section 5 employ 'Aryan' in the same way that Max Müller (1823–1900), an influential nineteenth-century philologist, used it, as an ethnological term about common linguistic roots of European, Iranian, and subcontinental Indian cultures. For Müller and Nietzsche alike, 'Aryan' refers broadly across the aforementioned ancient linguistic groups and only incidentally to any specific linguistic group. So when Nietzsche talks about the Aryans self-designating themselves as noble, he is talking about the evaluative practices found in members of any of the groups that spoke these ancient Aryan languages. 'Aryan' does not refer to modern linguistic, cultural, or ethnic groups, or, for that matter, biological races. Hence, when talking about Aryans, Nietzsche is not talking about modern Germans. Indeed, he notes later that there is scarcely a "an idea in common, let alone a blood relationship" (*GM* I 11) between modern Germans and the ancient barbarians from which they descended.[2]

Sections 6–9

The overall point of these sections is to isolate the priestly mode of existence and evaluation from the knightly-aristocratic mode of existence and evaluation, to reveal the priestly modality and then counterpose it

[2] This is not to say that 'Aryan' lacked racial connotations in the late 1880s. Influenced by Darwin's accounts of the origin of species, some authors had already begun using 'Aryan' to denote a biological type or race. Müller was aware of this semantic shift and warned in 1888 that "an ethnologist who speaks of Aryan race, Aryan blood, Aryan eyes

against the knightly-aristocratic mode. In so doing, he makes claims about specific priestly classes, in passing about Hindu ("Brahmanism" refers loosely to Hinduism) and Buddhist priests, and more directly about Jewish and Christian priests.

Contrasting knightly-aristocratic and priestly evaluative modes is interesting enough. The highest caste in ancient societies was not always the knightly-aristocratic caste, although that may have been the norm. In some ancient societies, priests, aristocrats, and warriors coexisted peacefully, in others they continuously bickered with one another, and in still others the priests held the highest caste. Whatever their relations to the warriors and aristocrats were like, the clergy always differed from them in crucial ways. The knightly-aristocratic mode of evaluation was simple and based on nothing more sophisticated than pronouncing themselves as being good, and then, as an

and hair, is as great a sinner as a linguist who speaks of a dolichocephalic dictionary or a brachycephalic grammar" (Müller 1884/2004, 120 ['dolichocephalic' means a skull that is unusually long and 'brachycephalic' means a skull that is unusually short]). Unfortunately, this racial sense of 'Aryan' eventually eclipsed the ethnological sense. By the 1920s, 'Aryan' was deposited in Nazi propaganda as a racial term that denoted the Teutons as exemplars of a biological type. Since Nietzsche was a hero to the Nazis, their puerile logic permitted them the immediate inference that he must also have been an early advocate of Aryan biological purity and that he must also have believed that modern Germans were the exemplars of the biological type.

For the racist use of 'Aryan,' the Nazis relied on Arthur de Gobineau (1816–1882) and Houston Stewart Chamberlain (1855–1927). We do not investigate their work here, but two points may be made. Gobineau argued that races are biologically defined categories and that biological differences determine psychological, sociological, and cultural personality characteristics. Inconveniently for the Nazis, Gobineau also thought that the Aryan race had by the nineteenth century become so diluted by intermarriage that the type remained only in isolated enclaves. As a result, his views were not championed in the early twentieth-century German *völkisch* ethnonationalist movement from which Nazism emerged after World War I. It is Chamberlain more than Gobineau who augured Nazism. English by birth, Chamberlain became a Germanophile after hearing Wagner in 1878. His fascination with Germany became so complete that he moved to Dresden, married one of Wagner's daughters, and became a German citizen. Chamberlain was polished, strange, and contemptible, and his military-class patina and erudition camouflaged deep paranoia and sadism. His thought was an important source for the blend of xenophobic Teutonic pride, vehement antisemitism, and reactionary anticapitalism that came to define Nazism. Chamberlain was one of Kaiser Wilhelm II's favorite thinkers, and with Wilhelm's seal of approval, his racist message spread into the *völkisch* movement and thence to Alfred Bauemler (1887–1968) and Alfred Rosenberg (1892–1946), on each of whom it had a lasting impact. It is generally accepted that Adolf Hitler (1889–1945) never read any of Nietzsche's books, instead relying on what others said about him.

offhanded "afterthought" (*GM* I 11), decreeing that the rabble was base or bad. The priestly elders, although also members of the nobility, emphasized purity and cleanliness and dismissed others as impure. Like the aristocratic-warrior distinction between good and bad, that between pure and impure was, as befits the period, "crude, coarse, superficial, narrow, direct and in particular *unsymbolic* . . . to a degree that we can scarcely imagine" (*GM* I 6). The term "pure" began as a self-designation used by those sanitary few who washed themselves regularly, refrained from eating certain foods and from engaging in sex with commoners, and had a horror of blood.

The conceptual transformation from self-reflexive social designation to self-reflective individual character description happened with 'pure' and 'impure' as well. Presaging what will be developed in the balance of *GM*, Nietzsche offers a brief description of priestly psychology, one that will be augmented in Essay II and Essay III. Habitually reluctant to take direct action against others and "partly brooding and partly emotionally explosive," the old clergy's obsession with cleanliness and purity led inevitably to digestive disorders, and so they turned to self-directed health regimes "of certain diets (avoidance of meat), of fasting, sexual abstinence, the flight 'into the desert'" and even of "self-hypnosis" (*GM* I 6). And, as argued below, they participated in customs and rituals that helped cultivate within themselves emotional regulation and attentional control.

Even if the priest's "*essentially dangerous*" form of existence was unnatural, we must also acknowledge that with them, humans became "*an interesting animal*" (*GM* I 6) for the first time, an admission that bears emphasis. Without the priests or some other goad, Europeans would have remained uncouth, simple-minded, superficial, and brutish. Thanks to the priests and those they "improved," everybody's psychology deepened, including that of the knightly-aristocratic masters, and with that additional depth we all became the tortured beings we are now.

Becoming interesting is not, of course, the same as becoming better. Wherever priestly castes gained influence over the knights and aristocrats, they inverted the master's equation of "good = noble = powerful = beautiful = happy" (*GM* I 7). The aristocrats and warriors designated themselves as good and thereby designated as good their flourishing health, their love of the other sex, their physical strength and happiness, their wealth and social status, their truth-telling, and all of the activities that preserved them. The priestly caste similarly designated their purity and cleanliness as good. But they valorized "the poor, impotent, lowly, . . . the suffering, deprived, sick, [and] ugly" and condemned the masters' actions as "cruel, lustful, insatiable and godless" (*GM* I 7).

All of this might, at least pending additional defense, be cautiously accepted as a set of etymological claims about certain ancient languages and empirical claims about certain psychosocial elements of the ancient aristocratic and priestly castes. This kind of analysis is what should be expected from a genealogist of morality such as Nietzsche, for it is implied by his claim that his explanation of the emergence of moral evaluation from of a state of nature is more accurate than the English psychologist's alternative, which projects back onto the state of nature contemporary moral evaluation and then claims to discover it there fully formed. He welcomes others to assess his historical hypotheses by examining other ancient societies to determine whether his hypotheses are supported or are disconfirmed.

Yet this is not all that Nietzsche says. Mentioning Hinduism and Buddhism briefly and ignoring Islam altogether, he names two priestly castes, the Jewish type and the Christian type that descended from it, and he thereafter focuses his discussion almost entirely on them. One reason he does this is that the topic of *GM* is European moral evaluation. Since Christianity is uniquely important for understanding European moral evaluation, and since Christianity grew out of the Judaism of the Second Temple period from 516 BCE to 70 CE, attention to it is vital. Had he been writing about and from within a society informed by, say, Buddhism, he would have written about the Buddhist priestly caste (as he in fact does briefly in Essay III, and more extensively in *A*).

What Nietzsche says about the old Jewish clerical caste here is frequently held up as evidence that he is an antisemite. A frequently cited passage is this one: "All that has been done on earth against 'the noble,' 'the powerful,' 'the masters,' 'the rulers,' is not worth mentioning in comparison with what *the Jews* have done against them: the Jews, that priestly people who in the end were only able to achieve satisfaction from their enemies and conquerors through a radical revaluation of their values, hence through an act of the *most spiritual revenge*" (*GM* I 7). Another:

> [F]rom the trunk of the tree of vengeance and hatred, Jewish hatred—the deepest and most sublime hatred moreover, capable of creating ideals and re-creating values, whose like never before existed on earth—grew something just as incomparable, a *new love*, the deepest and most sublime of all kinds of love: —from what other trunk could it have grown? . . . But we should certainly not suppose that it grew somehow as the actual negation of that thirst for revenge, as the opposite of Jewish hatred! No, the reverse is the truth! This love grew out of it as its crown, as the triumphant crown unfolding itself ever more broadly in the brightest daylight and fullness of sunlight, bent on the goals of that hatred, on victory. . . . This Jesus of Nazareth as the incarnate gospel of love, this "redeemer" who brought blessedness and victory to the poor, sinners, and the sick—was he not precisely seduction in its most uncanny and irresistible form, seduction and a detour to precisely those *Jewish* values and revisions of their ideal? (*GM* I 8)

It cannot be denied that Nietzsche thinks that the old Jewish priestly caste's hatred of and vengeance against Greek and Roman masters is the first important case of revaluing noble values. Nor can it be denied that he identifies the old priestly caste's alleged thirst for vengeance against the masters as the root cause of the Christian gospel of love. So if identifying the Jewish priestly caste as the first to revalue masters' values and for being at the root of the Christian doctrine of love is sufficient for being labeled 'antisemitic,' then Nietzsche must be included in the extension of the term.

However, what is even clearer in *GM* I 8, and especially in *GM* I 9, is that Nietzsche's primary target is not the Jewish priests at all; it is instead the Judeo-Christian religious complex and its attendant morality and moral psychology. The values of the masters have in the last two thousand years been supplanted by other values, and these other values are the product of priests and " 'the slaves,' or 'the rabble,' or 'the herd,' or whatever you prefer to call it" (*GM* I 9) who followed them. Whether we say that moral evaluation is being "jewified or christianized or rabbleized (what do words matter!)" (*GM* I 9), what is evident is that the "slave revolt in morality" (*GM* I 10) has been victorious in permanently transforming Europeans and, through their proselytizing and colonialist efforts, increasingly transforming other populations (the qualification is necessary because Nietzsche acknowledges in *GM* I 16 that the slave revolt in morality has not yet permeated moral thinking everywhere). The depth of the victory in Europe is so complete that even "free-thinkers" who might otherwise laugh at the "crude and boorish," even "repellent," practices of modern Christianity still willingly stomach the "poison" of its moral values that now courses through "the whole body of humanity . . . even though its tempo and pace, from now on, might tend to be slower, softer, quieter, calmer—there is no hurry" (*GM* I 9).

Section 10

Section 10 announces that "the beginning of the slaves' revolt in morality occurs when ressentiment itself turns creative and gives birth to values: the ressentiment of those beings who, denied their proper response of action, compensate for it only with imaginary revenge" (*GM* I 10). This passage introduces one of the most distinctive features of *GM*, the psychology of ressentiment and its role in generating moral values. Given that it occupies a dominant position in Nietzsche's analysis, it is more than a little disappointing that he does not define the term 'ressentiment' here, or, in fact, anywhere in *GM*, instead lifting the French word intact from Eugen Dühring's *The Value of Life* (*Der Wert des Lebens*), from 1865. Worse, the analysis of ressentiment in these sections is critically inadequate. Relevant supplemental discussion occurs later in *GM* III and, elsewhere, in *HH* and *BGE*. Since it is central to the genealogical project, a close description of the psychology of ressentiment and its role in the creation of values is necessary.

Part of the "essence of *ressentiment*" is that it reverses "the evaluating glance" by focusing on the "outside world instead of [turning the glance] back onto oneself," and that it "needs, physiologically, external stimuli in order to act at all—its action is basically a reaction" (*GM* I 10). Knightly-aristocratic evaluation "acts and grows spontaneously" and "seeks its opposite only so that it can say 'yes' to itself even more thankfully and exultantly" (*GM* I 10; see also *BGE* 260: "[T]the noble kind of human being feels *itself* to be value-determining"). On the other hand, ressentiment is fundamentally reactive. So, at a minimum, ressentiment is a psychological event, process, or episode that has causal antecedents. That is hardly a surprise: all psychological events, processes, and episodes have causal antecedents. Luckily, something more interesting than that is on offer. The masters, even if unreflective, brutish, and simple, were energetic and necessarily active, engaging their drives and engaged in their lives. They were yes-saying individuals, "strong, full natures in whom there is a superabundance of a power that is flexible, regenerative, healing," individuals who knew "not to separate action from happiness" and who could shake off with a shrug "many worms that would have burrowed deeply into others" (*GM* I 10). In comparison, the slaves were "impotent and oppressed" and "rankled with poisonous and hostile feelings" (*GM* I 10). They craved respite from their suffering, and for them happiness was a "narcotic, an anesthetic, rest, peace, 'sabbath,' relaxation of the mind and stretching of the limbs, in short something *passive*" (*GM* I 10).

Let us stop here. Without clarifying what the metaphors of "evaluating glance" and "saying 'yes' or 'no' to itself" mean and without knowing more about why the oppressed might desire anesthetizing affects, these initial descriptions of ressentiment are too enigmatic to reveal most of its dimensions and implications. So what follows describes ressentiment as a psychological event, process, or episode of a particular type that has a particular structure, feels a particular way, has particular causal antecedents and causal consequences, and is productive in certain ways.

Ressentiment's Status as an Instinct/Drive

Nietzsche is not such a fawning admirer of the old masters as to think they were free of ressentiment; nor does he credit its invention to the slave revolt in morality. Ressentiment was already found in societies predating the slave revolt, and he acknowledges in

GM I 10 that the old masters experienced it as well. He is also careful not to claim that ressentiment is determined by social class, so it is not a reaction whose content consists solely in countering noble values. Ressentiment is instead an "instinctive reaction" (*GM* I 11; see also *GM* III 15) found in all human beings and at all times in human history. As instinctive, ressentiment occurs naturally as an involuntary and largely unalterable set of physiological and psychological responses to certain kinds of inputs. So too, ressentiment's affective qualities—its phenomenological characters and the various emotions it prompts—are also involuntary and largely unalterable across individuals when prompted by any of that set of inputs. Those inputs and affects together cause other predictable cognitive, affective, and behavioral consequences.

Some exceptions to these generalizations may be admitted. For instance, at *A* 40, Nietzsche acknowledges that ressentiment can be brought under control and perhaps overcome (he even identifies the lesson of Jesus as being the overcoming of ressentiment, surprising for anyone who thinks that his disdain for Christianity extends without qualification to its spiritual touchstone). He also thinks that ressentiment is experienced less frequently and usually prompts different outcomes in the old masters than in the old slaves. Even if the masters experienced ressentiment, it did not "occur in countless cases where it is unavoidable for all who are weak and powerless," and when the masters did feel ressentiment, it was "consumed and exhausted in an immediate reaction" (*GM* I 10), such as directly challenging the offender to a combative trial of some sort.

Ressentiment as found in the slaves and priests is the focus of most of Nietzsche's attention, for as found among them, ressentiment reveals something that is familiar to most of us moderns (as discussed presently, ressentiment's expression in the priestly caste is somewhat different). Powerlessness, poverty, ill-health, unprotected social standing, and the unique kinds of suffering they caused, together entailed that the slaves could not engage in direct retaliation against insult and injury without immediate risk of losing either life or limb or whatever meager social status they had. Since direct response was barred, they had to settle for indirect retaliation, that is, they had to "compensate" for the impossibility of direct revenge with "imaginary revenge"

(*GM* I 10). One part of that imaginary revenge was the revolution that resulted in the revaluation of the masters' values.

Describing ressentiment as natural is but one of several descriptions of ancient individuals that emphasize what is natural in them. Consider:

> There is nothing strange about the fact that lambs bear a grudge towards large birds of prey: but that is no reason to blame the large birds of prey for carrying off little lambs. . . . It is just as absurd to ask strength *not* to express itself as strength, *not* to be a desire to overthrow, crush, become master, to be a thirst for enemies, resistance and triumphs, as it is to ask weakness to express itself as strength. (*GM* I 13)

If this general point is correct, it follows as a corollary that the masters were strong simply because they took physical actions against enemies and had desires to dominate others, to overthrow and crush them, while the slaves were weak simply because they refrained from physical combat and submissively accepted the masters' contempt for them. They may have tried to overthrow and crush enemies, and they may have tried revenge, but their weakness ruled out successful retaliation.

The masters behaved rather differently when they left the confines of society and went on adventures or on raids against other communities and tribes:

> [T]hey *return* to the innocent conscience of the wild beast, as exultant monsters, who perhaps go away having committed a hideous succession of murder, arson, rape and torture, in a mood of bravado and spiritual equilibrium as though they had simply played a student's prank, convinced that poets will now have something to sing about and celebrate for quite some time. At the center of all these noble races we cannot fail to see the beast of prey, the magnificent *blond beast* avidly prowling round for spoil and victory; this hidden center needs release from time to time, the beast must get out again, must return to the wild: —Roman, Arabian, Germanic, Japanese nobility, Homeric heroes, Scandinavian Vikings—in this requirement they are all alike. (*GM* I 11)

It cannot be denied that Nietzsche thinks highly of the masters and their "scorn for safety, body, life, comfort, their shocking cheerfulness and depth of delight in all destruction, in all the debauches of victory and cruelty" (*GM* I 11). So this passage might be taken to suggest that noble types of all ages and in all sociocultural contexts are justified in being as detached and blasé about their condescension and contempt of others as the masters were when they went on their campaigns of "murder, arson, rape and torture." Yet, despite the masters' obvious power, unthinking nonchalance, and wanton destruction, Nietzsche recognizes that from our modern perspective, they are "monsters," "shockingly violent," and "not much better than uncaged beasts of prey," with "hideous" behaviors that are "cold, cruel, lacking feeling and conscience, crushing everything and coating it with blood" (*GM* I 11). They were, after all, tribal barbarians, strong and brave but "mad, absurd and sudden" (*GM* I 11; see also *BGE* 257: "the noble caste always started out as the barbarian caste"). The only role the masters can play for us now is that they give an ancient example of a kind of human being that was impressive in its time. Other, modern examples of a "human being who justifies the human being, a stroke of luck, an instance of someone who makes up for and redeems the human being and enables us to retain our *faith in humankind*" (*GM* I 12) are now needed. (Note also that the list of old masters includes Romans, Arabians, and Japanese. None are blond Teutons. So the suspicion that membership in any noble class is reserved to Germans is again shown to be false.)

Ressentiment's Affective Character

Ressentiment erupts in our inner world as a combination of strong feelings including "agitation" (*GM* I 10), "pain" (*GM* III 15), "suffering" (*GM* III 15, 17), "misery" (*GM* I 14), "hatred" (*GM* I 10, 11, 14, 16), "hostility" (*GM* I 10), "vindictiveness" (*GM* I 13), "vengeful desires" (*GM* I 10, 11, 14, III 14, 15), "envy" (*GM* II 1, III 15), and "spite" (*GM* III 15). Note that this list segregates a set of affects that are caused by inputs but lack something or someone toward which they are directed (agitation, pain, suffering, misery) from a set of affects that are caused by inputs and have something or someone toward which they are directed (hatred, hostility, vindictiveness, vengeance, envy, and spite). Segregating the kinds of affect associated with ressentiment thus exposes it as a temporally extended and multifaceted psychological episode rather than a short-lived and unidimensional event or state. Ressentiment is initially experienced as an immediate, involuntary, and distressing reaction to certain kinds of currently unidentified inputs. Yet, in subsequent phases, it is a reaction complicated by other elements that load this direct and spontaneous distress with other recruited affective and cognitive dimensions and elements.

Compare ressentiment with defensive counters. Ressentiment is distinct from a "defensive return of a blow, a purely protective reaction, a 'reflex movement' in the case of any sudden injury or peril, such as that performed even by a headless frog to ward off corrosive acid" (*GM* III 15). Such behaviors are distinct from ressentiment because they reflexively prevent "further harm from being done" (*GM* III 15). Inanimate objects, plants, or nonhuman animals typically cause such defensive counters. Yet, even if another person injures us, we sometimes similarly act out of this kind of "self-preservation," and in doing so, we are thinking "not of the person who caused the injury, but only of oneself: we act thus *without* wanting to do harm in return, but only so as *to get out* with life and limb" (*HH* II *Wanderer* 33).

Nietzsche is not certain that defensive counterblows count as a form of revenge, but even if they do, they must be distinguished from a second kind of revenge. One distinctive feature of this second kind is that we "transfer [our] thoughts from [our self] to [our] opponent" and reflect "over the other's vulnerability and capacity for suffering: [we] want to hurt" (*HH* II *Wanderer* 33). Instead of preventing further pain with a defensive counterblow, the desire to cause suffering in others recruits other beliefs and affective states so as to displace or transfer our suffering onto another who is held causally responsible for it, thereby anesthetizing it. This more complex kind of revenge is characteristic of ressentiment. Ressentiment successfully anesthetizes suffering by redirecting sufferers away from the "true reason" (*GM* III 15) for their pain and onto some other cause for it. That fabricated cause is the "first available pretext.... 'Someone or other must be to blame'—this kind of conclusion is peculiar to all sick people" (*GM* III 15).

Ressentiment's anesthetizing affects are investigated presently. Here we note three facets of suffering on which Nietzsche relies. First, suffering is ubiquitous to life; it may be something we would love to ignore or paper over, perhaps even abolish (*BGE* 44), but it always remains. To try to abolish suffering would be to abolish life itself (*BGE* 44, 202, 225, 257; *EH* "Good Books" *Z* 8). Second, it is experientially axiomatic that suffering results in attempts to reduce it, and quickly (we will see in Chapter 5 that Nietzsche qualifies this categorical claim). Third, to curb it, the sufferer tries to self-diagnose its causes so as to avoid, defuse, or take vengeance against those causes. All of those who suffer have a causal drive (*Ursachentrieb*) for finding "a reason why we are in the particular state we are in—why we are feeling good or bad" (*TI* "The Four Great Errors," 4). The act of "familiarizing something unfamiliar is comforting, reassuring, satisfying, and produces a feeling of power as well" whereas "unfamiliar things are dangerous, anxiety-provoking, upsetting" (*TI* "The Four Great Errors" 5). The ways that ressentiment redirects and misdirects the sufferer, and the anesthetizing affects that it elicits, are key to unlocking its unique place in Nietzsche's psychological views of the slaves and priests and his explanation of their revolt against noble evaluation.

Ressentiment's Inputs

'Ressentiment' is composed of the French *sentiment* (feeling) prefixed by *re-* (again). So ressentiment is a temporally extended process that re-presents a feeling that was prompted by something in the past and now recalled in memory. The prompts for feelings recalled in ressentiment vary enormously, ranging from the purely physiological to the physiopsychological, to the more recognizably psychological, and, finally, to the psychosocial and social. At the physiological end of the spectrum are some quite specific causes, including "a disease of the *nervus sympaticus*, or an excessive secretion of bile, or a deficiency of potassium sulphate and phosphate in the blood, or abdominal strictures interrupting the blood circulation, or a degeneration of the ovaries and such like" (*GM* III 15). Other physiological causes include having bowel complaints and neurasthenia (*GM* I 6), a bad diet (*GM* III 17), practicing sexual abstinence and fasting (*GM* I 6), and malaria, syphilis, or other diseases (*GM* III 17). More frequently, general physiological conditions, disorders, ailments, and deficiencies are identified. So, for example, being filthy (*GM* I 6), weak (*GM* I 13, 14), impotent (*GM* I 7, 10, 13, 14), diseased, ill, and subject to inner disintegration (*GM* I 6, 11, III 15, 16), sick, upset, and leaden (*GM* III 16), obstructed, weary, and lethargic (*GM* III 17; *BGE* 260), and stunted, wasted, and poisoned (*GM* I 11) are all possible physiological causes of ressentiment.

Causes of ressentiment that straddle the physiological-psychological line include being failed, tired, and exhausted (*GM* I 11), mediocre and unedifying (*GM* I 11), cowardly (*GM* I 5, 13, 14), and timid and submissive (*GM* I 13, 14). Causes more plausibly characterized as psychological include suffering from 'psychic' disorders (*GM* III 16), and deep depression, heaviness, and black melancholy (*GM* III 17). And, finally, the psychosocial and social causes of ressentiment that Nietzsche focuses most on—they are the causes most tightly bound up in the slave revolt in morality—include being poor, powerless, and deprived (*GM* I 7; *BGE* 260), ugly (*GM* I 7), unhappy and pitiable (*GM* I 10), a slave worker and beast of burden (*GM* I 10), oppressed (*GM* I 10, 13; *BGE* 260), worm-eaten (*GM* I 10), downtrodden (*GM* I 11, 13), and ill-treated and violated (*GM* I 11, 13; *BGE* 260).

One thing that is immediately apparent is that ressentiment is a response fed by entirely natural "condition[s] of existence" (*GM* I 10) rather than otherworldly causes. It is important to re-emphasize here how thoroughgoing Nietzsche's naturalism is. That he commits himself to a naturalistic explanation of moral evaluation has already been established. Still, even if some of the causes of ressentiment are natural, there is no inconsistency in thinking that others might be otherworldly. However, Nietzsche rejects this mixed view. For him, all inputs to ressentiment are natural inputs and none are otherwise. Of course, persons experiencing ressentiment may believe that the cause of their ressentiment is an insult shown to God, but all that shows is that there is a difference between what people believe about ressentiment's causes and what those causes actually are, which in turn reveals that those who experience ressentiment are subject to self-deception.

The Cauldron of Ressentiment

Any one of the previously identified causal inputs, or any combination of them, can feed the cauldron of ressentiment, where they then mix with other affects, emotions, drives, desires, and beliefs about oneself and others. Recall that when felt, ressentiment in the old masters was immediately discharged in some trial of combat or display of courage and bravery. So even if it shares some of the same causes as those found in the slaves and priests, ressentiment in the masters resolved quickly and violently and did not persist long enough to recruit or mix much with other beliefs, affects, drives, and desires. However, deprived as they were of immediate physical opportunities to discharge their suffering, the stew of ressentiment in slaves and priests continued to churn, and to it other ingredients were added, making it more ruminative, more provocative and poisonous, more creative and imaginative.

Physiological causes are often easy to diagnose and, having once been diagnosed, they typically do not result in further reflection and so typically do not result in any kind of desire for revenge. Of course, if we smash a thumb with a hammer, we may curse the hammer and hurl it as far from us as possible. Similarly, when another person inadvertently elbows us in the ribs on the subway, we may shove the person's arm away. Both are protective counterblows to prevent further injury and do not include any desire to cause harm to anything or anyone else. We may also take our frustrations out on inanimate objects when we do something stupid, embarrassing, or clumsy. Tennis players sometimes smash their racket on the ground when they make a bad shot. In these and many other similar cases, desire to cause harm to inanimate objects exists even though we know that they do not feel pain and do not suffer. None are examples of ressentiment.

Most physiological, psychological, and social suffering is more involved than stubbing a toe or kicking a flat tire. To begin with, these knottier kinds of suffering may be difficult to diagnose because their causes are epistemologically opaque. We who suffer may not know enough to correctly self-diagnose debilitating headaches caused by brain cancer; we may be ignorant of the causal connections between eating sugar, cavity production, and toothache; we may be unconscious of some facial tic but be painfully aware that others find being in our presence unsettling; we may be blind to our own psychological shortcomings or self-deceived about our own character and yet may suffer from them on a daily basis; we may not be aware of the macroeconomic causes of economic oppression even while being dreadfully cognizant of our poverty and subjugation. In addition, many kinds of psychological and social suffering are difficult to neutralize even if their causes are known, either because those causes are unavoidable, or because they are recurring, or because they are uniquely salient, or because their resolution is so challenging.

Yet the need to diagnose suffering's causes continues even when we cannot identify them, and the need to end suffering remains salient even when we cannot see how to accomplish it. In these cases, those needs can recruit other affects, emotions, drives, and beliefs to discover or invent new causes of suffering and to conceive novel resolutions for it based on those discoveries and inventions. Here the creative productivity characteristic of ressentiment starts to express itself. Since we are all amateur sleuths of our own suffering, we continue to look for "a cause of distress; more exactly, for a culprit, even more precisely for a *guilty* culprit who is receptive to distress, —in short, for a living being upon whom [w]e can release . . . emotions, actually or in effigy, on some pretext or other" (*GM* III 15). This key passage contains four distinct claims. First, when we cannot easily find a cause for our distress, we often look for another animate being, usually another human being, to be a culprit of our misfortune. Second, other humans are culprits of our suffering because they are thought to be causally responsible for it. Third, since other humans are relevantly similar to us, culprits also feel pain and suffer. Fourth, we can release or transfer our suffering onto culprits, whether actually or indirectly "in effigy."

Especially when suffering is caused by weakness or impotence, we are prone to reidentifying the cause of our suffering as being some other person rather than some internal, social, or environmental condition. Having thus identified, or rather misidentified, a person as causally responsible, we seek to displace our suffering onto that person as a way of resolving it. This need to transfer or displace suffering onto a culprit who is believed to be causally responsible is a hallmark of ressentiment: ressentiment is a strong emotion that routinely attributes or misattributes blame to another in an attempt to deaden or at least muffle our ongoing distress. And one of the most astonishing features of our desire for revenge is that its narcotizing effect can be successful even if displacing suffering onto the newly minted object of our ressentiment, the culprit, is unsuccessful:

> [T]he release of emotions is the greatest attempt at relief, or should I say, at *anaesthetizing* on the part of the sufferer, his involuntarily longed-for narcotic against pain of any kind. In my judgment, we find here the actual physiological causation of *ressentiment*, revenge and their ilk, in a yearning, then, to *anaesthetize pain through emotion* . . . [T]he attempt is made to *anaesthetize* a tormenting, secret pain that is becoming unbearable with a more violent emotion of any sort, and at least rid the consciousness of it for the moment, — for this, one needs an emotion, the wildest possible emotion and, in order to arouse it, the first available pretext. "Someone or other must be to blame that I fell ill"—this kind of conclusion is peculiar to all sick people, and in fact becomes more insistent, the more they remain in ignorance of the true reason, the physiological one, why they feel ill. (*GM* III 15)

Granted, this is a gloomy psychological picture, but it is no less true for its bleakness. We can all identify episodes when we have tried to displace our frustration or anger with our own inadequacies onto others to avoid confronting them in ourselves.

Ressentiment's Productivity

Ressentiment's mixture of multifactored suffering, ignorance, self-deception, causal re- and misidentification, culprit invention, blame-throwing, and desire for revenge diverts attention away from distress that can otherwise feel intractable and redirects attention and suffering onto culprits who bear the brunt of our offloading attempts. Of course, the anesthetizing offloading of suffering onto others that ressentiment triggers takes many forms, most of them stupid but some of them scheming, explosive, or grotesque. One of the shrewdest and most fantastic is the slave revolt in moral evaluation.

Hatred, hostility, and the desire for revenge are among ressentiment's most fertile elements; they are certainly the elements to which Nietzsche most frequently attends. As we have seen, among the old masters, hatred and the desire for revenge were immediately expressed, directly and unmistakably aimed at an enemy, actively pursued until victory or defeat, and viscerally realized in tangible action. However, the more interesting case is hatred and the desire for revenge as found among slaves and priests, in whom they grow to uncanny proportions, not immediately but gradually, not directly and unmistakably but circuitously and deviously, not actively but passively, not viscerally and tangibly but deliberately and spiritually. These oblique, reactive, cunning, and otherworldly responses provide the genealogist with some of the most thought-provoking responses to distress and misery.

Festering ressentiment becomes creative in one way when causal responsibility for suffering is directed away from its actual cause onto a different object, a culprit who, like the sufferer, is also liable to pain and distress. This "release of emotions is the greatest attempt at relief, or should I say, at *anaesthetizing* on the part of the sufferer, his involuntary longed-for narcotic against pain of any kind. In my judgment, we find here the actual physiological causation of *ressentiment*, revenge and their ilk, in a yearning, then, to *anaesthetize pain through emotion*" (*GM* III 15). First, instead of identifying causal responsibility for suffering as something internal, we reidentify that cause as something external. Second, we bury the real causes of suffering and create human culprits on whom we can aim our hatred and focus our revenge. Third, the fabrication of a new target of ressentiment underwrites an imaginary reaction rather than direct action against that target.

The slaves witnessed the old masters' oppression regularly and their indifference daily, but the masters nonchalantly excused the suffering they caused and their indifference to it on the grounds that "the poets will now have something to sing about and celebrate" (*GM* I 11). Even when, as was also the case, the masters were not causally responsible for their suffering, the oppressed nonetheless reallocated responsibility to them, and in their attempt to do so they explored the nature of the culprits they identified, trying to isolate what about them might explain their oppression and indifference. At this juncture the priest's "far-sighted, subterranean revenge, which unfolds itself slowly and thinks ahead" (*GM* I 8) started to assert itself. Steeped in purity rituals that helped cultivate emotional regulation and attention diversion by performing rote motor behaviors loaded with significance, the priests were familiar with methods for cultivating self-control. Since they were members of an elite class, the priests occupied a unique position. They served their own ambitions for power by organizing the suffering found everywhere around them, and they galvanized ressentiment by offering to the oppressed an assessment of the warriors and aristocrats that explained their responsibility for suffering in a facile, if topsy-turvy, way. It was the warriors and the aristocrats who were to blame for everyone's misery because they chose to act despicably and did not care about the suffering they caused. Nietzsche investigates this facet of the slave revolt in Section 13, to which we turn shortly.

Here note that the slaves had a compelling reason for labeling the old masters as evil and themselves as good. The masters affirmed their flourishing lives and as an afterthought dismissed the slaves as bad. By doing so, they were able to dismiss slavish suffering as uninteresting yet required for realizing their own superiority. The slaves, unable to affirm their miserable lives, denounced that claimed superiority and as a consequence affirmed their own moral superiority. So, whereas the old masters self-designated themselves as good first and designated the rabble as bad second, the priest and the rabble designated the old masters as evil first and designated themselves as good in response to that contrast. That is, the old masters were active "yes-sayers" and the old slaves were reactive 'no-sayers.'

Sections 11–12

Sections 11 and 12 reveal why the psychology of ressentiment is so important for understanding the genealogy of moral evaluation. Ressentiment has, Nietzsche claims, been used "to breed a tame and civilized animal, a *household pet*, out of the beast of prey 'man'" (*GM* I 11). In this way, the mechanisms of ressentiment are "*instruments of culture*" by which "the noble races and their ideals were finally wrecked and overpowered" (*GM* I 11). Yet, even if instruments of culture, those in whom ressentiment festers are far from representing culture themselves. Indeed, the slaves and the priests represent the decline of humanity, not its growth. Breeding modern civilized humans has, after all, bred out of humanity what once made its exemplars admirable, even if frightening. Contemporary humans have become "a teeming mass of worms," "incurably mediocre and unedifying," and Europe is now dominated by "failed, sickly, tired and exhausted people" (*GM* I 11). What is needed is a "glimpse of a human being who justifies the human being, a stroke of luck, an instance of someone who makes up for and redeems the human being and enables us to retain our *faith in humankind*" (*GM* I 12). Without such humans, Europe's greatest danger is revealed: "[I]n losing our fear of man we have also lost our love for him, our respect for him, our hope in him and even our will to be man. The sight of man now makes us tired—what is nihilism today if it is not *that?*... We are tired of *humans*" (*GM* I 12).

Sections 13–15

Sections 13, 14, and 15 purport to be an analysis of how the slave revolt in morality advanced. However, if we expect a summary of violent clashes, riots, rebellions, and wars, or more etymological evidence about shifting reference for evaluative words over time, or evidence concerning the psychological dimensions of, and social relations between, ancient peoples, these sections will frustrate and disappoint. Section 13 merely describes a set of philosophical reflections on the nature of agency, the metaphysical seductions of language, and the status of the Kantian thing-in-itself; Section 14 offers an allegory describing a workshop where moral values and ideals are fabricated; and Section 15 describes the kingdom of heaven and recites, at length and in Latin, a description of the punishment of the damned from the early Christian Tertullian (155–220 CE).

When reading these sections, we should remember that the genealogy of morality is, among other things, interested in how the psychology of ressentiment is implicated in the slave revolt in morality. The focus is on the way that the poor, the sick, the powerless and downtrodden—what Nietzsche also calls 'the herd'—collaborated with the clergy to wage psychological war on the old masters. Their ressentiment became creative in part by manufacturing cognitive and affective devices that latched onto the high esteem in which the old masters held themselves and then sucked that esteem out (*A* 59). The slave revolt in morality proceeded by reconceiving what the old masters were, by using a suite of strategies on them—browbeating, persuading, coaxing, promising, humiliating, assuring, preaching, hoodwinking—until they accepted that reconfiguration.

As powerful, strong, self-confident, and happy as they might have been, the old masters were decidedly unreflective. One example of their coarseness is that they made no distinction between themselves as agents and the actions they performed: they were their actions, and so, since they were powerful, they could not but express their strength and power. As Nietzsche puts the point in *BGE*, each and every living organism has to "As Nietzsche puts the point in *BGE*, each and every living organism has to 'grow, spread, grab, win dominance—not out of any morality or immorality, but because it is *alive*, and because life *is* precisely will to power'" (*BGE* 259). Again, "'Exploitation' . . . belongs to the *essence* of being alive as a fundamental organic function; it is a result of genuine will to power, which is just the will of life" (*BGE* 259). The warriors and aristocrats embodied this will to power, this will of life, in what they did and affirmed, even if what they did oppressed the masses. We return to willing power and willing life in each of the next chapters.

The slaves were also dimwitted, but the priests who led and shaped them came from a pure elite and were adept at emotional self-regulation and attention control. They developed a strategy that proved to be profound in its consequences both for the slaves and for the aristocrats and warriors. Contrary to the old master's fusion of self and action, the priests introduced a metaphysical distinction between the subject and its actions. Just as the "common people separate lightning from its flash and takes the latter to be a *deed*, something performed by a subject, called lightning, popular morality separates strength from the manifestations of strength, as though there were an indifferent substratum behind the strong person who had the *freedom* to manifest strength or not" (*GM* I 13). The priests, committed to differentiating themselves from the masters and engaged in a multifaceted gambit against them, used the distinction between subject and action as a means for "gaining the right to make the birds of prey *responsible* for being birds of prey" (*GM* I 13). (For confirmation that Nietzsche is on the right track, think of the expression in many contemporary strands of Christianity that "God loves the sinner but hates the sin").

Not much more is offered here in defense of these extraordinary claims. We return to them below in the discussion section of this chapter; again when we discuss Essay II's analyses of responsibility, conscience, guilt / bad conscience, and power; and again when we discuss Essay III's assessment of the priests in cultivating and promulgating the slave revolt. What is of interest here is how that metaphysical distinction was used to valorize the slaves and poison the masters. The claim is twofold: first, under the direction of the priests, slaves came to think of their weakness as a choice rather than as a condition of their existence; second, in a parallel development, they started to slowly poison the masters into thinking that they too could avoid their displays of strength if they chose to do so.

Nietzsche describes the first half of the slave revolution clearly enough:

> When the oppressed, the downtrodden, the violated say to each other with the vindictive cunning of powerlessness: "Let us be different from the evil people, let us be good! And a good person is anyone who does not rape, does not harm anyone, who does not attack, does not retaliate, who leaves the taking of revenge to God, who keeps hidden as we do, avoids all evil and asks little from life in general, like us who are patient, humble and upright"—this means, if heard coolly and impartially, nothing more than: "We weak people are just weak; it is good to do nothing *for which we are not strong enough*." (*GM* I 13)

The weak came to think of their weakness as a virtuous choice of the soul rather than as a natural fact of their character. Their belief in a subject distinct from its actions has "facilitated that sublime self-deception whereby the majority of the dying, the weak and the oppressed of every kind could construe weakness itself as freedom, and their particular mode of existence as an *accomplishment*" (*GM* I 13). Pause long enough to grasp the significance of these claims. Weakness—"its *essence*, its effect, its whole unique, unavoidable, irredeemable reality"—transmuted from being something unlucky, involuntary, and unwelcome into something else, "a voluntary achievement, something wanted, chosen, a *deed*, an *accomplishment*" (*GM* I 13).

Nietzsche says nothing in Section 13 about the other half of the slave revolt, that which explains how victory over the masters was achieved by poisoning their self-image and self-evaluation. Nor does Section 14 provide any insight into this crucial element of the slave revolt (he does talk about these matters eventually, in Essay III, and we will investigate them there). Instead, Section 14 is a feverish and grating account of how the old slaves came to value themselves and to assemble their values. We might benefit best from an explanation of the various mechanisms used by the slaves and priests to implement their revolt against the old masters' mode of evaluation; instead, he invites "Mr. Nosy Daredevil" to look into the "dark workshop" of "how *ideals are fabricated* on earth" (*GM* I 14).

A key psychological ingredient in the workshop's activity of forging slave values is that while the weak desire revenge against those whom they hold responsible for their suffering, they cannot seek direct revenge against them, and, incapable of direct retaliation, they devise indirect kinds of revenge. Among others, they create the myth about themselves that they have chosen not to take revenge. In this way, "Not-being-able-to-take-revenge is called not-wanting-to-take-revenge" (*GM* I 14). Moreover, they take their ongoing misery as evidence not of their pathetic plight but as evidence that God chooses them. Their misery is "preparation, a test, a training, . . . something that will one day be balanced up and paid back with enormous interest in gold, no! in happiness" (*GM* I 14). And one of the slaves' refinements is to convert their hatred of the masters and their desire for revenge against them into what they call goodness and justice. "What they are demanding is not called retribution, but 'the triumph of *justice*'; what they hate is not their enemy, oh no! they hate '*injustice*,' 'godlessness' " (*GM* I 14).

Once the weak have become armed with the conviction that they are chosen by God, and their hatred of the masters has been converted into hatred of injustice, they further outfit themselves with ardent hopes that enlist divine justification for their revenge and posit divine realms where it is enacted: "[W]hat they believe and hope for is not the prospect of revenge, the delirium of sweet revenge, . . . but the victory of God, the *just* God, over the godless; all that remains for them to love on earth are not their brothers in hate but their 'brothers in love' "

(*GM* I 14). Since, as they claim is the case, they have made a choice (not because, as the case actually is, they have no choice), the wretched condescend to continue on so that they can "live 'in faith,' 'in love,' 'in hope'" (*GM* I 14) until God's justice is achieved.

Beneath these self-congratulatory affirmations, fictitious choices, and pious appeals to faith, love, and hope, something more malodorous fills the dark workshop. We need to pay attention to what the priests, "those black magicians who can turn anything black into whiteness, milk and innocence" (*GM* I 14), are saying. The weak "want to be the powerful one day, this is beyond doubt," but because they are weak, their power cannot be achieved in this world but will arrive only later: "[S]omeday *their* 'kingdom' too shall come—'the kingdom of God'" (*GM* I 15), and there finally the tables will be turned against the powerful. Of course, they and their priestly advocates advertise the existence of the kingdom of God with modest self-effacement, lest they draw attention to the long game they are playing. "[T]hey are so humble about everything! Just to experience *that*, you need to live long, well beyond death, —yes, you need eternal life in order to be able to gain eternal recompense in 'the kingdom of God'" (*GM* I 15). There in the kingdom of God reward and bliss await the faithful.

Even so, every so often, a religious spokesperson will drop the facade of humility and reveal what the talk about heavenly bliss is about. For instance, here is Saint Thomas Aquinas describing paradise's recompense: "'The blessed in the heavenly kingdom will see the torment of the damned *so that they may even more thoroughly enjoy their blessedness*'" (*GM* I 15). The sadism of this picture of heaven cannot be overstated. After all, the element of the faithful's heavenly afterlife that St. Thomas highlights is their glee in watching the damned being tortured for eternity. To ensure that this ghastly point is fully grasped, Nietzsche recites another early Christian, Tertullian, who rapturously describes the agonies awaiting the damned. Among the more heavenly sights and sounds that the saved will exult over are kings and governors "melting in flames more savage than those with which they insolently raged against Christians" and philosophers, poets, charioteers, and athletes, all screaming and "all red in a wheel of flame" (*GM* I 15). It will be the privilege of the saved to "cast an *insatiable* gaze on those who raged against the Lord" (*GM* I 15).

Sections 16–17

Disgusted by the workshop of moral ideals and horrified by its paradise, Nietzsche surveys the outcome from a contemporary perspective, from which it can be seen that "the two *opposing* values 'good and bad,' 'good and evil' have fought a terrible battle for thousands of years on earth" (*GM* I 16). The slaves call themselves and their behavior 'good,' and they call the masters and their behavior 'evil.' What under the noble evaluative regime was good becomes evil and what was bad becomes good. In this way, the priests managed to revalue a set of values, create new ones, and disseminate this new evaluative scheme to the herd, which accepts the scheme. This is the slave revolt in morality.

The fight between the two modes of evaluation can be stated simply: " 'Rome against Judea, Judea against Rome': —up to now there has been no greater event than *this* battle, *this* question, *this* contradiction of mortal enemies" (*GM* I 16). That the slave revolt has been victorious is beyond question. "Which of them has *prevailed* for the time being, Rome or Judea? But there is no trace of doubt: just consider to whom you bow down in Rome itself, today, as though to the embodiment of the highest values. . . . Without a doubt, Rome has been defeated" (*GM* I 16). More recent skirmishes between the herd and nobility only confirm the hypothesis. When, during the Renaissance, ancient cultural values reawakened, "as though from suspended animation," they were crushed by the "*ressentiment*-movement which people called the Reformation" (*GM* I 16). And, after that, "The last political nobility in Europe, that of the *French* seventeenth and eighteenth centuries, collapsed under the *ressentiment-instincts* of the rabble" (*GM* I 16). Finally, in the early nineteenth century, another gasp from the noble type emanated from Napoleon, "a man more unique and late-born for his times than ever a man had been before, and in him, the problem of the *noble ideal itself* was made flesh: . . . Napoleon, this synthesis of *Unmensch* (brute) and *Übermensch* (overhuman)" (*GM* I 16).

Section 17 closes the first essay not with a summary but with a suggestion and a request. First, we should all want to question whether we would like to renew the debate about the slave revolt's victory because, as Nietzsche admits, answering this question may not lead to "a speedy conclusion" (*GM* I 17). At least his own desires are clear: he explicitly wants to go beyond the herd's good and evil, and he implies that he wants not to go beyond some updated version of the noble's good and bad. Second, he reiterates his plea from the Preface for intellectual comrades from "philosophy, physiology, and medicine" (*GM* I 17) to continue his work on the genealogy of morality. What is needed "first and foremost" is a "*physiological* elucidation and interpretation, rather than a psychological one," of every "table of values, every 'thou shalt' known to history" (*GM* I 17). Those investigations, elucidations, and interpretations must be guided by metaethical questions about moral values, such as "[W]hat is this or that table of values and 'morals' *worth*?" and "*for what*" are values valuable? (*GM* I 17). For, as should by now be apparent, the genealogy of moral values discloses a long and protracted combat between what is noble and what is not, a battle that continues unabated. Philosophers and the sciences must now work together to "solve the *problem of values*" and to "decide on the *rank order of values*" (*GM* I 17). How this collaboration is to go forward is not further specified, but one obvious organization would be for the scientists to continue to study, as *GM* does, the values entrenched in our society and then for the philosophers to take the results of those studies as input for their legislative efforts of rank-ordering values and revaluing some of them. We will see in Essay III that this organization of tasks is complicated by science's own capitulation to the ascetic ideals entrenched in herd morality.

3.3 Discussion

If we are not dazed and perplexed after finishing the first essay, we have not been paying enough attention. Nietzsche's colorful tapestry of the slave revolt in moral evaluation is compelling but so incomplete that we should be worried that were we to start pulling on any of its threads we might unravel the entire argument. Two kinds of worries present themselves. The first is that much of what he offers in Essay I is incompletely described; the second is that some of what he says in Essay I is inadequately defended.

Here are five topics that Nietzsche introduces but incompletely describes in Essay I. First, he mentions custom more than once in his description of the constraints by which the masters bound themselves when interacting with each other but fails to elaborate. Second, he mentions but does not describe bad conscience / guilt in any detail. Third, he introduces but does not describe how ressentiment and justice are related. Fourth, he begins but does not complete his description of the priest's role in the slave revolt. Fifth, he asserts that the masters were brought to their knees by the slave revolt but does not begin to describe how that happened. We return to custom, bad conscience, guilt, and the relation between ressentiment and justice in the next chapter. Only after we better understand them can we approach the other two issues. Yet with custom, responsibility, conscience, bad conscience, and guilt in hand, we will better understand the role of ressentiment in justice, and that in turn allows us to return to the priest's role in the slave revolt in Essay III. And from that description we will then be able to explain how the masters came to their bitter end. As difficult as it may be, patience is the only alternative on these matters.

We may also wonder about some of what Nietzsche claims in Essay I. First, his exposition appears to equivocate on various uses of the term 'morality,' and that apparent equivocation may undermine his genealogical project. Second, more needs to be said about his contrast between master morality and herd morality. Third, he relies on a naturalized drive/affect moral psychology to underwrite the genealogical claim that herd morality layers new interpretations of our psyches onto other already existing ones, but he does not explicate this psychology. We discuss these three issues now.

Different Kinds of Morality and Moral Psychology

Nietzsche repeatedly uses the term 'morality' in *GM*, and scholars have noted that the term does not always refer consistently, referring on one occasion to one phenomenon and on another occasion to a distinct phenomenon. An example is that Nietzsche refers, among others, to master morality, slave morality, the morality of customs, herd morality, the morality of ressentiment, the morality of compassion, and Christian morality. Are these species of a single genus, or are they instead so disparate that they share no common core elements?

A second example is that he routinely criticizes moralities premised on certain moral values, such as compassion, while praising moralities premised on other moral values, such as courage. How can he do that consistently?

Different Senses of 'Morality'

In one way, using 'morality' to refer to distinct phenomena may be a superficial matter, no more serious a problem than that which attaches to terms such as 'bank,' 'foot,' and 'screen,' each of which also has multiple referents. So long as Nietzsche is clear that he uses 'morality' to refer to different phenomena, the problem dissolves. Still, since 'morality' does indeed refer to distinct phenomena, there may be nothing these phenomena share that merits bringing them under the scope of a single concept. Here let us introduce a distinction that, in one form or another, many scholars rely on when defusing this problem.[3] Nietzsche uses 'morality' to refer both to evaluative systems that are valuable in some sense and to evaluative systems that are not valuable in that sense. We can then gather the unworthy evaluative systems under the term 'morality in the pejorative sense,' and quarantine them under that term. Having done so, we can see that in *GM* Nietzsche's primary analytic focus is morality in the pejorative sense. This distinction allows 'morality' to refer generally to any system of evaluative practices, principles, and concepts governing human behavior, while recognizing that some species of the genus—those whose historical descent is Nietzsche's primary focus in *GM*—have features that disqualify them from being valuable systems. The trick, of course, is to recognize the distinct species and understand how they relate to one another. This is not always easy since we must distinguish worthy moralities from unworthy ones. Other philosophers would accomplish this by describing in detail what makes each a member of its class. Yet doing that is not Nietzsche's foremost task in *GM*.

[3] See Leiter 2002.

Two Kinds of Moral Psychology

If 'morality' refers plurally to different evaluative systems regarding human action, the clean and self-congratulatory ground of other histories of morality turns into something muddier and more humbling. The English genealogists "unsuspectingly stand under the command of a particular morality and, without knowing it, serve as its shield-bearers and followers, for example, by sharing that popular superstition of Christian Europe which people keep repeating so naively to this day, that what is characteristic of morality is selflessness, self-denial, self-sacrifice, or sympathy (*Mitgefohl*) and compassion (*Mitleiden*)" (*GS* 345). Contrary to the English, who think that 'morality' refers only to this evaluative system and who assume that all past moralities must be understood as variants of it, Nietzsche argues that 'morality' refers instead to diverse kinds of evaluative systems appropriate for different kinds of individuals. And contrary to the theologians and philosophers who affirm that the subject is free in all circumstances to choose to act in one way or another, Nietzsche argues that the subject and its actions are fused together in a way he has not yet described.

Nietzsche begins the genealogy of the moral system we have inherited—morality in the pejorative sense, herd morality, rabbleized morality, slave morality—by contrasting it with a distinct morality, master morality. We have already encountered the etymological evidence for the conceptual transformations that occurred when the masters converted self-reflexive praise of themselves into the evaluative scheme of good and bad, and when the herd reversed the master's evaluative scheme so that what the masters glorified as good became evil and what the masters dismissed as bad became good. However, the two-thousand-year history of Judeo-Christian theology, philosophy, and psychology charts how one of Europe's dominant social and intellectual institutions has slowly accumulated and advertised layers of interpretations about our moral psyches. Priests and ministers have dutifully simplified these sophistical reflections and spread them among the masses in sermons, counseling, and study groups, while the masses have reinforced them among themselves. Here, consider two of the reinterpretations—their descriptions of subjectivity and free-will-based agency—that helped operationalize these conceptual transformations.

Among the posits of Nietzsche's naturalism is a naturalized psychology, according to which nature bequeaths to us drives and affects in virtue of our being biological organisms. He thinks that various empirical discoveries in evolutionary biology, human physiology, and human psychology support his claims about these natural drives and affects, and that subsequent scientific investigation will corroborate these discoveries. One set of core drives are those concerned with "growth and expansion" (*GS* 349), cultivating our influence on the world by giving form to it. These core drives and their associated affects—Nietzsche identifies them all as exemplifying a "will to power" (*GM* II 12; *GS* 349; *BGE* 36)—are central to human health. Individuals who live fulfilling them are healthy while those who do not are weak, and those in whom they are robust are stronger than those in whom they are not. We discuss health and strength in greater detail below and discuss will to power in the next two chapters. Here note that it is precisely these drives and their affects against which the evaluative scheme of herd morality wages war:

> Impotence that doesn't retaliate is being turned into "goodness"; timid baseness is being turned into "humility"; submission to people one hates is being turned into "obedience" (actually towards someone who, they say, orders this submission—they call him God). The inoffensiveness of the weakling, the very cowardice with which he is richly endowed, his standing-by-the-door, his inevitable position of having to wait, are all given good names such as "patience," also known as *the* virtue; not-being-able-to-take-revenge is called not-wanting-to-take-revenge. (*GM* I 14)

This passage exemplifies one of *GM*'s main argumentative tactics, that of counterposing what is under one evaluative scheme dismissed as weak to what is valorized under another evaluative scheme as strength. Of course, we do not yet have what is needed to decide between the two evaluative schemes or assess Nietzsche's claim that one of them is more valuable than the other. Again, we will get to that in the next two chapters. Here the important thing is that, depending on the evaluative system we adopt, we can uniquely interpret and develop drives and affects that are common to all of us.

One of the slave revolt's most daring redescriptions augments its re-evaluation of strength and weakness through a reconception of the subject who is either strong or weak. Recall:

> The reason the subject (or, as we more colloquially say, *the soul*) has been, until now, the best doctrine on earth, is perhaps because it facilitated that sublime self-deception whereby the majority of the dying, the weak and the oppressed of every kind could construe weakness itself as freedom, and their particular mode of existence as an *accomplishment*. (*GM* I 13)

This puzzling argument requires additional premises before it can be assessed. These premises are added in Essay II. However, even without them we can appreciate the argumentative tactic of counterposing herd morality's supernatural description of subjectivity and agency to a naturalized description of subjectivity and agency. According to this naturalized description, the subject of action is fused with its actions. A strong person is one whose actions confront difficult conditions directly, while a weak person is one who acts to avoid challenging conditions, quickly capitulates to them, or dissembles and dithers about them. These kinds of subjectivity and agency were embodied in the old masters: they were healthy, affirmative, powerful, energetic, cheerful, spontaneous, and all the rest simply because that is how they acted day in and day out over a lifetime. They rarely reflected on whether they exercised free will to choose otherwise or even if they had free will because they rarely reflected on what their subjectivity was like or what the conditions of their agency might have been.

In herd moral psychology, the subject becomes untethered from its action, as if there were "an indifferent substratum behind the strong person who had the *freedom* to manifest strength or not" (*GM* I 13). This indifferent substratum is identified by Christianity as the soul and by philosophers as the subject. We discuss the soul/subject in greater detail in the next chapter. Here note that assuming there is such a detached soul outfitted with free will to choose to act in numerous ways in all circumstances licenses herd morality to direct attention away from actions and toward the soul, its choices, and its intentions. If there is a featureless subject, a soul, that has the freedom to choose one action rather than another, then even weak actions can be interpreted as freely chosen and intended. This gives herd animals the impression that their weakness actually expresses their strength, the strength to choose submission to others, to choose to turn the other cheek, to choose to obey God's mandates. If they were to adhere to a conception of themselves and their agency consistent with the conception the old masters embodied, herd animals might instead resist those who dominate them, and they might instead have a different view of their own worth when they do not resist.

Indeed, the soul's distinctness from all of its actions underwrites a key component of herd moral psychology. Since the subject is free to choose to act either bravely or cowardly, either proactively or reactively, either spontaneously or suspiciously, either confidently or diffidently, the herd animal's soul can retain inherent worth in God's eyes even when its life is a sequence of disastrous, disgraceful, demeaning, and otherwise deleterious actions that imply the contrary. As vulnerabilities, weaknesses, limitations, indiscretions, and transgressions (in a word, sins) pile up over a lifetime, the herd animal can always be consoled by the knowledge that God's unreserved compassion for its soul remains steadfast. We return to these matters in Chapter 4 and Chapter 5.

Drives and Affects

Although *GM*'s immediate topic is the genealogy of our inherited herd morality, it relies on and sporadically spotlights a genealogy of herd morality's presuppositions about human subjectivity and agency. The genealogy of moral evaluation will reveal that the twin presumptions that moral evaluation has a divine origin and that it applies universally are better understood as projections of certain psychological and social existence conditions onto a transcendental domain. Similarly, the genealogy of moral psychology will show that the twin presumptions that the moral subject is a substratum independent of its actions and an agent with free will are better understood as an interpretation that has developed with the existence conditions of certain human populations. Indeed, the two genealogies support each other: the genealogy of our inherited herd morality discloses the history of the evaluative principles and practices that apply to particular human populations, and the genealogy of herd moral psychology discloses the nature of the humans to which those evaluative principles and practices apply.

Nietzsche tries to stamp out every spark of the pretention that components of our psyche originate from something non-natural and therefore have a supernatural nature, and he likewise replaces those non-natural components with natural psychological components. We introduced these natural components—drives, instincts, and affects—in the last chapter. His argument is not just that natural drives and affects coexist with other non-natural psychological components, such as conscious thoughts, logical and rational abilities, and moral and religious injunctions. He thinks instead that even thoughts and their logical and rational properties are entirely natural, and his mature view is that thoughts and their logical and rational properties are also drives and affects.

These commitments permeate *GM*, although he rarely focuses on either drives or affects as categories, preferring instead to talk about individual drives and affects. But there should be no mistaking his ambition: he tries to understand all the complexities of human behavior and psychology by using drives and affects (we will see later that he adds memory, conscious thinking, sensory perception, and interoception) because they are either readily applicable to other organisms or developments from what is readily applicable to other organisms. Of course, he thereby incurs an obligation to show that these natural explanatory categories are sufficiently rich to explain everything he wants them to explain without having to reintroduce supernatural categories or reduce our complexities to something unrecognizable.

Masters and slaves alike descended from common ancestors and therefore shared a great deal physiologically and psychologically. Yet they were also importantly different from those common ancestors, and those differences demand explanation. Since both masters and slaves were drive- and affect-composed organic beings, Nietzsche's hypothesis must be that the physiological and psychological differences between masters and slaves in virtue of which the former were strong and healthy and the latter weak and sick are best explained by differences in their drives and affects. So, what are drives and affects? What might the differences between healthy and weak drives and affects be? And what implications do drives and affects have for our subjectivity and agency? According to Nietzsche, we supplement them with memory, promising, conscious thinking, responsibility, bad conscience / guilt, and will to power, which he adds in Essay II, and sensory perception and interoception, which he adds in Essay III.

In the most general terms, a drive (*Trieb*) is a long-standing, relatively stable, and (typically at least) subconscious activating—or impelling or urging—disposition that, given certain prompts, reliably and regularly tends to result in behaviors of specific kinds that temporarily satiate the prompts.[4] As such, drives are internal to and embodied in an organism, dynamically coupled with other suborganismic drives and with other suborganismic physiological and psychological states, processes, and episodes. Since they causally couple with other drives and other states, processes, and episodes, drives are not modular: while they may be identifiable as distinct from one another, drives do not simply chug away doing a single task, encapsulated and isolated from other drives. Rather, they constantly interact with other drives and with the other physiological and psychological states, processes, and episodes that make up an organism. Moreover, since organisms inhabit larger environments made up of other organisms, suborganismic drives dynamically couple with and embed themselves in those extraorganismic environments. The overall picture is energetic, incessantly stimulating, highly interactive, and ever-changing, not only between drives within organisms, but also between organisms and their environments and between organisms and other organisms.

Plants, animals, and humans all have drives. At least in *GM*, Nietzsche shows no interest in the drives of plants, fungi, protozoa, bacteria, insects, or sponges, focusing instead on drives found in birds, reptiles, and mammals, most importantly the human mammal. One of Nietzsche's background commitments in *GM* is that evolutionary

[4] See Richardson 1996 and Hales and Welshon 1999 for early defenses of this claim.

views of phylogenetic and ontogenetic human development describe biological drives accurately, at least for the most part (we will see below that he has certain reservations). Drives for sex and reproduction, for nourishment, for shelter and safety, and for self-preservation, flow from life's requirements to grow and expand. So they are in all of us in varying strengths, and are in that way basic. As we have already seen, however, the masters occasionally dismissed safety and self-preservation, and, as we will see, ascetics reject sex and even nourishment. So the picture even with basic biological drives gets more complicated in humans than in other animals. Understanding those complications is one of genealogy's tasks.[5]

Nietzsche also talks regularly and imprecisely about affect (*Affekt*), feeling (*Gefühle*), passion (*Leidenschaft*), mood (*Stimmung*), and emotion (*Gemütsbewegung*). Examples in *GM* show both his wide-ranging interest in the various psychological phenomena picked out by these descriptive categories and his cavalier indifference about describing any of them carefully. Among others, they include amusement, anger, attraction, awe, bitterness, boredom, calmness, contempt, contentment, cruelty, despair, depression, disgust, envy, exuberance, fear, fright, gratitude, greed, happiness, hatred, hope, horror, jealousy, joy, love, lust to rule, malice, pride, relief, ressentiment, revenge, sadness, self-satisfaction, sexual lust, shame, sorrow, spite, surprise, triumph, and worry. Of course, the list of emotions, feelings, passions, and moods—we will collect them here as species of the genus affect—is much longer than this. Nietzsche himself refers to hundreds of other affects in his published works and *Nachlass*.

[5] Moreover, Nietzsche expands the descriptive scope of the category drive well beyond biological drives. In the published works alone, he identifies, among many others, drives for curiosity, for certainty (*HH* I 16); for life (*D* 72); for love, to suicide, for quietude, and fear of shame (*D* 109); for distinction (*D* 113); for tenderness, humorousness, adventurousness, music, the mountains, annoyance, combativeness, reflection, and benevolence (*D* 119); for sacrifice (*D* 140); for knowledge (*D* 429); for the herd (*GS* 50); to doubt, deny, collect, and dissolve (*GS* 113); to laugh, lament, and curse (*GS* 333); for weakness (*GS* 347); for an enterprising spirit, foolhardiness, vengefulness, craftiness, rapacity, and lust for rule (*BGE* 20); for the power of the spirit (*BGE* 230); to doubt, deny, prevaricate, analyze, research, investigate, dare, compare, counterbalance, seek neutrality and objectivity (*GM* III 9); and for sentimentality, nature idolatry, the antihistorical, the idealistic, the unreal and the revolutionary (*TI* "Skirmishes" 49). He adds dozens more in the *Nachlass* notes.

All affective phenomena feel a particular way and have specific causal effects on the body. That affective states feel a particular way entails that we consciously experience them in characteristic ways.[6] Being worried is a different state than being relieved because feeling worried differs from feeling relieved; lusting after someone is a different state than envying someone because lust feels different than envy; sorrow is a different state than happiness because sorrow feels different than happiness. In addition, affective states have direct causal effects on the body, which entails that each affective state—that is, each affect—has a bodily modification as an immediate causal consequence. Disgust causes the nose to wrinkle, the upper lip to pull up, and the eyebrows to pull down; surprise causes the mouth to open, the pupils to dilate, and the eyebrows to pull up; depression causes lethargy, anxiety, and apathy; joy causes laughter, energy, and engagement.

These descriptions of drives and affects are deflationary: they take what might appear to be explanatory categories that presuppose purposes and redescribe them as categories that do not presuppose purposes. Unfortunately, these descriptions are too thin as stated to warrant some of the other claims Nietzsche makes on behalf of drives and affects. After all, plenty of long-standing and typically subconscious dispositions to behave are utterly innocuous (think of scratching an itch) and many affects are completely uninteresting (think of feeling the floor beneath our feet). This problem makes a dispositional account of drives and affects look too thin. Perhaps worse, Nietzsche routinely describes drives and affects in ways that appear to entail that drives and affects are conscious agents with purposes. Among other things, he claims that drives and affects evaluate and interpret, that they can be strong or weak, and that they can be healthy or sick. This problem makes drives and affects look too thick to be dispositions. Indeed, he appears to confront a dilemma: either he deflates drives and affects to dispositions and then cannot use them to explain some of what he wants them to explain, or he uses drives and affects to explain all of what he wants them to explain and must reinflate them beyond mere dispositions. Of course, Nietzsche can avoid one horn of the dilemma

[6] See Katsafanas 2018; Riccardi 2021; Richardson 2020; Welshon 2014.

by successfully defusing the problem posed by the other. We now show how he can avoid the bad consequences of the first horn by arguing that he does not have to reinflate drives and affects.

The second horn of the dilemma is a problem because reinflating drives and affects can entail the homuncularist fallacy.[7] The homuncularist fallacy is typically (although not necessarily) a certain explanatory failure that occurs when we try to explain how a person can do something by positing a subpersonal entity—a homunculus—that does that very thing. It is a fallacy because such an account only replicates on a smaller scale the need for an explanation prompted by something occurring at the larger scale. If, for example, we "explain" our ability to see by positing a subpersonal homunculus that sees, we are still as much in the dark as to what it is to see as we were before positing the seeing homunculus. Nietzsche would be guilty of this kind of homuncularist fallacy if he were to "explain" a person's ability to do something by positing subpersonal drives and affects that do that very thing.

Yet he appears to do just this. In *GM* alone, he claims that strength seeks out enemies and resistance, desiring to overthrow and crush, and that ressentiment reverses the evaluative gaze and anesthetizes pain through emotion. Elsewhere, he affirms that "it is our needs that interpret the world; our drives and their For and Against. Every drive is a kind of lust to rule; each one has its perspective that it would like to compel all the other drives to accept as a norm" (*KSA* 12 7[60]). Again:

> [A]nyone who looks at people's basic drives, to see how far they may have played their little game right here as *inspiring* geniuses (or daemons or sprites), will find that they all practiced philosophy at some point, —and that every single one of them would be only too pleased to present *itself* as the ultimate purpose of existence and as rightful *master* of all the other drives. Because every drive craves mastery, and *this* leads it to try philosophizing. (*BGE* 6)

[7] See Riccardi 2021.

If seeking enemies, crushing resistance, interpreting, evaluating, craving, and philosophizing can only be done by reflectively conscious agents, then it looks like Nietzsche attributes reflectively conscious agency to drives and affects, which looks like an instance of the homuncularist fallacy. So, if subpersonal drives and affects are not to be homunculi, there must be a way to explain how they seek, overthrow, evaluate, interpret, crave, and philosophize without entailing that they are reflectively conscious seekers, dominators, interpreters, and evaluators.

Evolution, Interpretation, and Evaluation

What must be added are dimensions of drives and affects in virtue of which they interpret and evaluate and can be assessed as strong or weak and as healthy or sick without entailing that they are reflectively conscious agents. A clue lies in their being products of evolutionary development: many drives and many affects have been naturally selected for because they increase our chances of surviving to reproductive age and thus increase the rate of our reproductive success. If so, we can say that a certain drive or affect in us is healthy when it functions to increase our chance of surviving to reproductive age and to improve the rate of our reproductive success, and sickly when it malfunctions and decreases our chance of surviving to reproductive age and the rate of our reproductive success. We can also say that a drive or affect is strong in us when it is more effective in increasing our chance of surviving to reproductive age and the rate of our reproductive success than it is in others and that a drive or affect is weak when it is less effective than in others.

That some drives and affects are evolutionary adaptations is helpful for Nietzsche in a number of ways. First, it ties our subjectivity down to natural forces and writes out non-natural forces as irrelevant. Second, it reveals the tight conceptual relation between drives and affects and their function in our life: drives propel us forward and affects communicate how things stand with us. Third, it provides a framework for understanding drives and affects that does not require conscious teleological explanations. As already argued, Nietzsche thinks that teleological explanations that appeal to conscious purposes or designs are superfluous fictions. An evolutionary approach to drives and affects licenses replacing conscious purposes and designs with adaptive functions and thereby provides a deflationary interpretation of drives and affects. On this deflationary approach, no reflective purposes or designs that explain why a drive has the function it has are ever required. Rather, drives are long-standing dispositions for certain kinds of behavior that have been naturally selected for in the past, that is, that have in the past led to increased chances of surviving to reproductive age and increased reproduction rates. Likewise, the purpose or design of affects is reconfigured as the naturally selected function of certain short-term conscious states to report on embodiment. In this deflationary context, drives and affects can still aim at or to an end, but that is because their ends are the evolved functions by which one drive or affect is distinguished from another drive or affect. The sex drive is the sex drive and not the food drive because it is a naturally selected disposition to engage in certain behaviors, such as seeking out a sexual partner, rather than other unrelated behaviors, such as seeking out food. So, too, for affects: revulsion prompts aversion from what is presented, while fondness prompts attraction.[8]

We have just noted that biological drives are distinguished from one another by the behaviors and actions characteristic of them and that affects can be either aversive or attractive. These features show that biological drives enlist various internal and external states of affairs to satisfy the drive and that affects are caused by various internal and external states of affairs. These features also reveal that drives and affects come loaded with saliency filters that make an organism variably responsive to the environment and enable that response to be environmentally plastic.

Consider these points in turn. First, the biological drive for food aims at providing calories to the organism and impels the organism to seek out food to satisfy the drive, thus structuring its experience of the environment. A simple example is the deer outside my office window. When it is driven by the need for calories, some items in its world are

[8] See Richardson 1996.

food.[9] Second, what food is eaten varies depending on environmental circumstances and hunger's intensity. When the deer is hungry and walks under the apple tree, it will eat an apple, but if it is in a meadow, it will eat grass. Likewise, the affect of hunger communicates the need for calories but can be caused by external or internal states of affairs. When the deer walks under an apple tree, its hunger may be triggered by the bouquet of ripening apples, but it can instead feel its stomach is empty. So the drive to do something results in certain kinds of action and behavior typical of the drive and in virtue of which it is distinguished from another drive, even if what in the world or in the organism is engaged by that action or behavior varies. Similarly, an affect communicates certain states of embodiment typical of the affect and in virtue of which it is distinguished from another affect, even if what in the world or in the organism causes the affect varies.

Drives and affects also often work together. Caloric need, a drive, triggers hunger, an affect, and savoring a meal, an affect, communicates that the need for calories, a drive, has been satisfied. Moreover, drives and affects of specific kinds work together with drives and affects of distinct kinds, sometimes canceling each other out, sometimes forming collaborations with each other, sometimes fighting each other. And these distinct internal battles and internal collaborations themselves must, if Nietzsche is correct, work together to comprise our subjectivity and agency. Unfortunately, in *GM* at least, Nietzsche does not provide many details about these complications beyond drawing attention to examples of them. This is a shortcoming. Nietzsche relies on the explanatory scope of a drive/affect psychology to back up his assertions about the variety of psychological phenomena implicated by the genealogy of morality, yet he only irregularly and incompletely displays how that psychology rises to the task. In part, this gap can be excused: his stated goal for *GM* was, after all, to provide a set of preliminary studies for the project of revaluing values, parts of which were, as the remaining outlines of that project demonstrate, to be devoted to these very issues. As the hundreds of *Nachlass* notes and occasional

[9] See Katsafanas 2018; Richardson 1996; Welshon 2014.

published passages in *GS*, *BGE*, *TI*, and *A* testify, the drive/affect psychology remained very much a work in progress.

We can excuse *GM*'s incompleteness by appealing to his expectation that he would soon return to what he knew were incomplete arguments and his restraint not to commit to print arguments he was still working out. Unfortunately, the result is that he never published any more than unevenly detailed descriptions and explanations of certain individual drives and affects (such as ressentiment, punishment, and willing), fragmented descriptions and explanations of others (such as those currently under discussion), and bits and pieces that have to be laced together with unpublished *Nachlass* notes. Scholars have been stitching these threads into something that resembles a cohesive whole. Some results are mentioned at the end of the chapter in "Further Readings."

That Nietzsche did not perfect his drive/affect psychology does not excuse us from trying to resolve the problem that homuncularism poses. To defuse that threat we must pull on two of his unfinished psychology's dangling threads. As we will see in the discussion of will to power and life in the next chapter and decadence in Chapter 5, it is crucial to Nietzsche's genealogical project that biological evaluation forms the basis of other kinds of evaluation, even if those other kinds of evaluation do not reduce to biological evaluation. Yet explaining how biological evaluation forms that basis requires explaining how a drive/affect psychology explains the way that biological drives and affects interpret and evaluate the world without entailing reflectively conscious interpreters and evaluators.

Here progress is possible. Recall that when an animal is hungry, it becomes tuned to its embodiment via affect, and its drives then structure experience so that the world becomes populated by potential food. Similarly, when an animal is driven to sexually reproduce, it becomes tuned to its needs via affect, and its drives then structure experience such that the world becomes populated by potential mating partners. As for other animals, so too for us. In *De Finibus*, Cicero attributes to Socrates the observation that "hunger is the best seasoning for meat and thirst is the best flavor for drink"; a quote attributed to Sade similarly observes that "lust's passion will be served; it demands, it militates, it tyrannizes."

Affective tuning and drive-structured experience can be interpretive and evaluative without having to be reflectively conscious. We and other animals experience both the internal milieu and the external world structured through the ways that drives and affects fix embodied salience hierarchies for satisfying or failing to satisfy a drive, for alleviating or exacerbating an unpleasant affect, or for heightening or deadening a pleasant affect. Biological drives and affects thus inform experience so that it is satisfying or unsatisfying, positive or negative, pleasurable or painful, delightful or distressing, attractive or aversive in ways peculiar to specific drives and affects. That is, drives and affects induce and structure valenced interoceptive and perceptual experience according to the saliency filters peculiar to specific drives and affects.[10] With some terminological generosity, fixing salience hierarchies and structuring valenced experience can be understood as kinds of interpretation and evaluation. If so, drives and affects provide a biological basis for simple kinds of interpretation and evaluation.

For example, Nietzsche claims that "our drives likewise do nothing but interpret nervous stimuli and, according to their requirements, posit their 'causes'" (*D* 119) Again: "[V]alue judgments are found in all the functions of organic beings" (*KSA* 11 25[72]). If we are prepared to extend this terminological generosity to Nietzsche, we are close to resolving the threat of homuncularism, for, as described here, fixing salience hierarchies and structuring valenced interoceptive and perceptual experience are prereflective dimensions of drives and affects. Hence, biological drives and affects are, at least in the loose way of speaking we are suggesting Nietzsche be allowed, interpreters and evaluators without being reflectively conscious interpreters and evaluators. Hence, drives and affects are not homunculi.

The other unresolved matter is how a drive/affect psychology can account for strong, weak, healthy, and sickly drives and affects without presupposing strong, weak, healthy, and sickly persons. Here again a solution presents itself. We have already seen that two constants in Nietzsche's thinking about drives and affects are that they are either healthy or sickly and that they are either strong or weak. Biological

[10] See Katsafanas 2018; Richardson 1996, 2020.

drives and affects provide a basis of shared physiological and psychological features against which health or sickliness and strength or weakness can be recognized and assessed. Consider health and sickliness first and consider them as they characterize drives (parallel points can be made about affects). Even if health and sickliness do not reduce survival to reproductive age and reproductive success, health and sickliness use the proper functioning of biological drives and affects to provide a base level of flourishing. A drive is healthy when its urging and its ensuing activities help an organism flourish in its environment, and a drive is sickly when its urging and its ensuring activities do not help the organism flourish in its environment. Similarly, a drive is strong when it controls other drives and a drive is weak when it does not control other drives.[11] A strong and healthy drive controls other drives to propel an organism to actions that help it flourish in an environment, while a weak but healthy drive fails to control other drives as the organism acts in ways that help it flourish. Similarly, a strong and sickly drive controls other drives to propel an organism to actions that do not help it flourish in an environment, while a weak and sickly drive fails to control other drives as the organism acts in ways that do not help an organism flourish.

Distinguishing drives by the criterion of whether they help an organism flourish in an environment leaves unanswered what flourishing consists in. To anticipate what is discussed in greater detail in Chapter 5: organisms flourish when they exercise will to power. But that just pushes the question back one step, for what is it to exercise will to power? This question is addressed in Chapter 4. Here it suffices to note that humans are animals, so we all have naturally selected biological drives and affects. Still, not all of our drives and affects are biological drives and affects or even reducible to them. Other drives and affects are sublimated, socialized, intellectualized, and spiritualized and have either completely replaced or have been superimposed on, emerged from, or superseded biological drives and affects. These phylogenetically recent drives are no longer subject to biological pressures but to social, intellectual, cultural, and religious pressures that began

[11] See Richardson 2004, 2020.

with the taming of the human animal and subsequently picked up steam with the development of custom, tradition, ritual, exchange relations, religions in general, and Christianity in particular. Some of these additional drives and affects are entirely novel, some remain consistent with our biological drives and affects, and some are contrary to biological drives and affects. In the next chapter, we encounter some of the drives and affects that make our subjectivity and our agency unique.

Further Reading

For more on the slave revolt in morality, see Conway 2008; Jenkins 2018; Leiter 2002; Loeb 2018; Migotti 1998; Morrisson 2014; Owen 2007; Reginster 1997; Snelson 2017.

For more on ressentiment, see Bittner 1994; Elgat 2017; Huddleston 2021; Jenkins 2018; Leiter 2002; Poellner 2011, 2015; Reginster 1997, 2006; Scheler 1961; Wallace 2007.

For more on drives and affects, see Alfano 2019; Anderson 2012; Dries 2017; Fowles 2020; Janaway 2007, 2009, 2012; Kail 2017; Katsfanas 2013b, 2015b, 2016; Knobe and Leiter 2007, 2019; Pippin 2006; Richardson 2004, 2020; Riccardi 2021; Welshon 2014; Williams 2006a.

For more on evolution, interpretation, and evaluation, see Clark 2013; Dries 2017; Johnson 2010, 2013; Katsafanas 2013b, 2016; Moore 2002, 2006; Riccardi 2001; Richardson 2004, 2020; Schacht 2013a.

4
Genealogy Essay II

4.1 Introduction

Essay II will be a surprise if we expect Nietzsche to provide additional argumentative and empirical support regarding the slave revolt in morality. Instead, Essay II reviews a long, multilayered history, from the emergence of distinctively human forms of subjectivity and agency to Christianity's invention of a God to whom we owe unpayable debts. The scope of this history extends beyond the slave revolt back to a more remote past. This earlier enculturation, achieved through what Nietzsche calls a 'morality of custom,' hammered rudimentary prudential responsibility, accountability, subjectivity, and agency into us. The depth of analysis he devotes to these matters is sometimes surprising. Over many sections, he details memory, forgetting, promising, micro- and macro-level exchange relations, and punishment before even starting the genealogy of conscience. These more basic psychological elements were already in place when Judaism and Christianity ushered in the slave revolt and began superimposing new interpretations onto them, thus creating new forms of subjectivity, responsibility, and agency, and inventing entirely new psychological phenomena like bad conscience / guilt. These facets of human psychology make us more interesting, more tormented, and more unnatural than other animals and even the old masters and old slaves.

In the discussion section, we investigate what Nietzsche's drive/affect moral psychology says about the development of the complexities found in our psychological nature. Doing so requires that we unpack what psychological cohesion and continuity, self-awareness and self-command, subjectivity and agency, and willing look like on this drive/affect psychology. We also analyze what Nietzsche says about power and willing power.

Nietzsche's On the Genealogy of Morality. Rex Welshon, Oxford University Press.
 DOI: 10.1093/oso/9780197611814.003.0005

4.2 Essay II by the Sections

Sections 1–3

Section 1 begins with an odd question: "To breed an animal with the prerogative to *promise*—is that not precisely the paradoxical task which nature has set herself with regard to humankind?" (*GM* II 1). Given that Nietzsche thinks the prerogative to promise is a paradox, he appears to set himself an impossible task. To defuse the paradox, he will have to sweep away theological and philosophical misperceptions we have about ourselves and dig deeply under them to uncover the psychological and social preconditions of promising. And uncovering the origins of promising and its preconditions is only propaedeutic for the larger task of understanding the origins of conscience and, more importantly, bad conscience / guilt.

Nietzsche introduces the discussion of promising by commenting on forgetting. Forgetting is not, as others have it, passive inactivity but an active psychological ability to squelch and censor. Thanks to it, much of what we experience stays as hidden to awareness as are the processes of digesting food. Active forgetfulness thus acts as a "doorkeeper or guardian of mental order" that sets aside as irrelevant all of "the noise and battle with which our underworld of serviceable organs work with and against each other" so that there is room left for "a little *tabula rasa* of consciousness . . . for something new, above all for the nobler functions and functionaries, for ruling, predicting, predetermining" (*GM* II 1). Active forgetting is utterly normal and results in a "necessarily forgetful animal, in whom forgetting is a strength, representing a form of *robust* health" (*GM* II 1). Of course, the healthy forgetful human animal also has memory, a "counter-device" (*GM* II 1) that suspends forgetfulness for promises.

Promising requires learning how to "distinguish between what happens by accident and what by design, to think causally, to view the future as the present and anticipate it, to grasp with certainty what is end and what is means, in all, to be able to calculate, compute" (*GM* II 1). These calculative and computational abilities require something equally fundamental. Humans needed both "to become *reliable, regular, necessary*" (*GM* II 1) and to think of themselves as such. It is only when we became, and moreover thought of ourselves as being, reliable, regular, and necessary that making a promise makes sense. Understanding how these features of this peculiarly human activity emerged and were shaped is the primary task of Essay II's first sixteen sections.

Claiming that memory is a product of breeding is a little odd. Surely, we might say, memory is a cognitive ability that develops on an ontogenetic schedule, part neurological, part psychological, part psychosocial. However, this worry misses what Nietzsche is trying to get at. He does not, and need not, deny that memory has a neurological basis or that it follows a particular developmental pathway. Indeed, he would likely be fascinated with recent advances in neuropsychology and ontogenetic cognitive growth. However, even if neurologically based, memory has in humans resulted in something more peculiar, a complex animal that can make promises. Producing such a strange animal requires that we acknowledge that humans must become "necessary, uniform, a peer amongst peers, orderly and consequently predictable" (*GM* II 2). We must also admit that uniformity and predictability developed only with effort, the history of which is "the long history of the origins of *responsibility*" (*GM* II 2). Nietzsche captures the protracted process for fostering predictability and responsibility by calling attention to the way that two of their preconditions, promising and memory, developed in a social milieu. And, of course, memory has also been "bred" into humans in the Darwinian sense that humans with reliable memory stores tended to survive to reproductive age more often and thus to have more offspring than those whose memory stores were not as reliable.

One ingredient in the process of nurturing promising and memory, and therefore predictability and responsibility, is what Nietzsche calls the "morality of custom" (*GM* II 2; the German *Sittlichkeit der Sitte* translates alternatively as "morality of mores").[1] Nietzsche mentioned

[1] Some translators and interpreters prefer translating *Sittlichkeit der Sitte* as "ethic of custom" because the dissimilarity between it and herd morality is so great that calling the former a kind of morality courts confusion. We have defused this concern in the previous chapter, where we acknowledged that there are distinct kinds of morality and that Nietzsche's primary interest in *GM* is in morality in the pejorative sense.

the role of custom in Essay I, where he noted that, compared to master morality and slave morality, a morality of custom is an "older and more original kind of morality" (*GM* I 4), but he left the claim undeveloped until now. Economic, cultural, and religious customs, traditions, and rituals helped install memory, emotion regulation, attention control, self-awareness, and a feeling of obligation to the community, each of which are elements of predictability and regularity, which are in turn elements of responsibility. Millennia before the slave revolt in morality began, the more primitive morality of custom established conventions that demarcated accepted behavior, distinguished it from atypical and impermissible behavior, and kept in mind "the perpetual compulsion to practice customs" (*D* I 16). All of the ritualized behavior and traditions stipulated by custom infiltrated education, marriage, farming, war, speech and silence, healthcare, and interactions with one another and the gods (*D* I 9). Their "minute and fundamentally superfluous stipulations" (*D* I 16) and frequent rehearsal hardened into habit and helped cultivate memory, emotion regulation, attention control, and a sense of obligation to the larger collective: "[W]ith the help of the morality of custom and the social straitjacket, humans were *made* truly predictable" (*GM* II 2). Soon we will meet two other mechanisms, exchange relations and punishment, that assisted in making humans predictable, regularized, and uniform.

We moderns find it difficult to have "any empathy with those vast stretches of the 'morality of custom' which pre-date 'world history' as the genuine and decisive main historical period that determined man's character" (*GM* III 9). In particular, we cannot comprehend how inescapable the compulsory dimension of a morality of custom must have been, but that is only because we have so internalized it that its initial novelty is no longer salient and millennia of later developments have papered it over. In a morality of custom, the most moral person was one "who obeys the law most frequently," someone "who obeys it even in the most difficult cases" and "who *sacrifices* most to custom" (*D* I 9). Those of us who now stand "at the end of this immense process where the tree actually bears fruit, where society and its morality of custom finally reveal what they were simply *the means to*" (*GM* II 2) are unlikely to recognize what the morality of custom entrenched and enhanced. Later, in Section 19, Nietzsche answers a question that the description of the morality of custom in Sections 1 and 2 leaves unanswered: Why did such a morality emerge in the first place?

Among the fruits on the slow-growing tree of the morality of custom are those who, liberated from the morality of custom, are "autonomous" and "supra-moral," individuals with their own "independent, enduring will, whose *prerogative it is to promise*" (*GM* II 2). Nietzsche describes these individuals who are aware of their "power and freedom" as being "sovereign" (*GM* II 2). A sovereign individual knows "the extraordinary privilege of *responsibility*," and is aware that "this rare freedom and power over himself and his destiny . . . has penetrated him to his lowest depths and become an instinct, his dominant instinct" (*GM* II 2). Acquiring the dominant drive of responsibility is an accomplishment that the sovereign individual names 'conscience.' Nietzsche introduces conscience here for the first time but leaves it unanalyzed beyond being the capacity to make and keep promises. We investigate conscience in more detail in Section 16. And we address who the sovereign individual is in greater detail in the discussion section of this chapter.

In Section 3, Nietzsche introduces "techniques of mnemonics," that is, mechanisms for embedding and cultivating memories. It is, he admits, a "terrible and strange" (*GM* II 2) history, for it is the history of punishment and inflicting cruelty. The "oldest (and unfortunately the longest-lived) psychology on earth," that "only something that continues *to hurt* stays in the memory" (*GM* II 3), governs these techniques. What follows is a sickening catalog: sacrificing children and virgins; castrating; stoning; breaking on the wheel; impaling on stakes; drawing and quartering; boiling in wine or oil; cutting out strips of flesh; coating the body with honey and leaving the sufferer to be bitten by insects and animals. Our past (and, in parts of the world, our present) is, in a word, brutal, filled with public and private procedures that burned into memory "five or six 'I will nots,' in connection with which a *promise* had been given, in order to enjoy the advantages of society—and there you are! With the aid of this sort of memory, people finally came to 'reason'" (*GM* II 3). Nietzsche also makes the offhand remark that, "in a certain sense, the whole of asceticism belongs here: a few ideas have to be made ineradicable, ubiquitous, unforgettable, 'fixed,' in order to hypnotize the whole nervous and intellectual system through these 'fixed ideas'" (*GM* II 3). We analyze this claim in the next chapter.

Sections 4–7

Nietzsche asserts here that his genealogy of conscience and bad conscience / guilt has etymology on its side. The German *Schuld*, which denotes the moral concept of guilt, descends from *Schulden*, which denotes the nonmoral concept of debt. Using this etymological clue as a crowbar, he pries open the long history of creditor-debtor exchange relationships and punishment and starts to poke around. His initial discovery, that "punishment, as *retribution*, evolved quite independently of any assumption about freedom or lack of freedom of the will" (*GM* II 4), is a reminder of the point already made in Essay I, Section 13, that the moralized description of subjectivity that separates subjects from their actions and thereby makes those actions freely chosen is a product not of a morality of custom, but instead of the later slave revolt. Both separating a subject from its action and a subject's freely choosing its actions carry in their train the abilities to distinguish "'intentional,' 'negligent,' 'accidental,' 'of sound mind' and their opposites" (*GM* II 4). Of course, these feature only in herd morality, so they are still far away during the period when punishment first appeared.

When punishment first appeared in societies, no distinction between subject and action existed. So the modern thought that we have always punished miscreants to cure them of their wicked choices presupposes far too much. "A *high* degree of humanization had first to be achieved" (*GM* II 4) before we can ascribe any such function to punishment. This point echoes a parallel point made in Essay I. Just as Essay I warned against projecting back to the origin of moral evaluation features of it that are found only in later expressions, so Essay II warns against projecting back to the origin of punishment what is for us now the obvious thought that "the criminal deserves to be punished *because* he could have acted otherwise," a thought that is actually "an extremely late and refined form of human judgment and inference" (*GM* II 4). For most of our history, punishment simply inflicted suffering on a wrongdoer who caused others injury, not, as we now think, because the wrongdoer is morally responsible for choosing to act intentionally. We return to the points made in this and the previous paragraph in the discussion section of this chapter.

For now, observe the equivalence between one party harming another party and the punishment reserved for the party who causes that harm. This "primeval, deeply-rooted" idea emerged from "the contractual relationship between *creditor* and *debtor*, which is as old as the very conception of a 'legal subject' and itself refers back to the basic forms of buying, selling, bartering, trade and traffic" (*GM* II 4). We might find the claim that the exchange relationships are the crucible of punishment implausible. However, trained as he was as a classicist and philologist, Nietzsche knew that archaeological evidence already demonstrated that buying, selling, bartering, trading, and wage labor predated the emergence of Greek culture, Second Temple Jewish culture, and early Christian culture, and therefore predated the slave revolt in morality.[2] So exchange and commercial relations are a candidate setting for the initial appearance of punishment, even if they are not the only candidates.

What is of interest are, first, the creditors who loaned money, sold goods, or supplied services and the debtors who borrowed, bought, or benefited from them, and second, what happened when the latter did not live up to contract terms with the former. On this account,

> [T]he debtor, in order to inspire confidence that the promise of repayment will be honored, in order to give a guarantee of the solemnity and sanctity of his promise, and in order to etch the duty and obligation of repayment into his conscience, pawns something to the creditor by means of the contract in case he does not pay, something that he still "possesses" and controls, for example, his body, or his wife, or his freedom, or his life. (*GM* II 5)

[2] Early examples of ideographic writing, from China in the 2300 BCE era and Mesopotamia in the 4000 BCE era, are tallies of goods (China) and workers' wages (Mesopotamia), so commercial activity and the arithmetic needed for it go back at least that far, farther still if forms of arithmetic that were not written down existed. Even if it is a little depressing to realize that accountants may have invented writing, it is evidence that Nietzsche is right that bartering and other economic relations were crucial for the development of humanity.

In short, if the debtor did not live up to the promise established by the contract with the creditor, "[T]he creditor could inflict all kinds of dishonor and torture on the body of the debtor, for example, cutting as much flesh off as seemed appropriate for the debt" (*GM* II 5).

The logic here is undemanding and gruesome. Instead of in-kind compensation, such as repaying loaned money with interest, forfeiting possessions, or sacrificing labor, the creditor had "the pleasure of having the right to exercise power over the powerless without a thought, the pleasure '*de faire le mal pour le plaisir de le faire* [to do evil for the pleasure of it]' " (*GM* II 5). This cruel pleasure allowed creditors to "take part in the *rights of the masters*" because, like the masters, they "shared the elevated feeling of being in a position to despise and maltreat someone as an 'inferior' " (*GM* II 5), even if this pleasure was later reduced to merely seeing the wrongdoer tortured or degraded after the authority to dispense punishment was transferred to legal or clerical officials.

The equivalence between harm received and pain inflicted remained even when those who dispensed pain were agents of the law or the gods: "[C]ompensation is made up of a warrant for and entitlement to cruelty" (*GM* II 5). The equivalence between receiving a harm and obtaining license to mistreat becomes entrenched because it is a psychological truth that "*to make* someone suffer is pleasure in its highest form" (*GM* II 6). Although it may be "repugnant to the delicacy . . . of tame house-pets (which is to say modern humans, which is to say us)" (*GM* II 6), we cannot, he thinks, avoid this awful truth. Even attempts to ground punishment and justice in utility and revenge, discussed in Section 11, presuppose this dark and underground truth, for seeking revenge itself leads right back to the disturbing idea that making someone suffer is satisfying. This is psychological bedrock for Nietzsche. He is convinced that "to see suffering does you good, to make suffer, better still—that is a hard proposition, but an ancient, powerful, human-all-too-human proposition" (*GM* II 6; see also *D* I 18).

In Section 7, Nietzsche summarizes Pope Innocent III's *De miseria humanae conditionis* (*The Misery of the Human Condition*), a graphic but immensely popular booklet published in 1195 that details unsavory specifics about the animality of human existence. We note three salient points. First, unlike us moderns, for whom "suffering is always the first of the arguments marshalled *against* life," our ancestors "could not do without *making* people suffer and saw first-rate magic in it, a veritable seductive lure *to* life" (*GM* II 7). Nietzsche adds to this claim in Essay III's discussion of asceticism. Second, it is a mistake to infer that we moderns are completely immune to the pleasures of suffering; we are not, even if they have over time become sublimated and more refined. Third, that we still take pleasure in suffering presupposes another hard and ancient truth, that the real objection to suffering "is not the suffering itself, but the senselessness of suffering" (*GM* II 7). Nietzsche expands on and defends this assertion in Essay III. Here note its corollary that suffering has always been a justification for creating gods who bear witness to it and thereby endow it with meaning: " 'All evil is justified if a god takes pleasure in it': so ran the primitive logic of feeling," and so thought the Greeks, who offered their gods "the joys of cruelty" as "a side-dish to their happiness" (*GM* II 7). So too does any form of Christianity wherein God is the unseen seer who looks down on us from above and sanctifies our suffering.[3]

Sections 8–11

Section 7 went off on a tangent, so Nietzsche opens Section 8 by reminding himself and us that the important job of mining the multifaceted creditor-debtor relationship, which sublimated responsibility, is still unfinished. Section 8 focuses on the micro-level relation between creditor and debtor, while Sections 9 and 10 introduce the homologous macro-level relation between members of a community

[3] These observations are coupled with two gratuitous generalizations, the first about sub-Saharan Africans, the second about educated women. There are no apologetics sufficiently nuanced to rid what Nietzsche says about sub-Saharan Africans being modern representatives of "prehistorical man" of the stench of racism. Nor can any amount of rhetorical ingenuity excuse his snide comparison of the pain endured by a "hysterical educated female" with "the total suffering of all the animals who have been interrogated by the knife in scientific research" of the charge of sexism (*GM* II 7). Although these passages praise the hardiness of sub-Saharan Africans and acknowledge the suffering of animals, claiming that nineteenth-century sub-Saharan Africans are primeval and that educated women are incapable of enduring pain is demeaning.

and the community of which they are members. These are crucial arguments for the rest of Essay II, since they add essential elements to the genealogy of responsibility and conscience and thus clarify the distinction between their genealogy and the more complicated genealogy of moral responsibility and bad conscience / guilt, presented in Sections 16 through 22.

The debtor-creditor relationship is the first interpersonal relationship where humans formally calibrated themselves against one another. The work of "fixing prices, setting values, working out equivalents, exchanging" was so preoccupying for the limited cognitive capacities of our earliest ancestors "that in a certain sense it *constituted* thought" (*GM* II 8). Impressed with themselves for being able to calculate but proceeding "with the ponderous consistency characteristic of the ancients' way of thinking," these early humans continued to put one foot in front of the other until they realized that "every thing has its price: *everything* can be compensated for," thus forging "the oldest, most naïve canon of morals relating to *justice*" (*GM* II 8). The raw ingredients of justice were therefore nothing more complicated than negotiating to settle disputes and enforcing settlements.

If the creditor-debtor relationship is among the earliest computing relationships known between individuals, the earliest relationship between these individuals and their communities was between obligated parts and an obliging whole. We have already touched on the obligation of individuals to their community when we noted that a morality of custom helped cultivate this sense of indebtedness. Here Nietzsche supplements the morality of custom with another mechanism that works with traditions and rituals to inculcate commitments to the social whole. When we live in a community, we enjoy certain benefits, chief among them "a sheltered, protected life in peace and trust, without any worry of suffering certain kinds of harm and hostility to which the man *outside*, the 'man without peace,' is exposed" (*GM* II 9). In exchange for those benefits, we share in the work of keeping the community secure and so commit to maintaining the various communal tasks that benefit members.

Here we encounter, for the first time and in a muted fashion, a thesis that Nietzsche will defend in Section 16, that our enculturation required redirecting what were initially outward primitive instincts, drives, and affects inward on ourselves. When we flout, feign, or conveniently forget promises or other commitments to the community, the community, acting now as cheated creditor, will exact penalties. The most important breach is not the particular harm done by the lawbreaking delinquent; rather, it is that "the lawbreaker is a 'breaker,' somebody who has broken his contract and his word *to the whole*" and all of the "valued features and amenities of communal life that have been shared up till now" (*GM* II 9). A community cannot tolerate individuals free riding when others contribute to sustain peace, safety, and trust; nor can it tolerate individuals defrauding, disparaging, or spurning the community's advantages and services. Once exposed, the lawbreaker is "not only deprived of all these valued benefits, —he is now also reminded *how important these benefits are*" by being cast out and forced to "return to the savage and outlawed state" of life outside community (*GM* II 9). The lawbreaker thus becomes a "hated, disarmed enemy who has been defeated, and who has not only forfeited all rights and safeguards, but all mercy as well" (*GM* II 9).

As the community's stability and power increases, its capacity to absorb unruly and injurious behavior also increases, eventually reaching a level of self-confidence so evident that the need to expel free riders, troublemakers, and criminals declines and the general public is no longer allowed to vent its rage against them. This crucial step in a community's growth occasions the invention of a legal system that enforces prohibitions against the "power of hostile and spiteful feelings" (*GM* II 10). A legal system has three interrelated benefits. First, it redirects attention away from personal injuries and onto the legal breaches that such injuries commit. Second, it protects wrongdoers from the injured party's desire for revenge and from the community's unchecked spiteful affects. Third, it encodes the maxim that "every offense . . . *can be paid off*," which, "at least to a certain degree," detaches the wrongdoer from his behavior (*GM* II 10). These insights justify Section 11's rejection of the alternative genealogy of justice proposed by those who try to ground justice in revenge and ressentiment. They thus prepare the ground for distinguishing conscience from bad conscience / guilt.

So long as a community's power and self-confidence grow, legal punishment becomes more lenient, but if that power and self-confidence come under threat, harsher forms of punishment will re-appear. Nietzsche states this functional relation succinctly as follows: "The 'creditor' always becomes more humane as his wealth increases" and "the *amount* of his wealth determines how much injury he can sustain without suffering from it" (*GM* II 10). In powerful and self-confident communities, increasing leniency can reach an upper limit in mercy, the self-sublimation of justice. Nietzsche lays out the reasoning for this startling conclusion by arguing that we can imagine a society that is "*so conscious of its power* that it could allow itself the noblest luxury available to it, —that of letting its malefactors go *unpunished*. 'What do I care about my parasites,' it could say, 'let them live and flourish: I am strong enough for all that!'" (*GM* II 10). We can even imagine a scenario in which "justice, which began by saying 'Everything can be paid off, everything must be paid off,' ends by turning a blind eye and letting off those unable to pay, . . . by *sublimating itself*" (*GM* II 10). This remarkable argument again shows the inanity of thinking that Nietzsche dismisses the benefits of social existence and the rule of law. Social existence is far from being an irredeemable calamity, and not everything that begins soaked in blood and violence must remain so. Even if justice began violently, it can under flourishing circumstances self-sublimate in the merciful renunciation of blood previously shed in its name.

Section 11 is another digression, but it contributes to Nietzsche's moral psychology by dismissing the alternative genealogical hypothesis that grounds justice in the desire for revenge and ressentiment. As noted in Essay I, Section 14, Christians try to "sanctify *revenge* with the term *justice*—as though justice were fundamentally simply a further development of the feeling of having been wronged" (*GM* II 11). However, it is not only Christians who advocate for this position. Others, such as the social scientist Eugen Dühring, also hypothesize that reactive emotions, such as hatred, envy, resentment, and revenge are fundamental, and that justice grows from them as a natural mediator between aggrieved and aggressor.

Nietzsche claims to the contrary that "life functions *essentially* in an injurious, violent, exploitative and destructive manner" and the active drives such as "lust for mastery, greed and the like" are fundamental (*GM* II 11). If so, then ressentiment cannot be the root of justice, first because it is reactive and derivative rather than active and original, second, because its vat of reactive responses inevitably redirects sufferers away from the real causes of their suffering onto new objects whom they misidentify as the culprits of their misery. This common but degenerate psychological process, described already in Chapter 3, emphasizes that those in whom ressentiment festers can "only place a false and prejudiced interpretation on the object of attention" (*GM* II 11). Those in whom the "active, aggressive, over-reaching" drives and emotions dominate are not disposed to such biased interpretations, so they have "a *clearer* eye, a *better* conscience" (*GM* II 11).

Nietzsche next shows how legal orders developed. The "senseless ravages of *ressentiment* [and] . . . spread of reactive pathos" (*GM* II 11) fueled by broken exchange relations and social obligations were the greatest threats to the strength, cohesion, and even existence of these early communities. Anyone familiar with honor-based murders of rape victims, honor-based female genital mutilation, and honor-based abuse, or who has studied the centuries-long rounds of vengeance found in and across certain communities, knows how horrific unchecked cycles of resentment and revenge have been and continue to be. The strong and powerful took the raw ingredients of creditor-debtor dispute resolution and custom-induced communal obligations in hand, created a legal system, and imposed it on the community, thereby pioneering justice as a set of communal restraints against the disorderliness of rampant ressentiment. Four mechanisms made up the legal order imposed by the old masters: first, it "lift[ed] the object of *ressentiment* from the hands of revenge" and delivered the miscreant into the hands of the law; second, it "substitute[d] for revenge a struggle against the enemies of peace and order," thus redirecting the revenge-seeker's attention away from any personal insult and onto the social damage taking revenge posed; third, it "work[ed] out compensation" between the injured party and the wrongdoer; fourth, it "promote[d] certain equivalences for wrongs into a norm which *ressentiment*, from now on, has to take into account" (*GM* II 11), thereby checking the temptation to act as a vigilante.

If this list of legal mechanisms looks familiar, that is because we have already met informal variants of them in earlier analyses of ressentiment and the creditor-debtor relationship. Legal mechanisms formalized features of creditor-debtor relations, and this formalization was the basis for identifying the permissible as the just and the impermissible as the unjust. Once implemented, the law put an end to the stupid cycles of revenge by introducing formal boundaries to permissible behavior, inculcating new and irreversible modifications in the procedures of punishment, and cultivating new psychological changes. Everyone then had to begin the long training of discovering "ever-more *impersonal* interpretation[s]" (*GM* II 11) of unruly and injurious behavior. Even aggrieved creditors, who were previously allowed to take pleasure in causing debtors pain, came under the scope of law, leaving them with only the muted pleasure of witnessing legally sanctioned punishment. At the upper limit of justice, there exists, as "a piece of perfection, the highest form of mastery to be had on earth," those just individuals whose "penetrating and merciful" conscience remains steadfast "even in the face of personal injury, of scorn and suspicion" (*GM* II 11). Such individuals are exceptionally rare, and they appear only, or at least most often, in societies with entrenched legal systems. But their rarity also shows what an exceptional achievement the law is itself.

We must take care not to undersell or misunderstand Nietzsche's point. As already noted, he does not decry the rule of law or the justice that comes in its wake. Rather, he rejects a particular hypothesis about the law's origin. That hypothesis holds that justice is a prelegal concept that names certain actions as "just *as such*" (*GM* II 11). If so, then "[E]very will should regard every other will as its equal" (*GM* II 11). However, since life is essentially violent, exploitative, and destructive, thinking that eliminating struggle is a benefit represents "a principle *hostile to life*" (*GM* II 11). Nietzsche asserts against this hypothesis that justice does not predate legal systems but appears only with their development. On this account, the law has never been "a means *against* fighting in general," but was and is "a means for use in the fight between units of power" so that we can create "greater units of power" (*GM* II 11). That is, the law is not primarily a set of social rules used to check exercises of power by some individuals against others. Instead, the law is a set of social rules used to aggregate power across individuals so that even greater power can be achieved. Justice, in turn, does not attach to actions that predate or exist outside of particular legal codes, but only to actions that occur within the scope of legal codes once they are established.

Sections 12–15

It may not be a coincidence that Section 12, the center of *GM*'s middle essay, contains Nietzsche's most extensive discussion of what genealogy theoretically presupposes. In Chapter 1, we introduced the method of genealogy by analyzing parts of this section. We need not repeat that discussion here. What is relevant for us now is genealogy's distinctions between origin and purpose, between emergence and usefulness, and between history and goals as they apply to the law and punishment. In Section 12, Nietzsche makes two preliminary points. In the next three sections, he addresses the myriad functions of punishment (Section 13), the arousal of feeling guilty as one of those functions (Section 14), and the causal effects of punishment on its targets (Section 15).

Two preliminary points bookend Section 12. The first is the now familiar one that the English psychologists' treatment of punishment, like their treatment of the origin of morality, is naive. "They highlight some 'purpose' in punishment, for example, revenge or deterrence, then innocently place the purpose at the start, as *causa fiendi* [the cause of something coming to be] of punishment, and—have finished" (*GM* II 12). The unsoundness of this kind of argument is plain. Just as the naive mistakenly think that a divine force made the eye to see and the hand to grasp, so the English psychologists naively claim that "punishment has evolved for the purpose of punishing" (*GM* II 12). Informed genealogists, knowing better than to argue in this fashion, start from the premise that "the origin of the emergence of a thing and its ultimate usefulness, its practical application and incorporation into a system of ends, are *toto coelo* [by the entire extent of the heavens] separate" (*GM* II 12). That is, informed genealogists know that no purpose existed already fully formed at the point in a society's history when punishment and then law first appeared and that another explanation of them, one that eschews purposes and designs, is available.

The second point, made at the tail end of the section, states one of Nietzsche's most notorious principles, that "the essence of life" is "its *will to power*," a "life-will" found in "spontaneous, aggressive, expansive, re-interpreting, re-directing and formative forces" (*GM* II 12). We have already encountered this principle, first in *GM* I 13's description of strength as the desire to overthrow, crush, become master, have enemies, resistances, and triumphs, second in *GM* II 6's description of cruelty as enjoyable, and third in *GM* II 11's dismissal of Dühring's attempt to ground justice in ressentiment. We will meet it again in Essay III. Here he assumes its truth to criticize Herbert Spencer's version of Darwinian evolution. Nietzsche does not deny that evolutionary adaptation occurs, and there is no clearer alignment to one of evolution's fundamental findings than Nietzsche's observation that the origin and emergence of something are distinct from the functions or purposes that thing comes to satisfy. Yet he thinks that something essential is missing from Spencer's description of evolutionary explanations. While evolutionary adaptation is in part a consequence of an organism's existing in an environment ill-suited to its health and strength, it is also in part a result of an organism's spontaneous and aggressive activities of imposing form on its environment that express its strength and maximize its health. Evolutionary advocates, such as Spencer, neglect this proactive and aggressive element and thereby reduce an organism's life to being nothing more than a reactive and passive process. Nietzsche thinks this ignores an organism's proactive drives and deeds to compel external circumstances to conform to its efforts. We expand on the roles that will to power plays in *GM* in this chapter's discussion section and again in Chapter 5.

Nietzsche applies these points about will power to punishment in Section 13. The act, the procedure, the ritual of inflicting punishment has been a permanent fixture in human history across its arc, but the various meanings, purposes, functions, and utilities we attach to punishment, which are after all nothing more than interpretations of the procedure, have changed repeatedly. So, contrary to naive genealogists of morality and the law—such as the English psychologists and Dühring—who think that the procedures of punishment were "*invented* for the purpose of punishment" (*GM* II 13), a clear-thinking genealogist counters that the procedure, that is, the act of punishment, antedates all of the purposes and meanings we have superimposed on it.

This is not to deny that punishment's various purposes and meanings have their own history. They do, of course, and over time they eventually "crystallize in a kind of unity that is difficult to dissolve back into its elements" (*GM* II 13). Nietzsche puts this crystalline unity under the flame of analysis to dissolve it back into its elements, and in the balance of the section he offers a compendium of punishment's purposes. We do not repeat them here. Revealing all of these distinct functions and purposes only strengthens his point that beneath the layers of interpretation that wrap punishment in brassy functions and sanctimonious purposes lie aggressive activities of compelling our companions to change.

However, one frequently touted purpose of punishment does bear emphasis. We moderns often think that we punish so as to arouse a "*feeling of guilt* in the guilty party" (*GM* II 14). To think this is true is to "violate reality and psychology even as it is today," not to mention as it was "for the longest period in the history of mankind" (*GM* II 14). Psychologically speaking, criminals only erratically feel the pang of bad conscience / guilt. Why is that? Nietzsche supplies four reasons. First, captured wrongdoers typically think to themselves only that something unexpected has occurred, not that they are guilty. Second, those who judge wrongdoers in courts of law typically target the wrongdoer's causal responsibility for the harm caused and try to find preventive measures that block the convicted criminal from causing more of it, but they rarely remain focused for long on whether the convicted criminal feels guilty. Third, judged and sentenced convicts typically feel sadness rather than guilt. Instead of thinking that they ought not to have done what they did, they more often accept their sentence as they previously accepted being caught, as if submitting to "illness, misfortune, or death, with brave, unrebellious fatalism" (*GM* II 15). Fourth, prison life itself does nothing to cultivate the pang of guilt in convicts. Prisons only make convicts "harder and colder" by concentrating and sharpening "the feeling of alienation" and "the power to resist" (*GM* II 14). In short, despite all of the pious nonsense suggesting otherwise, punishment does not facilitate the growth of bad conscience / guilt. Rather, it impedes it.

What remains of punishment once it is stripped of its purposes, intentions, designs, and functions are the durability of its methods and procedures and its causal consequences, its "actual *effects*" (*GM* II 15). Punishment achieves a "lengthening of the memory, in a will to be more cautious, less trusting, to go about things more circumspectly from now on," and an "increase of fear, the intensification of intelligence, the mastering of desires" (*GM* II 15). If to these psychological capacities we add the capacities for predictability, attention control, and promise-making discussed earlier, we can see that what Nietzsche has been doing in the first two-thirds of Essay II is describing the psychological prerequisites for, and thus the components of, prudential agency.

We henceforth use "prudential responsibility" to refer to the collection of these psychological capacities cultivated in human animals by custom, creditor-debtor relations, and punishment; we use "prudential agent" to refer to human animals who are thusly responsible; and we use "enculturation mechanisms" to refer to custom, creditor-debtor relations and punishment. Then, instead of having to say that the social mechanisms of custom, ritual, creditor-debtor relations, and punishment found in early societies made us more predictable, more in control of our emotions, desires, attention, and memories, increasingly capable of intelligent calculation, thinking about the future, and making promises, more circumspect and less trusting, and more indebted to the community, we can more succinctly say that enculturation mechanisms transformed primitive human animals into prudentially responsible agents.

Sections 16–18

Domesticating humans with prudential responsibility does not necessarily imply the psychological development of bad conscience / guilt. bad conscience / guilt has a more complex genealogy than prudential responsibility and agency, a genealogy that, depending on how one interprets these sections, either presupposes, works with, or lies side by side with prudential responsibility and agency.

Although Nietzsche uses 'conscience' throughout Essay II, he describes it only twice in *GM*. At *GM* II 2 he says that the sovereign individual calls the "knowledge of the extraordinary privilege of *responsibility*, the consciousness of this rare freedom and power over himself and his destiny" his "*conscience*" (*GM* II 2). Immediately after that, he adds that the "concept 'conscience'" as found in the sovereign individual is "to be answerable to oneself, and proudly, too, and therefore *to have the prerogative to say 'yes'* to oneself" (*GM* II 3). Then, at *GM* II 4, he notes that there is something distinct from conscience, "that other 'dismal thing,' the consciousness of guilt, the whole 'bad conscience'" (*GM* II 4). Luckily, these clues are enough to offer a first description of conscience. If, as *GM* II 4 asserts, bad conscience is being reflectively conscious of one's guilt, then, by parallel reasoning, conscience should also be reflective of something. And *GM* II 2 and *GM* II 3 suggest what that something is: it is being reflectively conscious of the prerogative of responsibility and promise-making and promise-keeping, of power over oneself, of being answerable and accountable to oneself and others, of being an agent.

Since promising, contracts, and customs worked together to create prudentially responsible agents, we can infer that conscience is being reflectively aware that one is a prudentially responsible agent. However, being reflectively aware of prudential responsibility is not the same as bad conscience, which is the reflective awareness of guilt and the accompanying qualitative affect of suffering, that is, feeling guilty. We should not expect to find such a late flowering phenomenon when its primitive progenitor first appeared, so it should be no surprise that as Nietzsche describes the first appearance of the ancestral feelings that lead to it, bad conscience / guilt is not present. The rest of Essay II describes how the primitive ancestral feeling grew with new interpretations into bad conscience / guilt as found in modern Christianized morality.

Nietzsche initially tells us that "bad conscience [is] a serious illness to which man was forced to succumb by the pressure of the most fundamental of all changes which he experienced, —that change whereby he finally found himself imprisoned within the confines of society and peace" (*GM* II 16). When primitive human first organized into communities, they found that they could no longer rely on the subconscious impulses and drives and qualitatively conscious affects that effortlessly guided survival and flourishing in precommunal existence. In this new, "unknown" world,

> The poor things were reduced to relying on thinking, inference, calculation, and the connecting of cause with effect, that is, to relying on their "consciousness," that most impoverished and error-prone organ! I do not think there has ever been such a feeling of misery on earth, such a leaden discomfort, —and meanwhile, the old instincts had not suddenly ceased to make their demands! But it was difficult and seldom possible to give in to them: they mainly had to seek new and as it were underground gratifications. All instincts which are not discharged outwardly *turn inwards*—this is what I call the *internalization* of man: with it there now evolves in man what will later be called his "soul." The whole inner world, originally stretched thinly as though between two layers of skin, was expanded and extended itself and gained depth, breadth and height in proportion to the degree that the external discharge of man's instincts was *obstructed*. Those terrible bulwarks with which state organizations protected themselves against the old instincts of freedom—punishments are a primary instance of this kind of bulwark—had the result that all those instincts of the wild, free, roving man were turned backwards, *against man himself*. Hostility, cruelty, the pleasure of pursuing, raiding, changing and destroying—all this was pitted against the person who had such instincts: *that* is the origin of "bad conscience." (*GM* II 16)

According to this passage, internalization—the mechanism that redirect instincts, drives, and affects inward on and into oneself by obstructing their outward discharge—is the root of bad conscience but not bad conscience itself. Nietzsche makes a similar claim in *EH*, where he notes that conscience and bad conscience have their roots in "the instinct of cruelty turning back on itself when it can no longer discharge itself outwards" (*EH*, "Why I Write Such Good Books, *GM*").

Recall that punishment was among the early community's tools for thwarting hostile, cruel, and destructive instincts and drives. Given outwardly directed instincts and drives as inputs, punishment projected them back onto, or, more accurately, introjected them into, the person who had those instincts and drives. Punishment and the other protective "bulwarks" these early communities had at their disposal—their enculturation mechanisms—thus worked together to domesticate the "wild, free, and roving" (*GM* II 16) human animal by minimizing opportunities for discharging instincts and drives on other conspecifics and the external world and multiplying opportunities for discharging them in the inner world and oneself.

The first product of internalizing outwardly directed instincts was a population of human animals tamed by custom and exchange relations, controlled by accompanying punishment regimes. These early humans still carried the physiological and psychological traces of their not-too-distant animal past, a past dominated by outwardly discharged instincts and drives that had been until recently the basis for their "strength, pleasure and formidableness" (*GM* II 16). With the self-laceration and "homesickness for the desert" that accompanied enculturation, the newly forged domesticated humans turned inward and made of themselves "a torture-chamber, an unsafe and hazardous wilderness" (*GM* II 16). Although not possessing bad conscience, they nevertheless became the host for affects that later mutated into bad conscience. Nietzsche briefly mentions that the invention of bad conscience laid the groundwork for "man's sickness of *man*, of *himself*" (*GM* II 16).

Note that the early humans who turned against themselves introduced "something so new, profound, unheard-of, puzzling, contradictory and *momentous* on earth that the whole character of the world changed in an essential way" (*GM* II 16). Never before envisaged possibilities now awakened for humans, "as though something were being announced through [them], were being prepared, as though [humans] were not an end but just a path, an episode, a bridge, a great promise" (*GM* II 16). We discuss these new possibilities in Section 24.

Section 17 names two assumptions for Nietzsche's hypothesis about the origin of the ancestral affect of bad conscience. The first is that human enculturation was so abrupt that it did not even cause ressentiment in newly domesticated populations. The second is that enculturation began with violence. The first organized societies "emerged as a terrible tyranny, as a repressive and ruthless machinery, and continued working until the raw material of people and semi-animals had been finally not just kneaded and made compliant, but *shaped*" (*GM* II 17). Describing this process as the activity of a unified and legally sanctioned political state would be inaccurate. What actually happened was that "some pack of blond beasts of prey, a conqueror and master race . . . [laid] its dreadful paws on a populace which . . . [was] still shapeless and shifting, creating thereby a structure of domination [*Herrschafts-Gebilde*] that *lives*, in which parts and functions are differentiated and related to one another" (*GM* II 17). As a sculptor imposes shape on a block of stone, so too did the early masters shape humans into domesticated animals fit for life in the community.

Since they imposed order on the herd, the old masters were necessary for bad conscience's emergence: without them, bad conscience would not have been possible. However, the first to experience the affects ancestral to bad conscience were those on whom order was imposed. When the old masters imposed form and order on the herd, violent oppression was unavoidable, and they either eliminated or "forcibly made latent" most of the rabble's freedoms (*GM* II 17). The remaining residue of freedom, "this *instinct of freedom*, forcibly made latent . . . this instinct of freedom forced back, repressed, incarcerated within itself and finally able to discharge and unleash itself only against itself: that, and that alone, is *bad conscience* in its beginnings" (*GM* II 17). Why should this be so?

Nietzsche provides an answer in the next section: the "*instinct for freedom* (put into my language: the will to power)" used the self "as a piece of difficult, resisting, suffering matter" and branded it "with a will, a critique, a contradiction, a contempt, a 'no' " (*GM* II 18). With external expression of will to power thwarted by imposed enculturation mechanisms, most humans in these early societies had no option but to turn inward on themselves. Henceforth, humans undertook the "uncanny, terrible but joyous labor" (*GM* II 18) of self-formation. Nietzsche calls this form-imposing labor on the self the "active bad conscience." It has been the "womb of ideal and imaginative events" and has "brought a wealth of novel, disconcerting beauty and affirmation to light, and perhaps for the first time, beauty *itself*" (*GM* II 18). However, active bad conscience is one, but not the only, form of bad conscience. Nietzsche introduces another form of bad conscience, that inculcated by religion, in Section 24.

We cannot ignore the parallel between what the old masters' and the clergy's activities accomplished on a social scale to forge a community and what enculturation and internalization accomplished on an individual scale to forge a subject. Just as the old knightly aristocrats and clergy foisted form and order on ragged bands of bartering individuals and molded them into communities of social animals overseen by customs, rituals, exchange relations, and punishment procedures, so the newly domesticated social animals began to impose form and order on themselves to make themselves sociable. It was that self-imposed form that prompted the first experiences of bad conscience in the masses, the feeling that they were not all they could be, that they were falling short of what they should be. From these reflections, Nietzsche draws a surprising inference: the activity of imposing order and inflicting cruelty found in the ancients grounds the pleasure that we moderns who now deny and sacrifice ourselves by acting selflessly feel when we act in unegoistic ways. Contrary to Schopenhauer and the English psychologists, it is "only bad conscience, only the will to self-violation [that] provides the precondition for the *value* of the unegoistic" (*GM* II 18). Hence, even if "bad conscience is a sickness," it is "a sickness rather like pregnancy" (*GM* II 19).

Condensed within these cryptic sentences is an argument against Schopenhauer. Recall from Chapter 1 that Schopenhauer argued that a selfless renunciation of willing and desire is the ideal liberated state for an individual, and that compassion is the fundamental moral response toward others. Schopenhauer justified these claims by arguing that only in this liberated state can we understand and feel benevolence for others who are also suffering from willing and desire. For Nietzsche, it is not ersatz states of psychological liberation from will and desire, but their opposites—violent and willful states of self-hatred found in bad conscience—that ground the value of compassion. Whatever value compassion may have, the causal antecedent of that value is the self-directed, self-willed contempt we have for ourselves. As such, compassion is not, as Schopenhauer thought, a value that expresses a transcendental moral ideal; it is instead a value that express an ancient dissatisfaction with our self. Compassion may still retain value after values are revalued, but whatever value it may then claim will, as its genealogy here shows, not receive support from the kind of arguments that Schopenhauer presented. We return to these evaluative matters in Chapter 5.

Sections 19–23

Sections 4 through 10 addressed the creditor-debtor relationship in prudential agents engaged in exchange dealings and in fulfilling obligations to the communities of which they were members. In Sections 19 through 23, Nietzsche reapplies the creditor-debtor model to cross-generational bonds between communities and their forebears, thereby adding other elements that help explain the development of bad conscience / guilt. The compressed arguments found in these sections can leave even seasoned scholars scratching their heads. It is clear that he assigns certain innovations to the psychological elaboration of conscience and bad conscience / guilt, but his description of these innovations is often puzzling. We are right to hope that he might organize his arguments carefully and present his claims directly. However, we are, as he has previously alerted us, nearing the end of the essay, so we are moving rapidly with "dreadful detonations" exploding all around us. Those of us trying to survive the din will find this warning cold comfort. We would benefit from careful exposition; he instead bombards us with a barrage of amplified rhetorical devices. We might desire soberness; he instead treats us to a charging, at times giddy, torrent of incomplete claims.

These four sections map two divergent psychological developments that followed upon humans creating gods. On the first, exemplified by societies under the Greek gods, conscience and even the active bad conscience of Section 18 never had the opportunity to curdle into moral guilt. Section 19, the first half of Section 20, and Section 23 describe this development. On the second trajectory, exemplified by societies that created a single God, appearing first in Judaism and then blossoming in Christianity, conscience and the active bad conscience went sour and decayed into something fetid, moral guilt. The second half of Section 20 and Sections 21 and 22 describe this development.

First Trajectory (Sections 19, 20, and 23)

For our primitive ancestors, "[T]he living generation always acknowledged a legal obligation towards the earlier generation, and in particular towards the earliest, which founded the tribe" (*GM* II 19), an obligation so profound that it extended to the tribe's debt to its predecessors for its very existence. With the tribe's growth and increased power, its indebtedness to its ancestors continued to increase, resulting in all kinds of festivals, tributes, shrines, sacrifices, rituals, customs, and traditions. So we finally have an answer to the question left hanging in Section 1: Why did a morality of custom arise in the first place in our primitive ancestors? The answer is now clear. A morality of custom began as a set of social measures that offered rituals and traditions for satisfying a community's debts to its ancestors and that had as one of its consequences the development of prudential responsibility.

Among primitive people, concern that their sacrifices were never enough grew "in proportion as the tribe itself [became] ever more victorious, independent, honored and feared," thus cultivating a "*dread* of the ancestor and his power" (*GM* II 19). The crude logic at play here led the strongest communities to transfigure their ancestors into heroes and gods. During what Nietzsche calls a "middle period,"[4] these strong and successful communities continued to grow, continued to "repay, with interest, their founders" (*GM* II 19), and continued to diversify their array of heroes and gods. So, as he notes elsewhere, "A people that still believes in itself will still have its own god. In the figure of this god, a people will worship the conditions that have brought it to the fore, its virtues—it projects the pleasure it takes in itself, its feeling of power, into a being that it can thank for all of this. . . . On this supposition, religion is a form of gratitude" (*A* 16). These heroes and gods conferred onto the community's noble castes, that is, its masters and clergy, the characteristics that, as we saw in Chapter 3, grounded control of the masses, warranted creation of orders of rank and evaluative concepts such as good and bad, and confirmed the knightly aristocrats and clergy as the meaning of society, the end in the service of which all others found meaning.

[4] Nietzsche's "middle period" may refer to the ancient cultures in the greater Levant between about 3000 BCE and the start of the Common Era, so after the invention of writing and arithmetic and before the appearance of monotheism. Among others, this time frame includes the dynastic Egyptians and Nubians up and down the Nile, the Amorites, Assyrians, Sumerians, Hittites, and Canaanites, and pre- and early classical Greeks.

In such a hierarchical social structure, slaves and serfs "adapted themselves to the divinity cults of their masters, whether through compulsion, submission or mimicry," so that the society's glory and feelings of indebtedness began to "overflow in every direction" (*GM* II 20). For evidence, we need look no further than the proliferation of Greek heroes and gods and the Greek legal codes, rank orders, competitive games, sacrifices, festivals, rituals, and traditions. It may be surprising to learn that Athenian society devoted a third of the days in a year to festivals of various kinds; in Rome, the number approached two-thirds. By incessantly reminding everyone about how lucky they were to be members of their society and about where they fit in it, these interlocking features kept ancient communities unified and strong.

Ancient gods played distinct psychological roles for the populace. The Greek gods, for example, were "reflections of noble and proud men in whom the *animal* in man felt deified, did *not* tear itself apart and did *not* rage against itself" (*GM* II 23). Just as the old masters enjoyed their active and lusty lives, and just as they discharged their will to power by imposing order on their own societies and by going on pillaging campaigns against others, their gods enjoyed themselves by demanding tribute and entertainment from humans, by imposing their fateful wills on all of humanity, and by squabbling and competing with one another, sometimes violently. Second, the gods were witnesses of, and thereby gave meaning to, suffering. So long as the gods existed, all earthly suffering, cruelty, and battlefield bloodletting became "festivals for the gods" that provided them the spectacle of suffering and cruelty as "a side-dish to their happiness" (*GM* II 7).

Greek gods were not simply spectators. They also commented on human foolishness, stage-managed us, and nobly accepted their responsibility for causing evil, as Nietzsche notes in this chatty passage:

> "How foolish they are" is what [a god] thinks when the mortals misbehave, —"foolishness," "stupidity," a little "mental disturbance." . . . But even this mental disturbance was a problem—"Yes, how is this possible? Where can this have actually come from with minds like *ours*, we men of high lineage, happy, well-endowed, high-born, noble and virtuous?"—for centuries, the noble Greek asked himself this in the face of any incomprehensible atrocity or crime

> with which one of his peers had sullied himself. "A *god* must have confused him," he said to himself at last, shaking his head. . . . This solution is *typical* for the Greeks. . . . In this way, the gods served to justify man to a certain degree, even if he was in the wrong, they served as causes of evil—they did not, at that time, take the punishment on themselves, but rather, as is *nobler*, the guilt. (*GM* II 23)

Nietzsche makes three distinct points in this passage. First, unruly and injurious behavior in ancient Greek society was the result of folly, stupidity, and mental disturbance, not, as found later in Christianity, a consequence of free choice. Second, human folly, mental agitation, and even madness were regularly the results of a god's ruse or joke, instead of a consequence of our own moral shortcoming. Third, humans, including those who tarnished themselves with crimes, routinely offloaded responsibility for their misdeeds onto the gods. It was the gods' wicked tricks rather than evil human nature that made people blunder into the troubles they met so regularly on earth. The gods' noble guilt thereby justified humanity, at least in part.

One way to put the difference between Greek and other middle-period societies from later Christianized societies is that for the former human folly was an epistemological rather than a moral shortcoming, a failure of knowledge rather than a failure of will. In Greek society, people usually did not know enough to know how to avoid getting into trouble. As a result of this foolishness, most people shambled around in an uninformed stupor, constantly colliding with other equally bumbling idiots. However, at least until Socrates, these pileups were not a reason for thinking that humanity was morally reprehensible or responsible for choosing to be ignorant. More importantly, these epistemological weaknesses implied that, since the gods were always at hand, any inward attempt to ground suffering in being guilty could be easily and definitively short-circuited. When the Greeks reflected and looked inside to discover why they were miserable, all they found were the consequences of a god's trickery or delight in human suffering. Since gods were not inside individuals—they were, after all, external beings—looking inside themselves never revealed to the Greeks that they were causally responsible for their suffering; rather, it was the gods who caused it. They used gods "to keep 'bad conscience' at bay so that they could carry on enjoying their freedom" (*GM* II 23). As now argued, Christianity changed what reflection discovered.

Second Trajectory (Sections 20, 21, and 22)

Nietzsche introduces the Christian God in *GM* II 20. This new god added certain innovations to the god blueprint as already found in the first trajectory. The first of these innovations was that the Christian God was "the maximal god yet achieved" and, therefore, instilled the "greatest feeling of indebtedness on earth" (*GM* II 20). Reading this, we might wonder why this should be so. After all, the Christian God was a god of the rabble, the herd, the slaves, serfs, and commoners, none of whom had debts to pay to the Roman gods since they existed to be the currency of repayment to those gods. Put otherwise, we must now try to understand why, since they had no reason to be indebted to the Roman gods for their miserable existence, early Christians should be indebted to any other god, much less be maximally indebted to the maximal god?

Part of the answer to these questions is that Christianity inherited its God from Judaism, and so inherited the Jewish sense of religious indebtedness to God for their flourishing as a society. Like a solar furnace, Judaism's novelty was to refocus a set of dispersed debts to a pantheon of gods onto a single point, making their god the only god to whom we owe all debts. This burning, maximal feeling of indebtedness to a single god is religious guilt. But guilt's religious expression is still not its moral expression. So long as bad conscience / guilt remained tied to indebtedness to God, it was still about an external entity, even if, as in the case of Judaism, it is God the maximal creditor. However, moral guilt concerns the self, so we still need other elements to explain how externally directed religious guilt became internally directed moral guilt.

Nietzsche's explanation of how we redirected externally directed guilt to God inward onto ourselves is opaque and confusing. Let us lay his account out charitably, if incompletely. Religious guilt, already maximal in Judaism, reached an apogee where we could no longer repay the debt owed to God. Since the debt was maximal and unpayable, remittance was "an iron impossibility," and this prompted " 'debt' and 'duty' to be reversed—but against *whom*?" (*GM* II 21). Nietzsche argues that debt and duty reversed against both the debtor and the creditor. Most important was the turn against the debtor, "in whom bad conscience now so firmly established itself, eating into him, broadening out and growing, like a polyp," eventually reaching a state in which debt became "*eternal* punishment" (*GM* II 21). However, there was also a turn against the creditor, as when we encumbered ancestors with original sin or converted nature into a fiendish evil or convinced ourselves that life itself is worthless. Here we have religious guilt universalized. What started as a sense of indebtedness to deified ancestors became in monotheistic religions such as Judaism a sense of unpayable indebtedness to God, which, since it was unpayable, rebounded back on and into the person and from there grew again outward to infect everyone around and then even past generations. Original sin stained every member of society, whether contemporary or departed. Accordingly, we all became equally deserving of punishment.

Christianity's advance over the Jewish God, its "stroke of genius" (*GM* II 21), was to concoct a mechanism that displayed our perpetual debt to God. God's son Jesus came down from heaven to forgive us for not being able to pay back our debt to God, but his crucifixion nailed our debt to eternity. No other religion had dared dream up the "horrible paradox of a 'God on the cross'" (*GM* I 8), of a "God sacrificing himself for man's debt," of a "God paying himself back . . . to redeem man from what, to man himself, has become irredeemable—the creditor sacrificing himself for his debtor" (*GM* II 21). The logic here is notable for its sheer nuttiness. If we have Judaism to thank for a debt focused on a single point, we have Christianity to thank for continuing to superheat that debt until nothing can douse it and it becomes eternal: "*God on the cross*—have people still not grasped the gruesome ulterior motive behind this symbol?—Everything that suffers, everything nailed to the cross is divine. . . . We are all nailed to the cross, consequently *we* are divine" (*A* 51). Christianity thus completed the logical development begun by Judaism. Judaism reached "its pinnacle" with the "'redeemer,' this apparent opponent of and disperser of Israel" (*GM* I 8). By fixing Jesus to the cross "so that 'all the world,' . . . could safely nibble at this bait" (*GM* I 8), Christianity infected every nibbler with religious bad conscience and moral guilt, and, as we will see in the next chapter, ascetic values and nihilism.

Nietzsche thinks that what he has just suggested is so obvious that we will have easily digested it and are now prepared to entertain his hypothesis that what is really going on is a "will to torment oneself, that suppressed cruelty of animal man who has been frightened back into himself and given an inner life . . . and has discovered bad conscience so that he can hurt himself, after the *more natural* outlet of this wish to hurt had been blocked" (*GM* II 22). Monotheistic religion uses God as a "presupposition in order to provide his self-torture with its most horrific hardness and sharpness. Debt towards *God*" (*GM* II 22). Since God is "the ultimate antithesis" of animal instincts, drives, and desires, his essentially transcendent and utterly antihuman existence served as justification for the clergy to reinterpret all of our instincts, drives, and desires as sins, as reasons for feeling guilty, as willful rejections of God's best hopes for humanity, as an "animosity, insurrection, rebellion against the 'master,' the 'father,' the primeval ancestor and beginning of the world" (*GM* II 22). Thereafter, God's ideal and the clergy's incessant reminders of that ideal condemn us. Worse, we condemn ourselves to "torture without end, as hell, as immeasurable punishment and guilt" (*GM* II 22) for being natural beings and for daring to think our drives and desires matter. Willing to find ourselves "guilty and condemned without hope of reprieve," we created God "in order to be palpably convinced of [our] own absolute worthlessness in the face of this ideal" (*GM* II 22). That is moral guilt, the most perverse expression of bad conscience, and with it, we "cut off the way out of this labyrinth of '*idées fixes*'" (*GM* II 22). Even if our insistence to suffer is interesting, our eagerness to wave off any escape from this fabricated maze so that we can remain lost inside it leads Nietzsche to experience a "black, gloomy, unnerving sadness," for "here is *sickness*, without a doubt, the most terrible sickness ever to rage" (*GM* II 22).

Sections 24–25

At the beginning of Section 24, Nietzsche announces that he will conclude Essay II with three questions. However, he adds another section after this one and asks seven questions, not three, so we may wonder which of the seven are the three to which he refers. The first question is easy enough to find. He asks three questions in quick succession, all of them thematically linked. Their common thrust is to wonder about the sacrifices needed to fix "how much reality always had to be vilified and misunderstood in the process, how many lies had to be sanctified, how much consciousness had to be troubled, how much 'God' had to be sacrificed" (*GM* II 24). We modern Europeans are the product of a process that despises our natural inclinations, so much so that they "finally came to be intertwined with 'bad conscience'" (*GM* II 24). We hate ourselves for being natural beings. Nietzsche argues instead that we should consider overcoming our Christianized "other-worldly aspirations," all the religious hopes and ambitions that are "alien to the senses, the instincts, to nature, to animals" and have made us "hostile to life and have defamed the world" (*GM* II 24).

Earlier, in Section 18, Nietzsche briefly referred to the active bad conscience. We wrote a promissory note there that we now redeem. The active bad conscience, that is, the willingness to treat oneself as an artist treats raw materials, is the "womb of ideal and imaginative events, [and has] brought a wealth of novel, disconcerting beauty and affirmation to light, and perhaps for the first time, beauty *itself*" (*GM* II 18). We now see that the active bad conscience is nothing less than the willingness to take who we are and subject it to experiments in self-formation. Nietzsche recommends that we take all that we have inherited from Christianity—its otherworldly aspirations, its gruesome imagery, its bad conscience, guilt, and self-hatred, its cultivation of a deep, tortured, and interesting self that is prepared to give form to itself—and subject all of it to experiments in creative reconfiguration.

Nietzsche next asks, "[W]hat is more deeply offensive to others and separates us more profoundly from them than allowing them to realize something of the severity and high-mindedness with which we treat ourselves?" (*GM* II 24). He does not doubt that few are able to recognize, much less realize, how demanding these experiments in self-reconfiguration will have to be. We need, as he suggests, spirits "for whom conquest, adventure, danger and even pain have actually become a necessity," spirits that are "acclimatized to thinner air higher up, to winter treks, ice and mountains in every sense," and most importantly, spirits who have "a self-assured willfulness of insight which belongs to great health" (*GM* II 24). He asks finally, "Is this at all possible today?" (*GM* II 24). Not only does he answer that it is possible, but he is confident that such a spirit will come. This "man of great love and contempt" will be able to redeem this world from "the curse which its ideal has placed on it up till now" (*GM* II 24). All of the upside-down and topsy-turvy Christian ideals, and the "great nausea, the will to nothingness, [and] nihilism" that have resulted from them, will be overturned when this "Antichrist and anti-nihilist, this conqueror of God and of nothingness" comes. That individual is "Zarathustra the Godless" (*GM* II 25).

4.3 Discussion

Certain topics left underdeveloped in Essay I get fuller treatment in Essay II. One of them is the role of custom in human psychological and moral development, bad conscience / guilt, and justice. However, Nietzsche again postpones discussion of the priest's role in the slave revolt in morality and the masters' subjugation. Moreover, he introduces new topics in Essay II that he does not explain until Essay III. These include asceticism and the ascetic ideal, religious arguments against life, the meaninglessness of suffering, and nihilism. Finally, after making a brief appearance in Essay I, the will to power reappears again in a central passage in Essay II, yet Nietzsche does not explain it in any detail or tell us why it is so important.

We defer explaining how the priests collaborated with the herd to undermine the old masters during the slave revolt until Chapter 5. We also defer explaining asceticism, religious arguments against life, the meaninglessness of suffering, and nihilism until then. Here we dig into the genealogies of subjectivity and agency, for although Nietzsche does not advertise it as such, a primary focus of Essay II is explaining how we became self-reflective and prudentially responsible and accountable subjects and agents. First, we show that a morality of custom, creditor-debtor relationships, and promising are crucial elements for the emergence of self-aware subjectivity, prudential responsibility and accountability, and agency. Second, we discuss the philosophical doctrine of free will, Nietzsche's rejection of it, and his own analysis of willed action. Third, we expand on what Nietzsche thinks power is, how he thinks power is related to life, and what he thinks willing power is. We defer discussing how will to power functions as an evaluative principle until Chapter 5.

Subjectivity, Continuity, Self-Awareness, and Self-Control

Philosophers, theologians, and English moral historians have tried to sell us a collection of fictions that we are one kind of subject and one kind of agent when we are instead a quite different kind of subject and a quite different kind of agent. By asserting that the subject is ahistorical, conscious, indivisible, and disembodied, and by claiming that agency is a God-given endowment for making conscious choices enacted by free will, they have misunderstood the nature of both subjectivity and agency. We are natural beings made up of drives and affects, and our subjectivity and agency are natural and social developments that are subjected to historical circumstances and work in human-all-too-human ways. Genealogies explain how we naturally and socially acquired prudential subjectivity and agency and how the philosophical and theological kinds of moral subjectivity and agency, despite being fictions, layered themselves over prudential subjectivity and agency in our self-understanding. Yet this standoff leaves us with little more detail about the kind of subject and the kind of agent Nietzsche thinks we are, and it leaves us wondering why his kinds are preferable to those he rejects.

Were we now, as other mammalian species still are, dominated only by subconscious biological drives and qualitatively conscious percepts and affects, we would even now be no more complex than they are. We would be, as they still are, dominated and propelled by caloric need, the need for shelter, the drive to reproduce, and various other drives for certain pleasures and the satisfaction of biologically fixed needs. Likewise, we would be, as they are, aware only of perceptions and affects of various kinds, as they variously are. As with other mammals who are qualitatively conscious of their perceptual and interoceptive states, there would be a way that things look, sound, feel, taste, and smell like to us and a way that hunger, pain, pleasure, thirst, and other internal states feel like to us. Finally, our behavior, like theirs, would be fully explicable by probing the interaction of drives and affects, as described in the last chapter. There be would no more to discover about us than whatever advances in evolutionary biology, evolutionary physiology, evolutionary psychology, and mammalian and primate ethology provide.

Nietzsche does not deny that we inherited these physiological, psychological, and ethological structures and perceptual and interoceptive awareness from our last common ancestor. However, our existence has come to include more complex drives and affects and more diverse kinds of drives and affects than those found in other primate species. We developed away from their kinds of existence into more interesting, more dangerous, more conflicted, sicklier kinds of socialized and communal beings. Thousands of years before the slave revolt, all of us, masters and commoners alike, were already significantly more complex than other primates, in large part because we already lived in complex and hierarchical social arrangements, interacted in ways assigned by custom and fixed by exchange relations, used language and mathematics, and bound ourselves to various social norms and regimes of punishment that secured ongoing peace and checked bad acting, free riding, and exploitation. Explaining the appearance and entrenchment of these additional complications to human drives, affects, subjectivity, and agency is a task of the first two-thirds of Essay II. Nietzsche's multifaceted story about memory, forgetting, customs, norms, rule-following, promising, exchange relations, and punishment is that explanation.

Another complication new to us is that even if, as in other primates, drives are still typically subconscious in us and provoke experiential saliencies and affects, our form of existence also includes being conscious of ourselves, our thoughts, our values, and our agency in novel ways. We think reflexively about our self, we think reflectively about past, current, and future events, we ruminate about what is valuable to us, we consciously make plans for the future and remind ourselves of past commitments, and we monitor our thoughts, drives, and affects. If so, then we are conscious in more numerous and additionally complex ways than our last common ancestors. Nietzsche's genealogy of subjectivity and agency has to capture the appearance and development of these complications as well. It is noteworthy, then, that in *GM* he never clearly identifies or elaborates on any of the developments in reflective consciousness.

Promising, Punishment, and Self-Awareness

Since we did not inherit promising from our last common ancestor, we have acquired it sometime after our split from them, and the abilities that comprise promising in turn helped us become prudentially responsible subjects and agents who have a conscience. These are in turn preconditions for bad conscience / guilt. Nietzsche's genealogical hypothesis is that promising plays a crucial role in cultivating the kinds of prudential subjectivity and prudential agency that host responsibility and conscience, and that because it plays this role, it thereby helps to underwrite bad conscience / guilt.

Promising is the ability to commit ourselves to one specific future rather than any other future. When we promise, we project ourselves into the future where we fulfill our commitment and remember ourselves from the past when we made the commitment. Of course, promising is more than a cognitive ability; it is also the practical ability to bind ourselves to our commitment even if in the future we are not disposed to do so. Making a promise entails avowing to ourselves and others that we are now who we will be in the future and that we are now prepared to override or inhibit our drives in the future so that we fulfill our commitment to that future. So when we make a promise, we avow to ourselves and others that we are prepared to take responsibility for controlling ourselves and our future engagements with others and the world. Just as the old masters commanded the slaves, so in promising we command ourselves, and just as the old masters ordered slaves about to help them satisfy their drives even if the slaves resisted, so we who promise order ourselves so that we satisfy certain of our own drives and desires even if other drives and desires resist.

To produce self-reflexive avowals such as promises, we had to become synchronically cohesive and reflexively self-aware (or, as we will also put it, synchronically self-conscious) of our cohesion:

> [M]an must first have learnt to distinguish between what happens by accident and what by design, to think causally, to view the future as

> the present and anticipate it, to grasp with certainty what is end and what is means, in all, to be able to calculate, compute—and before he can do this, man himself will really have to become *reliable, regular, necessary*, even in his own self-image. (*GM* II 1)

Second, we had to become capable of recognizing that who we have been in the past, who we are now, and who we will become in the future are related diachronically. That is, we had to become diachronically continuous and reflexively aware, through memory, of that continuity:

> [M]emory is . . . an active *desire* not to let go, a desire to keep on desiring what has been, on some occasion, desired, really it is the *will's memory*: so a world of strange new things, circumstances and even acts of will may be placed quite safely in between the original "I will," "I shall do" and the actual discharge of the will, its *act*, without breaking this long chain of the will. (*GM* II 1)

These points can be condensed as follows. First, without synchronic cohesion, promises would attach to no one when made; second, without diachronic continuity, promises would attach to someone else when enforced; third, without synchronic self-awareness, promises would not be recognized for what they are; and fourth, without diachronic memory, promises would be empty verbal exercises.

Punishment helped cultivate cohesion, continuity, self-awareness, and memory by causing other direct effects. Recall what Nietzsche says about the psychological effects of punishment:

> [T]he actual *effect* of punishment [is] primarily in the sharpening of intelligence, in a lengthening of the memory, in a will to be more cautious, less trusting, to go about things more circumspectly from now on, . . . a sort of improvement of self-assessment. What can largely be achieved by punishment, in man or beast, is the increase of fear, the intensification of intelligence, the mastering of desires: punishment *tames* man in this way. (*GM* II 15)

Making a promise thus included giving creditors permission to punish debtors were the debtors not to abide by their commitment. With fear of punishment in mind, the debtor was compelled to control desires, focus attention, and become more cautious and circumspect, to become, in short, dependable and predictable, which in turn helped cultivate self-awareness by introducing a cut between debtors and their desires and actions. Since "every offence [is] something that *can be paid off*, . . . at least to a certain degree, the wrongdoer is *isolated* from his deed" (*GM* II 10).

Indeed, both parties to a promise or contract needed to be dependable and predictable, the debtor so that the creditor could be confident that the debtor would not simply flee or claim amnesia when the debt came due, and the creditor so that the debtor could be confident that the creditor would not act capriciously to collect on the debt or act vengefully when the debt was not paid. By announcing and keeping to the terms of a contract, parties communicated to each other their expectation that the parties who made the terms would be continuous with the parties in the future who enacted the terms, that they would submit to those terms and endure punishment if they violated them, and that neither party would act on impulse nor vindictively beyond those terms. In short, promises and contracts promoted continuity, reliability, and regulated emotions in both creditor and debtor, and punishment enforced and reinforced them.

Custom, Punishment, and Self-Control

Exchange relations were not the only mechanisms for developing subjectivity and agency. Customs, traditions, and rituals did some of the same work for these early humans, and did other important work as well. Nietzsche claims that the "fearful pressure of 'morality of custom' under which all the communities of mankind have lived, many millennia before the beginnings of our calendar" (*D* I 14) were "the genuine and decisive main historical period that determined man's character" (*GM* III 9). We now show how customs, traditions, and rituals nurtured new psychological abilities, new social commitments, and a new sense of ourselves.

The inherent inanity of customs and rituals loaded meaningless motor behaviors with meaning, thus transforming behavior into action. Nietzsche calls this "the first proposition of civilization":

> Among barbarous peoples there exists a species of customs whose purpose appears to be custom in general: minute and fundamentally superfluous stipulations . . . which, however, keep continually in the consciousness the constant proximity of custom, the perpetual compulsion to practice customs: so as to strengthen the mighty proposition with which civilization begins: any custom is better than no custom. (*D* I 16)

By focusing on the motor elements of customs and rituals loaded with the meanings bequeathed to them by secular and clerical authorities, practitioners acquired abilities to recognize otherwise meaningless behavior as meaningful action and to endow their own behavior with significance. Again, by adhering to a ritual's schedule, practitioners cultivated enough predictability to carve out recurring intermissions in their lives for the ritual and sufficient emotional regulation to perform it. Moreover, since customs and rituals demanded attention to all of their petty details, practitioners also cultivated enhanced endogenous attention control and self-awareness of themselves as loci of action and thought. As with promising, these abilities helped embed and enhance in early human psychology a cut or pause between, on the one hand, ongoing engagement with others and the environment and, on the other hand, the demands of ritual actions. As with exchange relations and promising, this cut between self and action, between self and drive, between self and others, and between self and environment helped nurture self-reflection and agency.

Customs, traditions, and rituals also came loaded with penalties for failing to abide or practice them. The security found in obeying custom, reiterating tradition, and performing ritual was already compelling, but fear of punishment for not following a custom or not performing a ritual or not reiterating a tradition was equally compelling. Thus punishment made what were otherwise voluntary enhancements obligatory necessities. Moreover, punishment meted out in the name of tradition and custom began the process by which suffering was reinterpreted as valuable. Strangely enough, that value was calibrated as a direct function of punishment's severity and disutility to the individual. Tradition is a "higher authority which one obeys, not because it commands what is *useful* to us, but because it *commands*" (*D* I 9), and the amount early humans were prepared to suffer on behalf of tradition and custom by sacrificing what they held dear became a measure of their value as a community member. So, as noted already, in a morality of custom, the most moral human was the person "who obeys the law most frequently," who "obeys it even in the most difficult cases," who "*sacrifices* the most to custom" (*D* I 9). Indeed, the compulsion to obey fostered by sacrifice was not immediately useful for the individual at all. Sacrifice was instead a mandate for "the hegemony of custom, tradition [to be] made evident despite the private desires and advantages of the individual: the individual is to sacrifice himself—that is the commandment of morality of custom" (*D* I 9).

Through commandment, the other work that custom, rituals, and traditions did for early humans comes into view. By instituting orders through its traditions, customs, and rituals that decreed its preeminence, the community implanted a sense of membership in something supraindividual:

> [Tradition] is above all directed at the preservation of a *community*, a people; every superstitious usage which has arisen on the basis of some chance event mistakenly interpreted enforces a tradition which it is in accordance with custom to follow; for to sever oneself from it is dangerous, and even more injurious to the *community* than to the individual (because the gods punish the community for misdeeds and for every violation of their privileges and only to that extent punish the individual). (*HH* I 96)

Compelled to obey traditions, customs, and rituals, early humans became members of a community. As the community grew healthier, its enshrined traditions, customs, and rituals became markers for, and were interpreted as causes of, individual health. Of course, tradition required occasional personal sacrifice for the benefit of all because sacrifice embodied the community: "[E]ven if the individual suffers from an arrangement which benefits the whole, even if he languishes under it, perishes by it—the custom must be maintained, the sacrifice offered up" (*HH* II 89). And, thus, "[T]here creeps into the world the idea that *voluntary suffering*, self-chosen torture, is meaningful and valuable. Gradually, custom created within the community a practice corresponding to this idea: all excessive well-being henceforth aroused a degree of mistrust, all hard suffering inspired a degree of confidence" (*D* I 18). We develop the implications of these claims in Chapter 5 when we chart how the clergy and oppressed collaborated to bring down the old masters.

We now begin to see why Nietzsche thinks that theological and philosophical descriptions of subjectivity are not just alternative accounts but are instead wrongheaded fictions. Theologians and philosophers suggest that being a subject is a God-given condition of being human. Nietzsche's genealogy of subjectivity demonstrates that becoming a subject was instead an achievement resulting from enculturation mechanisms that chugged away for thousands of years, imposing and reinforcing uniformity, predictability, reliability, attention control, emotional regulation, self-awareness, cohesion, continuity, and self-sacrifice on what at the start were animals little different from our last common ancestors. As he notes, "[W]ith the help of the morality of custom and the social straitjacket, man was *made* truly predictable" (*GM* II 2). Otherwise put, enculturating mechanisms tamed and humanized us. As such, they may be existence conditions for the complicated beings we became, but they are far from being God-given conditions for being human.

Agency, Free Will, and Willing

Theologians and philosophers claim that the subject is ahistorical, indivisible, disembodied, unembedded, conscious, and distinct from its drives, emotions, and desires. This disembodied subject is also an agent, a subject that originates action. Theologians and philosophers have a particular account of agency, according to which the disembodied and detached agent reflectively deliberates about its drives, desires, and emotions and options for satisfying them. Undetermined by anything other than that reflective deliberation, the agent chooses the option that will best satisfy those drives, desires, and emotions and promptly acts on that choice. This is free will agency. Nietzsche rejects free will agency in any but a reappropriated sense of 'free will' and proposes an alternative account of agency. He argues that an agent is an embodied and embedded subject that comes loaded with subconscious drives and conscious affective states. He allows that this embodied and embedded agent sometimes reflects on which actions are likely to satiate drives and satisfy desires. However, he argues contrary to the theologians and philosophers that those reflections are determined by drives, affects, desires, and emotions. Hence, he thinks that the causal nexus between choice and action, even when it occurs, is tortuous and that free choice based on reflective deliberation alone is epiphenomenal.

Agency and Free Will

Agency, like subjectivity, has its origins in exchange relations and customs. Above we noted that making a promise entails that we are now and will continue to be prepared to modify, order, or inhibit specific drives and affects so as to fulfill our remembered commitment, to take responsibility for ourselves and our futures with others and the environment. Similarly, the morality of custom made early humans predictable, reliable, attentive, and emotionally regulated. Again, obeying tradition, submitting to custom, and practicing rituals all require self-inhibition, self-organization, emotional control, and endogenous attention control.

By making themselves exchange partners and by following tradition and custom or practicing rituals, early humans calibrated themselves against their commitments and learned how to inhibit themselves from following whatever drives and affects they had at the moment. They thereby became capable of controlling emotions, checking themselves against immediate inclination, and monitoring internal states and actions. Punishment ensured compliance when they demonstrated that they could not do so. Thus, again, either by their own doing or by being punished for not so doing, early humans came to introduce an interruption—a pause or cut—between themselves and the actions they might take or the immediate inclinations they might have: "[A] world of strange new things, circumstances and even acts of will may be placed quite safely in between the original 'I will,' 'I shall do' and the actual discharge of the will, its *act*, without breaking this long chain of the will" (*GM* II 1).

This pause introduced to humans the abilities to recognize that they were temporally continuous, to distinguish between immediate, short-term, and long-term inclinations, drives, and desires, to control and order their drives, desires, and emotions, and to originate action. Individuals may well have wanted to do one thing, but their commitment to ensure that in the future they would repay debts, collect loans, observe customs, and perform rituals required them to organize themselves and their actions so as to make those futures their futures. They were, as noted previously, becoming "*reliable, regular, necessary*, even in [their] own self-image" (*GM* II 1). They were becoming aware of themselves as being responsible for themselves and accountable to others, as being self-aware subjects whose control over drives and whose affective consistency warranted their dependability to themselves and others. In short, they were becoming prudential agents.

Developing prudential responsibility and agency occurred without free will. It is noteworthy that beyond rejecting it, Nietzsche mentions free will only rarely in *GM*. In Essay I, Section 13, he claims that we mistakenly think there is "an indifferent substratum behind the strong person which had the *freedom* to manifest strength or not." However, he discusses free will by name in only three passages, all in Essay II: Section 2, Section 4, and Section 7. Section 4 asks, "Have these genealogists of morality up to now ever remotely dreamt that . . . punishment, as *retribution*, evolved quite independently of any assumption about freedom or lack of freedom of the will?" (*GM* II 4). And Section 7 asks, "Might it not be the case that this extremely foolhardy and fateful philosophical invention, first devised for Europe, of the 'free will,' of man's absolute freedom [*Spontaneität*] to do good or evil, was chiefly thought up to justify the idea that the interest of the gods in man, in man's virtue, *could never be exhausted*?" (*GM* II 7). These passages state, first, that agents are never neutral and that they never freely choose from options (*GM* I 13), second, that punishment's role in cultivating subjectivity and agency does not require free will (*GM* II 4), and third, that free will is an invention that justifies a religious interest (*GM* II 7). We have discussed these claims already.

The most thorough discussion of free will in *GM* occurs at Essay II, Section 2. The section opens by rehearsing the role of custom in cultivating subjectivity and agency. Nietzsche asks us to think about the end product of these developments:

> Let us place ourselves . . . where society and its morality of custom finally reveal what they were simply *the means to*: we then find the *sovereign individual*, . . . having freed itself from the morality of custom, an autonomous, supra-ethical individual (because "autonomous" and "ethical" are mutually exclusive), in short, we find a man with his own, independent, enduring will, whose *prerogative it is to promise*—and in him a proud consciousness . . . of *what* he has finally achieved and incorporated, an actual awareness of power and freedom. . . . This man who is now free, who actually *has* the *prerogative* to promise, this master of the *free* will, this sovereign—how could he remain ignorant of his superiority over everybody who does not have the prerogative to promise or answer to himself, how much trust, fear and respect he arouses, . . . and how could he, with his self-mastery, not realize that he has necessarily been given mastery over circumstances, over nature and over all creatures with a less enduring and reliable will? (*GM* II 2)

This passage does not describe nineteenth-century Europeans or future humans, nor does it represent some kind of rarely attained human ideal.[5] Instead, it describes humans who, compelled by the straitjacket of various enculturation mechanisms, became so habituated to their continuity, predictability, emotional regulation, impulse inhibition, self-awareness, and memory that they could readily make and keep promises, fulfill contracts, and comply with custom and its rituals. They were competent at being responsible selves because they were, at least intermittently, masters of themselves. Their responsibility for themselves and self-mastery empowered them to be masters of others who were less competent at being responsible for themselves, that is, who were more irregularly and incompletely masters of themselves.

Those who became masters of themselves were liberated from the morality of custom whose commands had cultivated the abilities that

[5] See Leiter 2009 and Anderson 2021 for contrary interpretations of this passage.

resulted in their sovereignty. Obeying tradition and practicing rituals had, like promising, taught them how to bring their disparate drives and affects together into a temporary cohesion so that they could be prudentially responsible for themselves and accountable to others. When they told themselves or others they would do something, they and others knew they could and would do it; their word was surety of their action. Since they were prudentially responsible and accountable, they were reliable, and since they were reliable, they no longer needed the fear of punishment to compel them to do as custom demanded. Indeed, they no longer experienced custom as an external compulsory requirement at war with their drives and desires. Instead, their drives and desires became congruent with what custom required, so the deliberations those drives and affects informed came to embody custom. By embodying custom, they experienced the power of mastering themselves long enough to be "answerable" for their "own *future*" (*GM* I 1). They were ready for new internal wars.

Agency and Willing

We should take care, then, not to read too much into Nietzsche's assertion that those who have a prerogative to promise are "master[s] of the *free* will." Indeed, the free will mentioned in *GM* II 2 is not the free will that the theologians and philosophers attribute to us. In order to defend this claim, we first clarify what Nietzsche thinks willing is and then distinguish what he is prepared to acknowledge about willing from what philosophical and theological free will advocates attribute to us. It would be helpful, of course, were Nietzsche to tell us in *GM* what he thinks willing is, but he declines to do so. Instead, he characterizes wills in several ways and names various aims of willing.[6]

[6] For instance, he says that wills are strong and full (*GM* Preface 3); enduring or unenduring and reliable or unreliable (*GM* II 2); good (*GM* II 8, III 9); in bondage (*GM* II 221); mad (*GM* II 22); secret, hesitant, uncertain, and unacknowledged (*GM* III 3); excited, craving, and calming (*GM* III 6); and sick (*GM* III 14). Again, he identifies more than two dozen states of affairs that we will, that is, that we aim willing toward. These include knowledge (*GM* Preface 2); going against life (*GM* Preface 5); being human (*GM* I 12); baseness, abasement, levelling decline, and decay (*GM* I 16); life (*GM* II 11); power (*GM* II 12, III 14, 15, 18); caution (*GM* II 15); self-violation (*GM* II 18); self-torment, finding oneself guilty, and thinking of oneself as punished (*GM* II 22); infection and poisoning (*GM* II 22); setting up an ideal (*GM* II 22); nothingness (*GM* II 24, III 1, 14, 28); teaching something different (*GM* III 3); existence (*GM* III 7); remaining (*GM* III

We know that willing is not a decision to act based on uncaused reflective deliberation about options, for that requires that willing be free willing, and humans do not have free will. Our task is instead to make sense of Nietzsche's claims about willing in a world without free will. We simplify our task by focusing on the organismic level of willing and simplify it even more by focusing on Nietzsche's description of willing as it reflectively occurs in humans. We then subtract elements from that explanation to account for subpersonal human drives and affects and extend that streamlined account from humans and their drives to describe other species and their drives.

If willing does not rely on deliberation jumping uncaused into a sequence of events leading to action, what then does it rely on? By piecing together what has already been said about human subjectivity and human agency, and by reviewing what he says about willing elsewhere, an account emerges. By about three thousand years ago, humans were variably capable of being sufficiently cohesive at a time, continuous over time, emotionally regulated, attentive, and self-aware to be reliable, responsible for themselves and accountable to others. Those who had mastered themselves were more reliable, responsible, and accountable than those who lagged behind, zigzagging through their lives as rarely self-aware and barely cohesive bags of unordered and uninhibited drives and affects. In short, those who enjoyed the prerogative of promising had achieved a certain level of self-command and prudential responsibility that others lacked.

The self-command characteristic of these early humans continues to be pivotal for understanding what willing is. A passage in *BGE* describes the role of self-command in typical cases of human willing:

> [I]n every act of willing there is, to begin with, a plurality of feelings, namely: the feeling of the state *away from which*, the feeling of the state *towards which*, and the feeling of this "away from" and "towards"

7); the 'desert,' moderation, and simplicity (*GM* III 8); neutrality and objectivity (*GM* III 9); taking responsibility (*GM* III 10); contradiction and counternature (*GM* III 12); elimination of the will (*GM* III 12); reciprocity, forming a herd, a 'community,' a 'conventicle' (*GM* III 18); misunderstanding suffering (*GM* III 20); standing before facts (*GM* III 24); truth (*GM* III 24, 27); and deception (*GM* III 25). Our task is to make sense of this mélange.

> themselves. But this is accompanied by a feeling of the muscles that comes into play through a sort of habit as soon as we "will," even without our putting "arms and legs" into motion. Just as feeling—and indeed many feelings—must be recognized as ingredients of the will, thought must be as well. In every act of will there is a commanding thought, —and we really should not believe this thought can be divorced from the "willing," as if some will would then be left over! Third, the will is not just a complex of feeling and thinking; rather, it is fundamentally an *affect*: and specifically the affect of the command. What is called "freedom of the will" is essentially the affect of superiority with respect to something that must obey: "I am free, 'it' must obey"—this consciousness lies in every will, along with a certain straining of attention, a straight look that fixes on one thing and one thing only, an unconditional evaluation "now this is necessary and nothing else," an inner certainty that it will be obeyed, and whatever else comes with the position of the commander. (*BGE* 19)

Note how complicated Nietzsche thinks willing is. Willing is described as being a multifaceted and temporally extended, indeed protracted, subpersonal process made up of drives, affective reports and feelings about certain physiological and psychological states, endogenously controlled attention, reflective evaluations, commanding thoughts, internal organization, and certain affects and feelings, specifically (though not only) the commanding affect of superiority to compel obedience from resistant drives and affects and the coupled certainty that these resistant forces will obey.

This account of willing is inconsistent with what the theologians and philosophers have trained us to think about it. They think a human agent is a disembodied and synchronically unified subject that suspends the activating force of all of the drives and affects that comprise us; next inserts an act of deliberation about options into the chain of drives and affects; then decides to act based only on deliberation; and finally initiates some motor action simply by so deciding. Nietzsche counters that a human agent is an embodied and partially cohesive subject that never suspends the impelling force of all of the drives and affects that comprise us; only fitfully deliberates about options and then never without the uninterrupted urging of drives and affects; never decides to act only on deliberation; and never initiates action simply by deciding to act.

The cohesion of the subject who is an agent engaged in willed action is of particular importance, for it reveals the ongoing struggle between drives within any agent. Even if we are sufficiently cohesive to be predictable and capable of inhibition, we are still and always will be "both the one who commands *and* the one who obeys, and as the obedient one we are familiar with the feelings of compulsion, force, pressure, resistance, and motion that generally start right after the act of willing" (*BGE* 19). This is why willing is best characterized as evaluating and commanding rather than as deliberating and deciding: "[T]here is will only where the effect of command, and therefore obedience, and therefore action, may be *expected*" (*BGE* 19). Take a moment to reflect on this sentence. We are, as we now know, comprised of drives and affects. Since there are always struggles between drives and between affects, some drives and affects will always have to command others. That other drives and affects resist entails frequent, sometimes chronic, slippage between what some of our drives command and what actually occurs. Yet, under the tutelage of the theologians and philosophers, we have become accustomed to think that we have free will, and that is in part why "we are in the habit of ignoring and deceiving ourselves about this duality by means of the synthetic concept of the 'I'" (*BGE* 19). We conceive of ourselves as fully unified subjects and erroneously (albeit understandably) think that deliberation and decision necessitate action, that "willing *suffices* for action" (*BGE* 19).

Action consistent with self-command and self-obedience does happen, but only so long as nothing internal continues to impede us and nothing external imposes itself on us. In such cases when action occurs, the internal command/obedience episode succeeds, which is to say that certain drives and affects or sets of them manage to organize and control other drives and affects, and internal resistances are overcome long enough to act. Successful self-command, in turn, prompts the "feeling of pleasure as commander," the "feeling of power that accompanies all success," and "the feelings of pleasure from the successful instruments that carry out the task," which include our own body, that "society constructed out of many 'souls'" (*BGE* 19). We can, with some charity, say that strong wills are commanding-obeying episodes that result in overcoming resistances, whereas weak wills are commanding-obeying episodes that fail to overcome resistances. Again, with some charity, we can attribute to subjects the capacity to successfully execute self-command when one set of drives and affects commands and another set of drives and affects obeys. We can even reappropriate the term 'freedom of the will,' not as a term that refers to a non-natural causal faculty but as a term that gives a name to "the multi-faceted state of pleasure of one who commands and, at the same time, identifies himself with the accomplished act of willing. As such, he enjoys the triumph over resistances, but thinks to himself that it was his will alone that truly overcame the resistance" (*BGE* 19).

This account of reflective human willing describes it as a temporally extended process that is every bit as complex and protracted as ressentiment. In humans anyway, reflective willing is a process that takes diverse drives, desires, and affects as inputs. Those inputs are endogenously attended to and evaluated by calibrating them with others so as to promote a certain future. And some drive or set of cooperating drives commands others to realize that future and then monitors the ensuing obedience or disobedience of the others and the cooperation or interference from the external environment. What bears emphasis is that the pleasure of command that accompanies a single stage in the process does not replace the other nodes in that process. Theologians and philosophers mistakenly think that it does.

Nor can willing be reduced to the reflective evaluation of options by a disembodied and detached subject that the theologians and philosophers think is the core of free choice and free will. Again, contrary to them, at no point in the process of human willing does undetermined deliberation jump into the process to suspend the impelling force of drives and affects; at no point does a disembodied and detached agent introduce a freely chosen option into the process; and at no point is any such free choice alone sufficient for action. These are the fictions that transform how willing happens into the myth of free willing. Of course, that free willing is a myth has not stopped the theologians and philosophers from claiming it is real. They have been happy to spread the fantasy that free will is a gift from God that we all equally possess. After all, they thereby strengthen their story about why the old masters are evil, explain away the slaves' slavish nature, and implant the cancer of irredeemable indebtedness to God, which metastasizes through our psyches as moral guilt and its attendant ascetic moral values. We return to these issues in the next chapter.

We can now fulfill a promise made earlier at the beginning of this subsection. Instances of reflective human willing as described in *BGE* 19 include endogenous attention and reflective evaluation as elements of a process and the affect of pleasure that accompanies successful command and obedience as another element of that process. We can and frequently do attend to our drives and affects and evaluate our futures, and we sometimes do feel the pleasure of command. However, Nietzsche also allows that much of our own willed activity lacks this pleasure and one or both of these reflective elements. He also allows that subpersonal drives and nonhuman actions are instances of willing that do not have any reflective elements in their causal etiologies. So even if some episodes of human willing include these elements as parts, many other episodes of human willing do not, and where members of another species lack one or more of them, their willing will likewise be explained without reference to any reflection. If so, then these other elements must explain how those other instances of willing are still sufficiently similar to one another to categorize them as kinds of willing.

Recall that drives come loaded with saliency filters that structure valenced interoceptive and perceptual experience. Recall too that affects are valenced qualitative experiences that report on an organism's status. If so, then drives and affects can fulfill interpretive and evaluative functions in instances of suborganismic willing without being reflective. Since they fulfill the functions that in episodes of reflective willing are fulfilled by endogenous attention, evaluation, and commanding, subconscious interpretation and evaluation and qualitative affect are elements of willing episodes at the subpersonal human level and at the suborganismic level of other drive-comprised but nonreflective organisms. Moreover, drives and affects also have ends, namely those evolved functions by which one is distinguished from another so that the organism is prompted to feel a certain affect, such as lust or hunger, and so that the organism is disposed to engage in certain behaviors, such as seeking out a sexual partner or finding food.

Since nonreflective drives and affects fulfill the impelling, interpretive, and evaluative functions of willing and can do so in the absence of endogenous attention, reflective evaluation, and reflexive command, we may well wonder whether the reflective elements are completely superfluous. This issue is an area of an active scholarly debate that focuses on Nietzsche's convoluted, sometimes vexed, claims about the role of reflective consciousness in human and animal agency. The suggested readings at the end of this chapter point to discussions of these intricate matters. Here it suffices to note that all animals, and hence the reflectively conscious human animal, are dynamic agents whose willing spontaneously reinterprets, redirects, and imposes form on its own drives and affects, other conspecifics, and the environment. We are not only passive recipients of information from our bodies, others, and the environment that are compelled to adapt to changes; we are also agents that compel ourselves, others, and the environment to change so that we can flourish.

Power and Willing Power

Occasionally and at what appear to be crucial points in *GM*, Nietzsche unexpectedly drops will to power into an argument. Most of these occurrences are in Essay II, Section 12, but at other places in *GM* he uses related phrases, such as "lust for power" (*GM* I 7), "power-will" (*GM* III 11), "feeling of power" (*GM* III 7, 14, 19), and "path to power" (*GM* III 7). Since the word 'power' appears elsewhere in *GM* more than two hundred times, and since will to power is one of Nietzsche's most notorious contributions to philosophy, it is an easy inference that power and will to power are important. So it is galling that he rarely describes power or will to power and that the descriptions he does provide are vague. We turn now to clarify these matters. First, we state what power is and show how power relates to life. Second, we clarify what is involved in willing power.

What Power Is and Why Life Is Power

The most sustained descriptions of power in *GM* are these, all from Essay II, Section 12:

> [E]verything that occurs in the organic world consists of *overpowering*, *dominating*, and in their turn, overpowering and dominating consist of re-interpretation, adjustment, in the process of which their former "meaning" [*Sinn*] and "purpose" must necessarily be obscured or completely obliterated. (*GM* II 12)

> The essence of life, its *will to power*, [is] spontaneous, aggressive, expansive, re-interpreting, re-directing and formative forces. (*GM* II 12)

> [E]very purpose and use is just a *sign* that the will to power has achieved mastery over something less powerful, and has impressed upon it its own meaning of a use function. (*GM* II 12)

Four things are noteworthy. First, these descriptions are extraordinarily general: power is the "essence" of life, achieving "mastery over something less powerful," "impressing a meaning" on something less powerful, and "spontaneous, aggressive, expansive, re-interpreting, re-directing and formative forces." Second, his use of the word 'force' (*Kräft*) in one of the passages recalls *GM* I 13, where he claims that "a quantum of force is . . . a quantum of drive, will, action—in fact, it is nothing but this driving, willing and acting." Third, he identifies power as a set of living forces, not as a set of physical forces.[7] Fourth, he identifies a specific set of life forces with will to power without specifying what life is. He states neither what orders of life he is talking about nor whether he extends power to all or only some orders. Nor does he specify the levels at which power is found. Perhaps every level of life from the micro level up is a level of power; perhaps power starts only at levels at or higher than suborganismic components of life, such as molecules and cells; perhaps it starts only at or above the level of suborganismic physiological systems, such as organs and tissues; perhaps it is found only at or above the level of suborganismic drives and affects, such as the sex drive and the affect of lust; or perhaps it exists

[7] In *GM*, Nietzsche does not extend will to power to nonorganic physical forces (except indirectly in the quoted *GM* I 13), but he does so elsewhere, both in published works (as at *BGE* 36) and in many *Nachlass* notes. We acknowledge but do not consider these extensions here.

only at or above the level of organisms that have drives and affects, such as sheep and humans, and supraorganismic collections of them, such as flocks, societies, and species.

In *BGE*, *TI*, *A*, and the *Nachlass*, Nietzsche expands on power and life in ways that help clarify these matters. For instance, he argues that we can explain our life "as the organization and outgrowth of one basic form of will (namely, of the will to power, which is *my* claim)" and that we can "trace all organic functions back to this will to power and find that it even solved the problem of procreation and nutrition (which is a single problem)" (*BGE* 36). Again, he suggests that a living organism tries to "incorporate new experiences,' to classify new things into old classes, —which is to say: it aims at growth, or, more particularly, the *feeling* of growth, the feeling of increasing strength" (*BGE* 230). Similarly, he argues that "life itself is *essentially* a process of appropriating, injuring, overpowering the alien and the weaker, oppressing, being harsh, imposing your own form, incorporating, and at least, the very least, exploiting . . . life *is* precisely will to power. . . 'Exploitation' . . . belongs to the *essence* of being alive as a fundamental organic function; it is a result of genuine will to power, which is just the will of life" (*BGE* 259). In this same passage, he extends this assessment beyond organisms to societies. In a *Nachlass* note, he reinforces the equivalence of power and living: "[A]ll expanding, incorporating, growing is a striving against what resists. . . . What do the trees in a jungle fight each other for? For 'happiness'?—For *power*" (*KSA* 13 11[111]). And in *A*, he condenses his claims about life and power into a catchphrase: "I consider life itself to be an instinct for growth, for endurance, for the accumulation of force, for power" (*A* 6). Similarly in *TI*: "[T]he overall condition of life is . . . a state of . . . abundance, opulence, even absurd squandering. Where there is a struggle, it is a struggle for power" (*TI* "Skirmishes" 14).

According to these passages, then, power is a set of spontaneous and insistent drives and activities implicated in growth, expansion, striving against resistance, exploitation, oppression, appropriation, and incorporation. All of these different drives and activities are condensed at *GM* II 12 into the general type of overpowering or dominating, which, as noted, consists in reinterpretation, adjustment, overcoming resistance, and imposing form and meaning. These passages also state that life and the will to life are will to power, that exploitation is the essence of being alive, and that life is an organism's instinct (that is, drive) for growing, for enduring, and for accumulating power. Finally, these passages locate four levels of life where power is found: suborganismic physiological processes, suborganismic instincts and drives, organisms, and societies made up of human organisms. That is enough for us to proceed.

Willing Power

If willing is a temporally extended and command-obedience process as previously described, and if power is a set of spontaneous and insistent drives and activities implicated in growth, expansion, exploitation, oppression, appropriation, overcoming resistance, and incorporation, then willing power is that complex process and involves these spontaneous and aggressive drives and activities. However, what that involvement amounts to is not at all obvious.

We begin by reinforcing a previous claim. Recall that Nietzsche takes reflectively willing power as a special case of willing power, that is, as a species of a larger genus. We have shown how to subtract reflective elements of willing from cases of willing as they appear in subconscious human drives and in species of animals that do not engage in reflective cognition at all. This applies in the case of willing power as well: being reflective is not necessary for willing power. Even if reflectively willing power includes endogenous attention control, reflective evaluation, and whatever other accoutrements (e.g., deliberation) we think necessary to accurately describe the species of willing with which we are most familiar, other species of willing power that lack these elements also occur and do so regularly.

The more salient issues are understanding what, if anything, willing power adds to other instances of willing, and second, understanding how the heterogeneous ways that power is willed can be consistent with gathering all of them under the concept of willing power. Nietzsche does not explain himself in *GM*. Indeed, he is even elsewhere not as clear about these matters as we might hope, for he makes at least three distinct claims about the logic of willing power.[8] According to

[8] See Richardson 1996, 2020; Reginster 2006; Riccardi 2021; Katsafanas 2016.

the first, willing power is a first-order psychological episode that has the same structure as willing anything else. Willing power is thus one among other first-order instances of willing with the determinate aim of power, existing alongside all the other first-order kinds of willing he identifies in *GM* (recall the list earlier in this chapter). According to the second, willing power is the metaphysical basis or ground of all willing on which all instances of willing supervene and to the end of which all other first-order kinds of willing are means. Willing power is thus what all first-order kinds of willing have in common because it is the root kind from which all kinds of willing devolve, in terms of which all kinds of willing are to be understood, and the fundamental or ultimate end of all kinds of willing. According to the third, willing power is a structuring feature, or set of features, of all first-order kinds of willing. Willing power is thus a property of first-order kinds of willing with no determinate aim of its own.

At various points, Nietzsche writes on behalf of each of the alternatives. First, he sometimes suggests that animals and humans will power just as they will other states of affairs. Representative passages are found in *GM*. For example, he affirms that "the strongest, most life-affirming impulse . . . [is] the *will to power*" (*GM* III 18). Again:

> Every animal . . . instinctively strives for an optimum of favorable conditions in which to fully release his power and achieve his maximum of power-feeling; every animal abhors equally instinctively, with an acute sense of smell that is "higher than all reason," any kind of disturbance and hindrance that blocks or could block his path to the optimum. (*GM* III 7)

These passages can be interpreted as saying that an animal's days are taken up by a never-ending cycle of willing episodes, some of which command growth, expansion, exploitation, oppression, appropriation, and incorporation, in short, power.

While such episodes do occur, they do not exhaust willing power. All animals, including human animals, routinely engage in activities that fall within the scope of what Nietzsche otherwise describes as willing power but which do not involve power as a first-order future. And if willing power were just one among other first-order kinds of willing, then it might be argued that they exist side by side with those other kinds without being any more important or fundamental than they are. However, if no kinds of willing are more valuable or more fundamental than others, then Nietzsche's evaluative assessment that those kinds of willing that are vengeful, ressentimentful, decadent, or antilife are bad, while those that are strong, proactive, or pro-life are good cannot be sustained.

These problems suggest that the second alternative, that according to which willing power is the ground of and ultimate end of all willing, is preferable. On this way of thinking about things, willing power is the undifferentiated basis on which all kinds of willing are grounded and the end to which all kinds of willing are means. Nietzsche sometimes talks of willing power in this way as well. Recall:

> [E]verything that occurs in the organic world consists of *overpowering*, *dominating*, and in their turn, overpowering and dominating consist of re-interpretation, adjustment, in the process of which their former "meaning" [*Sinn*] and "purpose" must necessarily be obscured or completely obliterated. (*GM* II 12)

> [E]very purpose and use is just a *sign* that the will to power has achieved mastery over something less powerful, and has impressed upon it its own meaning of a use function. (*GM* II 12)

And here again is *BGE*:

> Assuming, finally, that we succeeded in explaining our entire life of drives as the organization and outgrowth of one basic form of will (namely, of the will to power, which is *my* claim); assuming we could trace all organic functions back to this will to power and find that it even solved the problem of procreation and nutrition (which is a single problem); then we will have earned the right to clearly designate *all* efficacious force as: *will to power*. (*BGE* 36)

If these passages get the logic of willing power correct, then all first-order willing episodes are grounded in one basic kind of willing, will to power. If so, then willing power is not one first-order kind of willing among others, for if all first-order willing is an "outgrowth" of willing power, then each kind of first-order willing is a development out of the basis of willing power. Moreover, it is tempting to think that since every kind of first-order willing is willing power, every first-order kind is exercised as a means in the service of the ultimate or fundamental end of willing power.

However, Nietzsche does not always consider the relation between will to power and other kinds of willing as described by this alternative. He typically thinks of willing power as a feature of willing episodes rather than as the fundamental basis of all willing episodes, and he typically denies that various first-order kinds of willing are only a means to the fundamental end of power. Rather, first-order willing episodes typically have their own aims and some such episodes are not simply a means to the end of power. So this view also appears to pose problems.

The third way of thinking about willing power is to think of it as a feature of a particular sort instantiated by first-order kinds of willing.[9] We can appeal to the plasticity of drives to understand what this might mean. Recall from Chapter 3 that drives can be satisfied by engaging in any of a number of activities distinctive to the drive and can be directed toward any number of futures. For instance, the sex drive seeks discharge by engaging in any number of activities—going to a real or virtual bar, meeting people at school, work, or online, attending church social mixers, joining clubs, and so forth—and can be satisfied by coupling with any of a number of partners.

The suggestion under consideration is similar. Just as first-order kinds of willing engage drives, affects, and activities distinctive of the kind and aim at futures distinctive of the kind, so willing power engages diverse kinds of first-order willing and aims at growing, expanding, enhancing, or developing the drives, affects, and activities distinctive of those kinds. Willing power grows and develops the drives, affects, and activities distinctive of first-order kinds of willing by willing any of a number of, or some conjunctive set of, changes to them: exploiting, oppressing, appropriating, and incorporating them, or reinterpreting and adjusting them, or overcoming their resistances

[9] Clark (1990) initially adumbrated the view, and Richardson (1996) first spelled the view out in detail. See also Reginster 2006; Riccardi 2021; Katsafanas 2016.

and giving new form to them. In this way, willing power structures all the diverse drives, affects, and activities engaged by the diverse kinds of first-order willing. We can then say that willing power is a structuring feature of first-order willing. Therefore, willing power is not always one kind of first-order willing among other such kinds with its own aim, nor is it the basic kind of willing that supplies the fundamental end to which all first-order kinds of willing are means. Instead, willing power inherits aims from the first-order kinds of willing it structures.

Suppose we adopt this view of willing power as a second-order structuring of first-order willing kinds. And suppose we couple this view with the idea that while initially directed toward satisfying biological drives in a natural environment, willing power has over the last five thousand years structured increasingly diverse and complex psychological and social drives. We can then say that willing power has also become a way to structure first-order psychological and social willing episodes so that they facilitate growth, development, flourishing, and overcoming resistances in these diverse and complex environments. In psychologically intricate and systematically socialized humans who are turned both inward and outward toward others, willing power structures our experience of ourselves, our conspecifics, and the world's nonhuman inhabitants. Once we will power within and on ourselves, we acquire new abilities to organize our drives and affects so that they become unified in increasingly complex and creative ways. Willing power can thus fundamentally alter our ambitions for ourselves.

Recall that one of the markers of the old masters' coarseness was that they directed willing power primarily on other humans either equal or lower in social rank. We can now understand what thousands of years of the morality of custom, Christianity, socialization, and internalization have wrought in us and why the old masters are but a few developmental steps beyond wild animals and no longer an exemplar for us:

> [T]he material on which the formative and rapacious nature of this force vents itself is precisely man himself, his whole animal old self—and *not*, as in that greater and more eye-catching phenomenon, the *other* man, the *other* men. This secret self-violation, this artist's cruelty, this desire to give form to oneself as a piece of difficult, resisting,

> suffering matter, to brand it with a will, a critique, a contradiction, a contempt, a "no," this uncanny, terrible but joyous labour of a soul voluntarily split within itself, which makes itself suffer out of the pleasure of making suffer, this whole *active* "bad conscience" has finally—we have already guessed—as true womb of ideal and imaginative events, brought a wealth of novel, disconcerting beauty and affirmation to light, and perhaps for the first time, beauty *itself*. (*GM* II 18)

And again in *BGE*:

> If genuine proficiency and finesse in waging war with himself (which is to say: the ability to control and outwit himself) are inherited and cultivated along with his most powerful and irreconcilable drives, then what emerge are those amazing, incomprehensible, and unthinkable ones, those human riddles destined for victory and for seduction. (*BGE* 200)

In these passages, willing power structures reflective experience of ourselves by revealing that we are an internal battleground of "powerful and irreconcilable drives" that we must "give form to" by "branding" ourselves with a "will, a critique, a contradiction, a contempt." If we dare, we impose on ourselves regimens of self-discipline for overcoming internal resistances, regimens of first-order kinds of willing that promote the internal changes necessary to overcome who we have been so that we might become who we are. As Nietzsche colorfully puts it: "Slavery, in both the crude and refined senses of the term, seems to be the indispensable means of disciplining and breeding even the spirit" (*BGE* 188). These regimens organize our drives, affects, desires, emotions, and activities in ways that other animals are incapable of even attempting, for they require all of what our enculturation, religious inculcation, and internalization have made possible. As we will see in the next chapter, internalizing will to power is the source of both the greatest promise and greatest threat to ourselves and our species.

Thinking about the logic of willing power as a second-order ordering of first-order willing episodes has found favor recently among some scholars because it avoids the flattening consequences of power being one among other kinds of willing and the metaphysically loaded assumptions of power being the ground and ultimate end of all willing, while still promising something that is psychologically fertile and explanatorily rich. Let us grant these benefits. However, it must also be admitted that every scholarly effort to better understand power and willing power is hampered by Nietzsche's vague, ambiguous, and imprecise descriptions of them. For categories as pivotal as power and willing power are, these shortcomings are conspicuous.

Consider two obvious problems that arise from what Nietzsche says about power and willing it (there are others). Throughout *GM*, *BGE*, *TI*, and *A*, he asserts both that power is domination and exploitation of an environment and its inhabitants, and alternatively that power is growing and overcoming resistances presented by an environment and its inhabitants and experiencing the affects affiliated with growing and overcoming resistances. These conceptions of power are arguably distinct, and on two dimensions. On the first conception, power is an achievement of domination and exploitation, while on the second, power is an activity of growing and overcoming resistance, accompanied by feelings that flow from such activity. But some domination and exploitation does not result from activities that require growing or overcoming resistances. Think of someone born into economic privilege who may dominate or exploit an environment and its inhabitants without lifting a finger, much less by overcoming any resistances. Likewise, some growing and overcoming resistances activities do not result in achieving domination or exploitation. Consider someone born into economic oppression who may overcome many resistances and grow without dominating or exploiting an environment and its inhabitants. So what is sufficient for exercising power differs for the two conceptions: for the one, growing and overcoming resistances and experiencing that activity's affects are sufficient for having power, while for the other, achieving domination and exploitation is sufficient for having power.

A second problem is that, given the above tensions about what power consists in, tensions will also attach to what willing power consists in. It is, for example, one thing to will a future state of affairs that is an achievement; it is something else to will a future state of affairs that is an activity. Again, willing domination and exploitation differs from willing growing and overcoming resistances and the affects affiliated with such activity. Now, a counter to these tensions might be to argue that growing and overcoming resistances cannot be willed without willing domination and exploitation and that willing domination and exploitation cannot be willed without growing and overcoming resistances. However, assuming that this entailment holds for what willing power consists in is as open to counterexample as claiming that it holds for what power consists in. Suffice it to say, Nietzsche's concepts of power and willing power require additional interpretation, elaboration, and clarification before any conclusions about their plausibility can be inferred. For those interested, the suggested readings provide direction into this productive region of scholarship.

Further Reading

For more on the ethic of custom, creditors and debtors, and bad conscience / guilt, see Janaway 2007; Leiter 2002; May 1999; Migotti 2013; Mulhall 2011; Reginster 2006, 2011, 2021; Richardson 2020; Ridley 1998; Risse 2001.

For more on subjectivity, self-awareness, and self-control, see Janaway 2009; Katsafanas 2016; Mulhall 2011; Reginster 2006; Riccardi 2021; Richardson 1996, 2020; Welshon 2014, 2015.

For more on willing, free will, agency, and the sovereign individual, see Acampora 2006c; Alfano 2019; Anderson 2013, 2021; Doyle 2011; Clark and Dudrick 2009a; Gemes 2009b; Janaway 2007, 2012; Katsafanas 2013a; Leiter 2009, 2011; Migotti 2013; Owen 2007; Poellner 2009; Riccardi 2015, 2021; Richardson 2020; Ridley 2009, 2021; Risse 2007.

For more on power and willing power, see Clark 1990, 2000; Clark and Dudrick 2012; Janaway 2007, 2012a; Katsafanas 2016; Loeb 2015; Owen 2000; Poellner 1995, 2013; Reginster 2006; Riccardi 2021; Richardson 1996, 2020; Schacht 2000; Soll 2012; Strawson 2015.

5

Genealogy Essay III

5.1 Introduction

Essay III is the most philosophically ambitious of *GM*'s three essays. It is also the most heartbreaking and maddening. Nietzsche finally answers previously unanswered questions about the slave revolt in morality, particularly those about the priest's role in that revolt, resolving matters left dangling from the first and second essays. He also develops new arguments about the ascetic ideal, ascetic values, and decadence, the nature and value of science, the nature and value of knowledge, the nature and value of truth, meaningful and meaningless suffering, and nihilism. As much as he does to make himself understood about these matters, these arguments prompt questions that he does not answer.

In the discussion section, we address some of the unresolved issues raised during the essay. The first set of topics revolves around the perspectivity of sensory perception and interoception and the resulting perspectivity of science, knowledge, and truth. We then analyze the relativistic implications of perspectivism and its paradoxical nature. Next, we examine the evaluative dimensions of will to power that to this point have been generally shrouded by Nietzsche's use of it as a biological and psychological explanatory principle. With those evaluative dimensions added, we scrutinize asceticism and decadence. Finally, we use asceticism and decadence to understand Nietzsche's claims about meaningless suffering and nihilism.

Nietzsche's On the Genealogy of Morality. Rex Welshon, Oxford University Press.
 DOI: 10.1093/oso/9780197611814.003.0006

5.2 Essay III by the Sections

Sections 1–5

The first five sections of Essay III examine ascetic values as found in artists, making straightforward points and taking predictable ad hominem shots against Wagner. We can afford to be brief. The ascetic ideal is a set of values identified as "compassion, self-denial, self-sacrifice" (*GM* Preface 5) and "poverty, humility, chastity" (*GM* III 8). Elsewhere, he adds "selflessness" and "self-renunciation" (*EH* "Why I Am a Destiny" 8; see also *GS* 345). These values mean different things for artists, philosophers, women, priests, saints, and those who suffer chronically. What is apparent across the uses to which they have been put is that humans prefer to will something rather than not will at all, even if what they prefer is "to will *nothingness*" (*GM* III 1), that is, even if what they prefer to will is contrary to life and, therefore, nihilistic. Since ascetic values are contrary to what makes most lives worth living, trying to realize them in our lives typically requires us to be moved by drives, have desires, hold beliefs, and do things that are inconsistent with our flourishing. How, then, can achieving them be elements of a flourishing life? Answering that question is one of Essay III's topics.

Nietzsche tries to understand why artists appeal to ascetic values. Predictably, his candidate artist is Wagner, and the ascetic value he examines is chastity (or purity). Wagner's espousing chastity in his later work is a puzzle, especially since his earlier life had been notoriously immodest and his earlier operas had been dedicated to "the *highest intellectualization and sensualization*" (*GM* II 2). He must have come to think that sensuality and chastity were antithetical. Nietzsche counters that "all healthy, cheerful mortals" know that chastity and sensuality need not be contradictions, and that even where they are thought to be so, "such 'contradictions' are what make life so enticing" (*GM* II 2). Perhaps *Parsifal*, an opera that "return[s] to sickly Christian and obscurantist ideals" (*GM* II 3), was meant not to be taken seriously but as a joke, for thinking that it was intentional is depressing.

Nietzsche admits that this criticism is ad hominem and that it would be better to "avoid the confusion . . . of thinking [the artist] is identical with what he can portray, invent and express" (*GM* II 4). If we do separate Wagner the artist from his work and consider the work seriously, *Parsifal*'s triteness becomes even more glaring. How could an artist as great as Wagner have fallen so far as to espouse Christianity in his art and do it so unartfully? Nietzsche's heartbreak over his old friend's feeble end is apparent: he wishes that Wagner "had taken leave of us and of his art in some *other* manner, . . . in a more triumphant, self-confident, Wagnerian manner—in a manner less deceptive, less ambiguous with regard to his general intent, less Schopenhauerian, less nihilistic" (*GM* II 4). That he did not reveals the sad truth that artists are always too dependent on their milieu to be able to understand the philosophical implications of their own work. They are too often "courtiers of their hangers-on and patrons and sycophants with a nose for old or indeed up-and-coming forces" (*GM* III 5), and they need a philosopher as a "front man" (*GM* II 5) to provide intellectual heft and warrant for their creations. We might therefore find a better answer to our question about the meaning of ascetic values by understanding what they mean for philosophers.

Sections 6–10

In Sections 6 and 7, Nietzsche offers more ad hominem comments about ascetic values as found in Kant and Schopenhauer, then in Sections 8, 9, and 10, he turns to the philosophical type's instrumental use of ascetic values for providing a productive working environment and supplying camouflage in a hostile social environment.

Music was for Schopenhauer the supreme artistic form for expressing the essence of the world. He became a "mouthpiece of the 'in itself' of things, a telephone to the beyond" (*GM* III 5), and what he gleaned from his conversation with the metaphysical was that the pleasure of beauty was unique among all pleasures because it was pleasure without "interest" (*GM* II 6). This, Nietzsche thinks, is fascinating but wrongheaded. He counters that we are driven, desiring, and feeling creatures and that our lives are recurring sequences of discharging drives, quenching desires, overcoming resistances, and creating form in ourselves and the external world, on the one hand,

and, on the other, suffering from hindered drives, frustrated desires, and failed endeavors. Satisfaction and discontent are, thus, a direct function of drive, desire, and will: the more we discharge drives, pursue what we desire, and impart form, the more we flourish. Kant and Schopenhauer held to the contrary that aesthetic pleasure is severed altogether from desire and will. Kant understood beauty in just these terms: " 'Something is beautiful if it gives pleasure *without interest*' " (*GM* III 6, parsing Kant's *Critique of Aesthetic Judgment*, Section 2). Nietzsche chuckles at this definition's naivete. The idea that "under the charm of beauty, *even* naked female statues can be looked at 'without interest' " is, he thinks, so preposterous that "we are entitled to laugh a little" (*GM* III 6).

Nietzsche hypothesizes that Schopenhauer's reason for not being able to escape Kant was that for him beauty and aesthetic contemplation "counteracts *sexual* 'interestedness' " (*GM* III 6). To confirm this hypothesis, Nietzsche quotes Schopenhauer's rhapsody about the " 'painless condition which Epicurus praises as the greatest good and as the condition of the gods; we are, for that moment, relieved of the base craving of the will, we celebrate the sabbath from the penal servitude of volition, the wheel of Ixion stands still' " (*GM* III 6, quoting *World as Will and Representation* I, 231). Schopenhauer's reference to Ixion confirms the hypothesis. According to Greek myth, Ixion killed his father-in-law and was exiled to the wilderness. Zeus saw him and invited him to Olympus to join the gods for a meal. While still at the table, Ixion openly lusted after Zeus's wife Hera, thus violating hospitality customs. Angered, Zeus created a cloud that looked like Hera and tricked Ixion into mating with the cloud. The offspring of that coupling, Centauros, subsequently mated with the Magnesian mares to create the half-human, half-horse Centaurs. Zeus then expelled Ixion from Olympus, struck him with a thunderbolt, and had him tied to a burning wheel that was set spinning for eternity. The wheel of Ixion thus represents the repetitious churn of sexual desire.

Much more plausible than beauty occasioning disinterested pleasure is Stendhal's claim that the beautiful is "*une promesse de bonheur* [a promise of happiness]" (*GM* III 6, quoting Stendhal's *De l'amour*, Chapter 17). For Stendhal, who was a "more happily adjusted personality," it was "precisely the *excitement of the will* ('of interest') through beauty" (*GM* III 6) that made the experience of beauty so important. We can see, then, that Schopenhauer misunderstood aesthetic experience and misapplied Kant's understanding of it to his own case. After all, he sought relief from his irksome sex drive, so aesthetic pleasure was for him an intimately interested means to psychological health. While it cannot be denied that beauty was pleasing to Schopenhauer, it was so for a "most private interest possible: that of the tortured person who frees himself from his torture" (*GM* III 6). This is not to diminish the "*main strength* in his nature (the strength to contemplate and penetrate deeply)" (*GM* III 8), of which Nietzsche remained in awe until the end. Rather, it is to suggest that "sensuality is not suspended as soon as we enter the aesthetic condition, as Schopenhauer believed, but is only transfigured and no longer enters the consciousness as a sexual stimulus" (*GM* III 8).

Generalizing, Nietzsche hypothesizes that philosophers exploit ascetic values to liberate themselves from various kinds of internal torture and to find "an optimum of favorable conditions in which to fully release [their] power and achieve [their] maximum of power-sensation" (*GM* III 7). In a passage that unsurprisingly depicts his own life, he details what ascetic values look like in philosophers:

> [F]reedom from compulsion, disturbance, noise, business, duties, worries; clear heads; the dance, bounce and flight of ideas; good, thin, clear, free, dry air, like the air in the mountains, in which all animal existence becomes more spiritual and takes wings; peace in every basement; every dog nicely on the lead; no hostile barking and shaggy *rancune*; no gnawing worms of wounded ambition; bowels regular and under control, busy as a milling mechanism but remote; the heart alien, transcendent, expectant, posthumous. . . . A deliberate obscurity, perhaps; avoidance of self-confrontation; an aversion to noise, admiration, news, influence; a small position, daily routine, something that hides more than it uncovers; occasional association with harmless, happy animals and birds, which are refreshing to behold; mountains for company, not dead mountains, though, ones with *eyes* (by which I mean lakes); in some cases even a room in some crowded, run-of-the-mill hotel where one can be sure of not being recognized and can talk to anyone with impunity. (*GM* III 8)

As lonely as this life appears to be, it provides philosophers what they must have so they can achieve what they must do. By bringing ascetic values to bear on themselves, they provide the conditions needed to "bridle their unruly and tetchy pride or their wanton sensuality" and check their "inclination towards luxury and finery or . . . their extravagant generosity" (*GM* III 8). They thereby earn the open space populated by their beloved ideas, which they joyfully observe, follow, capture, inspect, analyze, research, test, distill, organize, and eventually present to others.

Importantly, philosophers do not conceive of themselves as acting virtuously. Philosophers who use ascetic values as "prerequisites for their *best* existence and *finest* productivity" abide by them because their "*predominant* instinct, which impose[s] its demands on all other instincts" (*GM* III 8), commands them to do so. Unlike morality, which presumes to bind everyone under the unconditional values of meekness, sexual moderation, and material simplicity, philosophers use them instrumentally and impose them only on themselves. Philosophers are often humble, but that is simply because, sure of themselves, they "speak softly" (*GM* III 8) and recoil from the spotlight; they are often poor because "their slogan is, 'who possesses, is possessed' " and refrain from entrapping themselves with gewgaws and ornaments; and they are often chaste because "their dominating instinct, at least during periods when they are pregnant with something great," demands it (*GM* III 8). They welcome "peace, coldness, nobility, distance, the past" and look for "places where [they] can be relieved of the necessity of thinking *about* [*themselves*]" so they can achieve what the philosophical muse, their "supreme master," demands (*GM* III 8).

Nietzsche supplements these reflections with an analysis of the social milieu in which philosophers first emerged and the challenges they faced. The argumentative thread through Sections 9 and 10 is frayed, but the overall point is that for centuries, philosophers have embodied such an outrageous and fundamentally dangerous kind of existence that they have had to hide behind the skirts of asceticism just to survive. The essential problem that philosophers pose to society is that their intellectual drives to "doubt, deny, prevaricate, analyze, research, investigate, dare, compare, and counter-balance," and their insistence on "neutrality and objectivity" and "every '*sine ira et studio*' [without anger or partisanship]" are contrary "to the primary demands of morality and conscience for the longest period of time" (*GM* III 9) and so pose a threat to social cohesion.

Before the slave revolt in morality, the morality of custom codified what was acceptable and what was forbidden, and it established enforcement mechanisms that secured obedience to its edicts. Those who thought like philosophers were ill-suited to such a life, for their delight in thinking rationally, in questioning, doubting, denying, analyzing, and adopting a noncommittal stance to all sorts of claims led inexorably to raising doubts about all of custom's rituals and traditions whose authority had to stay unquestioned if they were to bind ancient communities together. These early philosophers recognized that their penchant for reason was incongruent with the compulsory demands of custom, and they likely felt that they were themselves "the embodiment of '*nitimur in vetitum* [we incline toward that which is forbidden]' " and might actually have "guarded [themselves] 'from feeling,' from being aware of [themselves]" (*GM* III 9). We moderns who flaunt our hubris and "rape nature with the help of machines and the completely unscrupulous inventiveness of technicians and engineers" and who "experiment on ourselves in a way we would never allow on animals" (*GM* III 9) may find it difficult to imagine a time when "well-being was viewed as danger, curiosity as danger, peace as danger, compassion as danger, being pitied was viewed as disgrace, work as disgrace, . . . *change* was viewed everywhere as being unethical and ruinous as such!" (*GM* III 9).

Since ancient communities and societies were steered by custom, tradition, and ritual, and since they were hardened by war, cruelty, and adventure, the warriors and aristocrats derided and mistrusted contemplatives' reflection, intellectual curiosity, and encouragement of peaceful coexistence. The suspicion expressed for contemplatives extended even to how contemplatives thought of themselves. In a violent and tradition-bound society, those who advocated peace, reasoned thought, and investigation "had no other remedy than to conceive a pronounced *fear* of themselves" and to encourage others to "learn to *fear* them" (*GM* III 10). They thus created "imaginative forms of self-mortification" (*GM* III 10) and masqueraded as priests, sorcerers, and soothsayers, using such disguises to signal that their exotic intellectual innovations and shocking ways of thinking were worthy of fear and respect. And since they already disguised themselves as seers and magicians, contemplatives and early philosophers found it easy to adopt ascetic values as additional camouflage for surviving in a world antagonistic to them, as a necessary "outward appearance, as a precondition of existence—[they] had to *play* that part in order to be a philosopher, [they] had to *believe* in it in order to be able to play it" (*GM* III 10).

Sections 11–14

Nietzsche turns in Section 11 through Section 22 to the crucial and dangerous matters of Essay III, the discussion of priests, the unhealthy and weak, and their commitment to the ascetic ideal. These are justly well-known analyses; they are also dense and convoluted. We impose order on the arguments of these sections as follows: Sections 11 through 16 analyze how the ascetic ideal, despite appearances, has to be consistent with life, while Sections 17 through 22 analyze how damaging the ascetic ideal is for any but the desperate and how hurtful it is even for them.

With the priest, ascetic values are no longer a philosophical pose or an artistic passion but something consuming and compositional, an ideal that marks out a type. For ascetic priests, life, nature, the world, in fact "the whole sphere of what becomes and passes away" becomes fodder for their hostility and ressentiment and for their "unfulfilled instinct and power-will that wants to be master, not over something in life, but over life itself" (*GM* III 11). Their "monstrous method of valuation" that life is a "wrong path," a "mistake which can only be set right by action," is contemptible and should evoke only derisive laughter when encountered; surprisingly, it is "one of the most wide-spread and long-lived facts there are" (*GM* III 11), both in Europe and in Asia. Indeed, asceticism is so common that, seen from space, the easiest inference would be that "earth [is] the ascetic planet *par excellence*, an outpost of discontented, arrogant, and nasty creatures who harbor a deep disgust for themselves, for the world, for all life and hurt themselves as much as possible out of pleasure in hurting" (*GM* III 11).

Generally speaking, ascetic lives embody a living conflict that "*wills* itself to be conflicting, that *relishes* itself in this affliction and becomes more self-assured and triumphant to the same degree as its own condition, the physiological capacity to live, *decreases*" (*GM* III 11). Instead of exuberantly expressing themselves and taking pleasure in living, ascetics fixate on and celebrate "failure, decay, pain, misfortune, ugliness, voluntary deprivation, destruction of selfhood, self-flagellation and self-sacrifice" (*GM* III 11). This is all highly paradoxical. How can there be an ideal for living that is a contradiction of life itself? Moreover, why should those who, by endorsing and personifying this ideal try to live a self-contradiction, be so prevalent across social classes, cultures, and eras?

These perplexing questions are pursued to their conclusion in Section 13 (we return to Section 12 presently). As he does in previous essays, Nietzsche responds that the paradox is only apparent and is instead an expression of something that is not a paradox at all, that "*life itself must have an interest* in preserving such a self-contradictory type" (*GM* III 11). If so, then the ascetic ideal can be seen as a "trick for the *preservation* of life" (*GM* III 13), more precisely, a trick for the preservation of a particular kind of life. Those safeguarded by endorsing the ascetic ideal live futile or decaying lives and use the ascetic ideal to justify and preserve themselves and protect against further decline. Their miseries being second only to their heartbeats, they clutch the ascetic ideal as a last hope, and by doing so they continue living a "life [that] struggles with death and *against* death" (*GM* III 13). For their part, ascetic priests serve the "herd of failures, the disgruntled, the under-privileged, the unfortunate, and all who suffer from themselves" by "instinctively placing [themselves] at their head as their shepherd" (*GM* III 13), providing the herd a diagnosis of their suffering, a prognosis for its future course if left untreated, and a prescription regimen to treat it. In the process, ascetic religion becomes one of the "great *conserving* and *yes creating* forces of life" (*GM* III 13), sustaining those who need strength just to be able to sidestep the pit of despair and continue living.

We are now in a better position to consider Section 12. As opposed to philosophers who think that their tasks are best accomplished by living ascetically, ascetic philosophical thought expresses all of the eerie strangeness inherited from the priest's negative evaluation of life and promotion of values that champion its denigration. Ascetic philosophizing looks for systematic—that is, philosophical—errors "precisely where the actual instinct of life most unconditionally judges there to be truth" (*GM* III 12) so as to sow doubt about life itself. Hinduism and Buddhism, exemplars of ascetic philosophy, not only "demote physicality to the status of illusion" and dismiss "pain, plurality, the whole conceptual antithesis 'subject' and 'object'" as erroneous, they go even "renounce faith in one's own ego, deny one's own 'reality' to oneself" and assert that while "there *is* a realm of truth and being . . . reason is firmly *excluded* from it'" (*GM* III 12). Even Kant's domain of things as they are in themselves is not exempt from setting reason against itself; after all, the thing-in-itself's "'intelligible character' means . . . a quality about which all that the intellect can comprehend is that it is, for the intellect—*completely incomprehensible*" (*GM* III 12). Of course, Nietzsche does not side with those who think we can know about the entities beyond the realm of sensory experience; instead, he rejects the existence of such a realm altogether.

The asceticism found in so much of philosophical thought should not be conflated with disparaging the dangerous possibilities of the philosophical drive to "*want* to see differently," to want to "use the *difference* in perspectives and affective interpretations for knowledge" (*GM* III 12). As famously stated here, the drive to multiply perspectives is the crucial virtue for realizing intellectual greatness and the most salient standard of intellectual discovery: "[T]here is *only* a perspectival seeing, *only* a perspectival 'knowing'; the *more* affects we are able to put into words about a thing, the *more* eyes, various eyes we are able to use for the same thing, the more complete will be our 'concept' of the thing, our 'objectivity'" (*GM* III 12). Perception and cognition are intrinsically perspectival because drives and desires are inherently interpretational, inescapably indexical, and unavoidably evaluative. Thus, to the extent that philosophers proliferate perceptual and cognitive perspectives, increase affective interpretations, and multiply evaluations, to that extent do they learn more about things and events and even themselves. We return to perspectivism in the discussion section of this chapter.

Unfortunately, propagating perspectives is not how ascetic philosophers think knowledge improves. To the contrary, they suggest that objectivity is "contemplation without interest" and claim that the subject of knowledge is a "pure, will-less, painless, timeless" (*GM* III 12) substratum that uses dispassionate reason. In the hands of Schopenhauer and Kant, ascetic philosophical thought tries to subdue and extirpate the perspectivity of instincts, drives, and emotions as knowledge is pursued. However, just as they were mistaken to hold that aesthetic pleasure is disinterested, so too is it a mistake to think that objectivity is the perspective-free product of a disinterested rational epistemic subject. It is impossible to conceive of an eye "turned in no direction at all, an eye where the active and interpretative powers are to be suppressed, absent, but through which seeing still becomes a seeing-something" (*GM* III 12). Of course, the impossibility of disinterested knowledge will never dissuade ascetic philosophers from trying to achieve the impossible; after all, one of their distinctive characteristics is trying to purge themselves of emotions, drives, and affects, which is the most absurd gamble of all. Even if, *per impossible*, they managed to "eliminate the will completely and turn off all the emotions without exception," they would thereby "*castrate* the intellect" (*GM* III 12).

Section 14 is packed with fuming rebukes and repetitious venting, becoming more than a little tedious. Luckily, scattered amid the invective are crucial clues about how the old masters came to be vanquished and how slave values came to entrench themselves. We start by acknowledging that humans are "*the* sick animal" because we have "dared more, innovated more, braved more, and challenged fate more than all the rest of the animals taken together," and we are "more ill, uncertain, changeable and unstable than any other animal" (*GM* III 13) as a result of our ruthless self-experimentation. Given the prevalence of sickliness, we rightly honor "the unusual cases of spiritual and physical powerfulness, the *strokes of luck*," yet all too often the sick and the weak envy these strokes of luck and work assiduously to undermine and demoralize them, thus injecting "skepticism into our trust in life, in [humanity], in ourselves" (*GM* III 14). For, as we have already seen, the self-contempt common in the herd engenders a predictable redirection of suffering onto guilty culprits, thus breeding hatred of those who are healthier, stronger, and more powerful and successful. Unable to escape their own failure and suffering from themselves, the herd's hatred infects the successful with countless "small doses of poison, pinpricks, spiteful, long-suffering looks, . . . interspersed with the *loud* gesture of the sick Pharisee playing his favorite role of 'righteous indignation'" (*GM* III 14).

The most effective toxin in the stockpile of ressentiment is a contaminating agent that transforms a healthy conscience that takes pleasure in being physiologically and psychologically healthy, strong, powerful, and successful into the bad conscience / guilt. Nietzsche's description of how this slow-motion corruption works is lurid and uncompromising:

> These worm-eaten physiological casualties are all men of *ressentiment*, a whole, vibrating realm of subterranean revenge, inexhaustible and insatiable in its eruptions against the happy, and likewise in masquerades of revenge and pretexts for revenge: when will they actually achieve their ultimate, finest, most sublime triumph of revenge? Doubtless if they succeeded in *shoving* their own misery, in fact all misery, *on to the conscience* of the happy: so that the latter eventually start to be ashamed of their happiness and perhaps say to one another: "It's a disgrace to be happy! *There is too much misery*!" . . . But there could be no greater or more disastrous misunderstanding than for the happy, the successful, those powerful in body and soul to begin to doubt their *right to happiness* in this way. (*GM* III 14)

Look around contemporary Europe, he suggests, and what will be found is a horde of individuals full of envy, spite, hatred, and ressentiment, many of them embedded in social organizations, universities, and religious institutions. All of them are dedicated not to alleviating suffering and misery, but to preserving and proliferating suffering and misery as evidence of guilt, hailing them as virtuous responses to guilt, and convincing those who live joyfully without guilt to be ashamed. These unwholesome and nasty creatures "promenade in our midst like living reproaches, like warnings to us—as though health, success, strength, pride and the feeling of power were in themselves depravities for which penance, bitter penance will one day be exacted" (*GM* III 14).

Sections 15–16

At the head of the ressentiment multitude is the priest, "shepherd and defender of the sick herd" (*GM* III 15), who cares for his flock with diverse strategies, some of them directed against the herd's envy of the healthy and powerful, some of them directed on relieving their suffering, and some of them directed against the healthy and powerful themselves. Some work is needed to untangle the coils of Nietzsche's thinking in these sections, so we consider each of these strategies in turn.

Wounding the Herd

Nietzsche does not unequivocally condemn the ascetic priest. It is beyond doubt that he eases the suffering found in the herd by smearing the "ointments and balms" (*GM* III 15) of religion over their distress. Of course, the priest "first has to wound so that he can be the doctor; and whilst he soothes the pain caused by the wound, *he poisons the wound at the same time*" (*GM* III 15). The intricacy of the priest's comforting is crucial for understanding the appeal and danger of ascetic religions. That the priest helps the suffering redirect their suffering onto culprits and that his rituals and traditions tranquilize despair by substituting other strong emotions are familiar points by now. The priest also adds new wounds that he then offers to heal, and in healing the wounds he has caused he injects further poison. Just being close to a priest "necessarily makes everything that is healthy sick, and everything sick, tame" (*GM* III 15). The priest supplies narcotics to those who suffer, thus habituating them to the sedatives he has introduced into their systems, ensuring their dependence. Worse, he infects the healthy as well.

At this point, we must ask two questions. First, why does the priest further wound those whose lives are already full of suffering? Second, how does the priest succeed? Recall that priests in the period before the advent of Christianity (Nietzsche's "middle period") were members of the nobility and that their societies were war ridden and tradition bound. Although less directly belligerent than the old master class of aristocrats and warriors, the priests were nonetheless driven by power and prone to squabbling with other nobles. Knowing that they would likely lose any direct confrontation with the old masters, the priests instead invested their form-imposing energy, that is, their will to power, on to the mission of reigning over the herd. The priest's chosen strategy to effect rule over his bedraggled minions, a strategy later perfected by Christianity and still in use, was to convince them that they were their own worst enemies and that he alone could cure them of themselves. Thus is the first question posed above answered: the priests were prepared to wound those who were already suffering because doing so furthered their drive to impose form on others, which in turn strengthened them as they fought the old aristocrats and warriors for power.

The priests were in fact uniquely situated in these middle-period societies, and their unique standing explains how they were able to wound and poison the herd, thus answering the second question. Since priests were consumed by a ressentiment that could be neither directly nor quickly discharged, they were intimately familiar with the herd's festering envy and ressentiment. As Nietzsche notes, the priest "must be sick himself, he must really be a close relative of the sick and the destitute in order to understand them, —in order to come to an understanding with them" (*GM* III 15). On the other hand, priests were also members of the nobility and in charge of religious traditions, so they witnessed how effective ritual and custom were in directing and redirecting attention, regulating emotion, and making people predictable, not just for other nobles but for the rabble and themselves as well. The priest was therefore both "a close relative of the sick and the destitute" and "more master of himself than of others, actually unscathed in his will to power," a singular mixture that enabled him to both understand the herd and use what he knew about the herd "to come to an understanding with them" (*GM* III 15). He inspired the herd's confidence that the priestly diagnosis of their suffering was correct, that priestly explanations of it were sound, and that priestly remedies were effective in alleviating it. Thus did the priest gain "the trust and fear of the [herd] and [become] their support, defense, prop, compulsion, disciplinarian, tyrant, God" (*GM* III 15). So the first element of explaining how priests succeeded in wounding the herd is that priestly psychology was so familiar to the members of the herd that they trusted priests, not despite but because of their nobility.

The sufferer's character cannot be ignored when explaining how the priests succeeded in wounding and poisoning the masses. We have discussed ressentiment already in Chapter 3, so we are already familiar with some of what Nietzsche says about it here in Section 15. For our purposes here, the crucial factors of that analysis are, first, the sufferer enthusiastically redirects attention away from themselves onto culprits who might instead be held causally responsible for their suffering, and second, they cultivate a voracious appetite for anesthetics to ease the suffering that those culprits are thought to have caused. Regarding the first point, Nietzsche notes how creative suffering can be:

> [S]ufferers, one and all, are frighteningly willing and inventive in their pretexts for painful emotions; they even enjoy being mistrustful and dwelling on wrongs and imagined slights: they rummage through the bowels of their past and present for obscure, questionable stories that will allow them to wallow in tortured suspicion, and intoxicate themselves with their own poisonous wickedness—they rip open the oldest wounds and make themselves bleed to death from scars long-since healed, they make evil-doers out of friend, wife, child and anyone else near to them. "I suffer: someone or other must be guilty"—and every sick sheep thinks the same. (*GM* III 15)

This mistrustful and suspicious psychology of acrimonious displacement characterizes herd humans from all eras. And, just as they are eager to redirect their suffering onto a culprit, they also long for relief from suffering, which in the end means relief from themselves.

Seeing needs going unmet, ascetic priests offered a diagnosis of suffering. To herd humans, they whisper, " 'Quite right, my sheep! Somebody must be to blame: but you yourself are this somebody, you yourself alone are to blame for it, *you yourself alone are to blame for yourself* " (*GM* III 15). Nietzsche does not doubt that this diagnosis is wrong from the start, or that priestly explanations are preposterous, or that their prognoses are irrational, or that their prescriptions are toxic. He does admit that "at least one thing has been achieved by it, the direction of *ressentiment* is . . . *changed*" (*GM* III 15). By redirecting ressentiment back onto the sufferer, the priest changed the culprit held responsible for suffering, thus wounding every last member of the herd. It was no longer their weakness, unhealthiness, powerlessness, or oppression that caused their suffering, but nor was it the old masters' cruel domination or casual indifference. Instead, the priest's novel diagnosis was that something else inside humans, all humans, was the cause of suffering. What, then, was it about all of us that the ascetic priest identified as the culprit responsible for suffering? And what did naming this inner culprit achieve for the sufferers and the ascetic priests?

Poisoning the Wound

The priests offered an entry-level nonreligious explanation of suffering and then linked it to a religious explanation. The herd required defense both against the old masters' "crude, stormy, unbridled, hard, violently predatory health and mightiness" and, perhaps surprisingly, against their own "envy of the healthy" (*GM* III 15). Priests accepted this two-pronged mission, and its dual focus required that they move along different fronts simultaneously, protecting the herd from the old masters and protecting the herd from itself. This made priests a "more delicate" animal, one that "despises more easily than it hates" (*GM* III 15).

Consider, first, the introductory nonreligious explanation of human suffering. The herd's festering ressentiment, and the "wickedness, malice, and everything else characteristic of all those who are diseased and sick," continuously threatened both rebellion against the old masters and "anarchy and . . . inner disintegration" (*GM* III 15) within the herd itself. Ressentiment is a dangerous explosive, primed to explode at any time, but in these middle-period societies, its risks were magnified by the old masters' coarse psychology and their penchant for solving problems with violence and cruelty. The priest saw a different solution for defusing the herd's ressentiment of the powerful. His trick was to "detonate this explosive material without blowing up either the herd or the shepherd" (*GM* III 15) by wounding them with the belief that they were the culprit responsible for their own suffering, thus changing ressentiment from an outwardly directed affect to an inwardly directed affect.

The groundwork for the priest's redirection of ressentiment back onto and into those who suffer was already set by internalizing drives and the prudential precursors of bad conscience that punishment and earlier religious rituals had helped install. Christianity improved on these measures. The innovation of the Christian priest was to adulterate internalization and incipient forms of bad conscience with guilt about sin, original sin being the most profound. By introducing belief in sin into the wound, the Christian priest infected it and then rediagnosed it as the deepest and most damning injury possible, the cure for which only he had. Thus, while previous priests had inflicted and contaminated a wound, rediagnosed the infection as a novel spiritual sickness, and then taken charge of curing the malady they had introduced, the Christian priest named the cause of that spiritual sickness as sin. Of course, the entire conceptual framework of sin and guilt is gobbledygook: sin "is not a fact, but rather the interpretation of a fact, namely a physiological upset . . . seen from a perspective of morals and religion" (*GM* III 16). Were one to protest Nietzsche's diagnosis by suggesting that feeling guilty proves the existence of sin, the rejoinder is immediate: feeling guilty no more entails sin than feeling healthy entails being cancer-free.

The Christian priest's cure for suffering was, of course, submission to God and to his servants, God's earthly advocates. The priest's doctrines explained the herd's suffering, consoling them for its inescapability in this life while promising them that it would be transformed into bliss in the afterlife. Until that blessed day, his teachings and rituals supply that steady dose of guilt, gratitude, compassion, faith, and submission that deadened unruly nonreligious emotions and drives such as lust, greed, spite, wickedness, malice, envy, and, of course, ressentiment. Awestruck by religious spectacles and soothed by the priest's living example, the enthusiastic flocked together and organized in churches for mutual support. In these hothouses of disinformation, distracting rituals, and diversionary emotions, the consistency of the ascetic ideal with life was fully revealed. Deploying the "paradoxical and paralogical concepts as 'guilt,' 'sin,' 'sinfulness,' 'corruption,' 'damnation'" on the herd is nothing less than a strategy for keeping the most abject alive: by introducing a wholesale psychological reorientation that "makes the sick *harmless*" and redirects their ressentiment, the ascetic ideal "*exploits* the bad instincts of all sufferers for the purpose of self-discipline, self-surveillance and self-overcoming" (*GM* III 16).

Conquering the Old Masters

One of the unanswered questions from Essay I was this: how were the old master castes of warriors and aristocrats brought to their knees by the slave revolt in morality? Here in Essay III, Nietzsche finally says enough about how Christian priests and the herd used the ascetic ideal to explain how the old masters were vanquished. Put in general terms, the answer has two elements.[1] First, fueled by their pathos of distance, convinced of their superiority, and pleased with their happy lives, the old aristocrats and warriors had every reason to isolate themselves from the herd and relinquish the unpleasant task of mingling with it to others. They were delighted that the priests accepted the job, for with the priests in charge of the herd, the old aristocrats and warriors could continue to ignore them, as they were predisposed to anyway. Second, the priests made the old masters pay for taking on this disagreeable job. The priests took what they had learned about the mutability of ressentiment and what they had developed for reigning over the herd and turned it against the old masters. In the process, they sowed discontent within the old masters, made them feel ashamed about living happily and without bad conscience / guilt, and convinced them that otherworldly powers were greater than any earthly power.

We saw in Essay I that the old aristocrats and warriors held the slaves—the herd—in contempt and that their pathos of distance buttressed their contempt by establishing values that reflected their superiority. As early Christian priests organized their flock into a religious organization and social movement, ascetic values unfavorable to the old aristocrats and warriors spread quickly. What Section 14 says about contemporary Europe applies equally to every point along the road leading forward from the initial appearance of organized

[1] See Anderson 2011; Migotti 1998.

Christianity: "That the sick should *not* make the healthy sick . . . ought to be the chief concern on earth: —but for that, it is essential that the healthy should remain *separated* from the sick, should even be spared the sight of the sick so that they do not confuse themselves with the sick (*GM* III 14). Nor should the healthy be tempted to help the herd by becoming "nurses and doctors" (*GM* III 14), for that would entail debasing themselves. Rather, for the healthy of all eras, "[T]he pathos of distance *ought* to ensure that their tasks are kept separate . . . for they alone are *guarantors* of the future, they alone have a *bounden duty* to man's future" (*GM* III 14). After all, their health and excellence propel society's advances, and comforting or healing the sick would deter them from their duty. In brief, the healthy self-segregate from the herd so they can breathe "good air" and remain uncontaminated by the "evil fumes of inner corruption and the secret, worm-eaten rottenness of disease" found in the "madhouses and hospitals of culture" (*GM* III 14). Only by self-segregating can healthy humans defend themselves against "the two worst epidemics that could possibly have been set aside just for [them]—against *great nausea at man*! Against *deep compassion for man*!" (*GM* III 14).

The priest's battle with the old masters on behalf of his flock was a relentless "war of cunning (of the 'spirit') rather than of force" (*GM* III 15). To achieve victory over the predators, the priest had to "make himself into a new kind of predator, or at least *signify it*" (*GM* III 15) by becoming as inexorable as a bear, as nimble as a tiger, and as cunning as a fox. These traits were necessary for the priests because the old masters were not nearly as receptive to their teachings as the herd. Unlike the herd, the old masters were healthy, powerful, strong, open, honest, and active, even if they were cruel, violent, self-absorbed, suspicious of cleverness and reason, and neglectful and condescending toward the herd. Nonetheless, so long as they flourished as the cream of society, the old masters could afford to dismiss the priest as an annoyance. In response, the priest adopted all manner of camouflaging tactics, so that when he mingled with the old masters he acted with "bearish solemnity, venerable, clever, cold, deceptively superior, as the herald and mouthpiece of more mysterious powers" (*GM* III 15). Having caught the attention of the old masters, the priest sowed "suffering, division and self-contradiction on this ground wherever he [could], only too certain of his skill at being master of the *suffering* at any time" (*GM* III 15).

To be successful against the old masters, the priest had to convince them that their social standing, their happiness, and their pathos of distance were unjustified, in short, that they were no different than the herd. Most importantly, the priest had to convince them that they too suffered because they too were guilty. And here the Christian priest excelled as no earlier priests had. First, this priest was much cleverer than the old masters and therefore capable of levels of dialectical finesse that flummoxed them. Second, the priest carried a sack full of ingenious doctrines that bred shame within the old masters: an immaterial soul that God gifted to each of us; a free will that was equally distributed to each and every one of God's human creations; a promise of power and happiness that the old masters never dreamed of achieving, that of everlasting life in heaven; and a focusing of gratitude onto a single God who had sacrificed himself for all of us and left all of us saddled with original sin and its attendant guilt. Recall:

> [W]hen will they actually achieve their ultimate, finest, most sublime triumph of revenge? Doubtless if they succeeded in *shoving* their own misery, in fact all misery, *on to the conscience* of the happy: so that the latter eventually start to be ashamed of their happiness and perhaps say to one another: "It's a disgrace to be happy! *There is too much misery*!" (*GM* III 14)

Nietzsche's explanation is, then, that the priest used his greater cleverness, his mastery of dialectic, and his collection of religious doctrines to seduce the less reflective old masters into feeling guilty about themselves and to "doubt their *right to happiness*" (*GM* III 14).

Sections 17–22

In these sections, Nietzsche digs deeply through the polluted soil of ascetic religion and exposes its representatives' and adherents' harmful behavior. Although he focuses attention on Christian priests and Christians, he also mentions Buddhism, Sufi fakirs, and various other representatives of asceticism. These are lengthy and intricate discussions and are not easily summarized. Ascetic religion presents six diagnosable dangers. First, it narcotizes emotions in its attempt to thwart depression (Section 17). Second, it advocates mechanical activities and small pleasures as methods for alleviating depression (Section 18). Third, it addicts the sufferer both to the priest's diagnosis of sin and guilt and to his cures for them, thus ensuring an ongoing dependency on religion (Section 19). Fourth, it introduces a treatment protocol that adds suffering to suffering, thus compounding rather than abating it (Section 20). Fifth, its emphasis on sin inures sufferers to the priest's orgies of feeling, thus desensitizing them to the pleasures of living and habituating them to hating what life has to offer (Section 21). Sixth, it stipulates that its teachings should be spread as far and wide as possible, thus corrupting not just others who suffer but the healthy as well (Section 21). Section 22's hostile review of the New Testament adds so little to the previous five sections that we can, and will, pass over it.

Narcotizing Depression and Hypnotizing the Psyche

Section 17 is *GM*'s longest single section and contains Nietzsche's most detailed assessment of depression sedation. He first announces that his fundamental objection to ascetic religions such as Christianity is that their balms and ointments combat "only suffering itself, the discomfort of the sufferer, . . . *not* its cause, *not* the actual state of being ill" (*GM* III 17). Since priests treat only a symptom of suffering, namely, its affective feeling, their medications "cannot possibly yield a real *cure* of the sick in the physiological sense" (*GM* III 16). So the priest's self-image as a doctor of the soul is fraudulent from the start. Nevertheless, priestly affective medications are inherently thought-provoking. One of the most intriguing is how they counteract depression through consolation and spiritual sanctification. All ascetic religions engage in these hoaxes, but Christianity is an absolute "treasure-trove of the most ingenious means of consolation, so much to refresh, soothe and narcotize is piled up inside it" (*GM* III 17). Nietzsche argues to the contrary that religious consolation and spiritual sanctification are tantamount to physiological hibernation and psychological hypnosis.

After Jesus died, the early Christian priests quickly learned that they had to adjust herd emotions "in order to conquer the deep depression, the leaden fatigue and the black melancholy" (*GM* III 17) the herd lived with on a daily basis. One of its key moves was to show those who suffered how, through self-surveillance and self-discipline, they could overcome their suffering by reducing their lives to the bare minimum required to continue existing. By deadening their desires and emotions so there was "no more wanting, no more wishing, . . . no loving, no hating; equanimity; no taking of revenge; no getting rich; no working; . . . if possible, no consorting with women," the herd could avoid "everything that arouses the emotions and 'blood'" (*GM* III 17) and achieve a state of comprehensive relief. As in practical matters, so also in spiritual matters. With "Pascal's principle '*il faut s'abêtir* [one must make oneself stupid]'" (*GM* III 17) as a succinct statement of their case, the priests recommended that sufferers psychologically lose themselves and thereby morally purify themselves of sin and sanctify their soul. Of course, the results of these procedures were physiological states akin to hibernation in which "a minimum of expenditure of energy and metabolism" occurs and psychological states akin to hypnosis in which "life can just about be maintained without actually entering consciousness" (*GM* III 17). By walling drives and desires off from awareness and snuffing out emotion, the herd could indeed starve out the "deep, physiological depression" (*GM* III 17) that attends their existence. That the price for bringing Schopenhauer's burning wheel of Ixion to a standstill was so extraordinarily high only validated the worth of the gift of relief.

Nietzsche is convinced that the "interpretation placed on these states by those subject to them has always been as fanatically incorrect as possible," but he admits that "we should not overlook the tone of the most convinced gratitude resounding in the mere *will* to such a kind of interpretation" (*GM* III 17). Those who enter this state of "total hypnosis and silence" describe it as "mystery as such, which even the supreme symbols are inadequate to express, as a journey home and into the heart of things, as a liberation from all delusion, as 'knowledge,' 'truth,' 'being,' . . . as a beyond good and evil" (*GM* III 17).[2] It

[2] Nietzsche is fascinated by ascetics whose "intention to starve out physicality and desire" leads to "all sorts of spiritual disturbances" (*GM* III 17). Sufi fakirs, Orthodox Hesychasts, Saint Theresa of Avila, and certain Buddhists are all exemplars of the perverse lengths to which religious ascetics will go in their effort to express their indebtedness to

is noteworthy that those who claim to achieve Christian salvation or Buddhist enlightenment describe the states similarly across traditions; it is even more noteworthy that they are beyond good and evil, a goal that Nietzsche advocates. This is a surprising admission, but one that Nietzsche affirms for the adherent of Buddhism and even for those who emulate the way Jesus lived, so long as that is not conflated with the priest's teachings and the organized social institution of Christianity.

The argument that Buddhists go beyond good and evil, outlined in *A*, is direct. Buddhism is, Nietzsche argues, "a hundred times more realistic than Christianity" because "the idea of 'God' had already been abandoned before Buddhism arrived" and because "it has stopped saying 'war against *sin*' and instead, giving reality its dues, says 'war against *suffering*,'" and by doing so, "it has left the self-deception of moral concepts behind—it stands, as I put it, *beyond* good and evil" (*A* 20). A more intricate argument on behalf of Jesus going beyond good and evil is also presented in *A*. Nietzsche notes that "Jesus could be called a 'free spirit', using the phrase somewhat loosely" because for him "the word kills, everything solid kills" (*A* 32). For Jesus, "the experience of 'life' as only he knew it, repelled every type of word; formula, law, faith, or dogma," so much so that "he saw everything else, the whole of reality, the whole of nature, language itself, as having value only as a sign, a parable" (*A* 32). Indeed, Jesus's glad tidings lacked cognitive content altogether; instead, "his bequest to humanity was a *practice*," one that demonstrated that "he loves *with* those, *in* those people who did him evil" (*A* 35). The way Jesus lived showed how to "love without

the divine, evoke divine sanctification, and subdue their emotions. He is also fascinated by the psychological training programs we subject ourselves to and the self-directed tortures we pursue in order to achieve internal reorganization. Across *D*, *BGE*, *GS*, *GM*, *TI*, and *A*, he identifies dozens of psychological reorganization regimens, most affiliated with moral codes and religious demands. Consider only the regimens affiliated with the ascetic ideal mentioned in *GM*. He identifies at least twenty: self-denial and self-sacrifice (Preface 5); self-hypnotism (I 6); abstinence, dieting, self-abasement, self-depreciation (I 11); self-deception (I 14); self-torture (II 8, 22); self-consciousness (II 10, III 9); self-tyranny (II 18); self-negation and self-elimination (III 3); self-mortification, self-martyrdom, self-misunderstanding (III 10); self-contempt and self-annihilation (III 17); self-belittling (III 25); and self-critique (III 25). Even if these programs and their curricula turn us against ourselves and into kinds of selves that are usually sick, decadent, and resentful, exceptional individuals can use them.

exceptions or rejections" (*A* 29), how to live without "contradiction," "negation," or "dialectic" (*A* 32), without "guilt and punishment" (*A* 33), and without *ressentiment* (*A* 40), a life in which the " 'kingdom of heaven' is a state of the heart—not something lying 'above the earth' or coming 'after death' " (*A* 34).

Of course, Christianity and Buddhism are contrary to life, that is, both are "religions of *decadence*" (*A* 20) at their cores. For both, a state of thoughtless, quiescent inertness during which living is suspended or deferred is to be cultivated in the service of relief from suffering. This "*deep sleep* [in] people so weary of life that they are too weary even to dream [is] the entry to Brahma, as a *unio mystica* with God *achieved*" (*GM* III 17). We return to these matters in the discussion section. It is enough to emphasize that with its rejection of God and its laser focus on human suffering, "Buddhism is a hundred times more realistic than Christianity" (*A* 20), and that even within Christianity we must distinguish the captivating but decadent example of Jesus's ressentiment-free life from the social movement organized around ressentiment that sprang up after he died. Jesus was undeniably a decadent, but his was a distinctive species that conjoined compassion with a complete absence of ressentiment, resulting in a type that mixed "sublimity, sickness, and childishness" (*A* 31) and that was completely foreign to the strategic, dishonest, and *ressentimentful* compassion characteristic of the Christian priest and his flock.

Transforming Work and Forming Congregations

For those ill-suited to the rigors of life without drives, desires, or feelings, Christianity obliged with more mundane and practical, but also more transitory, solutions for suffering. Nietzsche identifies them in Section 18 as mechanical activity and small pleasures. The mechanical activity of daily work and ritual can alleviate suffering because it "diverts the interest of the sufferer from the pain" (*GM* III 18). Moreover, the mundane mechanics of ritual and the daily orderliness of work both impose so much "regularity, punctuality, [and] mindless obedience" on sufferers that their entire life is "fixed once and for all" with "time-filling, a certain encouragement, indeed discipline, to be 'impersonal,' to forget oneself, to be in a state of '*incuria sui*' [lack of concern for self]" (*GM* III 18). Accomplishing all of these diversionary tactics was easier for priests than one might suppose. After all, when they treated "the suffering of . . . work slaves or prisoners (or women: who are, after all, mostly both at the same time, work slaves and prisoners)," they did little more than "switch names round a bit . . . so that in the future they would view a hated thing as a benefit, as relative happiness" (*GM* III 18).

The inventive priests did not stop at introducing abundant religious ritual into the herd animals' life and redefining their appalling plight as a blessing. They also urged their flock to fight off depression with routine acts of "*giving pleasure* (as doing good, giving gifts, bringing relief, helping, encouraging, comforting, praising, honoring)" (*GM* III 18). So doing aroused "the strongest, most life affirming impulse, albeit in the most cautious dose—the *will to power*" (*GM* III 18), expressed by the gift-giver's happiness of being superior to the recipient, even if only in some small way and for a brief time. These small gifts have other benefits as well. If, for instance, we investigate the history of early Christianity we find that "mutual do-gooding was deliberately nurtured" (*GM* III 18) because forming a herd induced a feedback loop that tightly bound isolated sufferers into a community of like-minded individuals dedicated to winning the battle against depression, lethargy, and hopelessness. As the Christian community congregated in churches and grew in dedication and self-confidence, "[A] new interest [was] kindled for the individual," that of cultivating the community's health and power as opposed to its members' sickness and weakness. As with all traditions and customs, the individual was thereby given the opportunity to overcome "the most personal element in his discontent, his aversion to *himself*" (*GM* III 18). The priests were delighted to groom the individual acts of charity and the collective commitment to the congregation's upkeep. After all, they profited both from the gifts they agreed to manage on behalf of the congregation and from the congregation's ongoing health, and they nurtured their drive to impose order on the herd and undermine the power of the old masters, who were "as naturally inclined to strive to be *apart* as the weak [were] to be *together*" (*GM* III 18).

Entrenching Sin, Adding Guilt, and Addicting the Suffering Sinner

To this point, Nietzsche has focused on the priest's "innocent means in the fight against listlessness," a set of tactics "concerned with one thing: some kind of *excess of feeling*, which is used as the most effective anaesthetic for dull, crippling, long-drawn-out pain" (*GM* III 19). Of course, priests and their religions have sprayed morality over all suffering, thereby introducing layers of misinterpretation and "moralistic mendaciousness" that have by now become so habituated that "everyone who feels himself to be a 'good person' today is completely incapable of approaching anything except . . . in a way that [is] mendacious right down to its very depths" (*GM* III 19).

What demands attention is not the ascetic priest's appropriation of intense emotions and drives—an appropriation that, Nietzsche admits, the priest undertakes in good conscience—but something that the priest is the acknowledged expert with, his "utilization of the *feeling of guilt*" (*GM* III 20). Following familiar points about the origins of bad conscience and the internalization of cruelty, he notes a nuance of guilt not previously mentioned. As the priest's sermonizing about sin, guilt, and punishment wormed its way into their psychology, herd animals became addicted to the priest's "cures" for the sickness he had caused. We are all born in original sin, sin constantly thereafter, and are rightly guilty and so deserve punishment—so say Christianity and its sales force, the priests. Since Christian sins are nothing more than effects of unavoidable and largely inalienable affects, desires, and drives, when herd animals accepted the priest's interpretation of affects, drives, and desires as sins, they became trapped without a means of escape from what they could not but do and from the priest's insistence that they must. The priest's tenacious hectoring only intensified their torment, which in turn drove them back looking for the relief he had assured them he could provide. Sadly, these treatments provided only temporary respite from drives and desires that are as natural and unavoidable as sensory perception. So the treatments had to be repeated over and over, thus making the herd animal ever sicker, eventually resulting in "a shattered nervous system" (*GM* III 21).

As sin, punishment, and guilt were "applied on the largest and smallest scale, with individuals and with masses," the addiction to priestly treatments spread through the herd, so that "[the] the ascetic ideal and its sublimely moral cult, this most ingenious, unscrupulous and dangerous systematization" (*GM* III 21) eventually sapped their health. Addicted Christians thus became a fixed type, and their contrived syndrome—the ongoing "condition of punishment" (*GM* III 20)—became baked into the psychology of most Europeans. Inured to the "sight of this invalid, of "the sinner," for a couple of millennia" (*GM* III 20), the type no longer even strikes us as bizarre. Worse, we are unlikely ever to rid ourselves of the type until Christianity's asceticism and all that it has bequeathed to humanity are overcome. Until that day comes, the legacy of Christianity's diagnosis of suffering as sin, punishment, and guilt, its shameless compounding of suffering, and its treatment regimen—"the hair shirt, the starving body, contrition; everywhere, the sinner breaking himself on the cruel wheel of a restless and morbidly lustful conscience; everywhere, dumb torment, the most extreme fear, the agony of the tortured heart, the paroxysms of unknown happiness, the cry for 'redemption' " (*GM* III 20)—will continue unabated. It is "the *real catastrophe* in the history of European health" (*GM* III 21).

Ascetic religion is, then, an interpretation imposed on a widespread preexisting condition, that of being sick of oneself and of life. This interpretation (i) proposes topsy-turvy etiologies of the condition; (ii) builds on those mistakes by misdiagnosing the condition's symptoms and dimensions; (iii) compounds those errors with a specious prognosis; (iv) prescribes addictive treatments that at best address surface symptoms rather than the condition itself; and (v) makes the sick sicker. By doing so, it also (vi) redirects the herd animal's ressentiment back onto and into itself; (vii) defuses ressentiment's more explosive tendencies; (viii) cultivates the herd animal's self-discipline, self-surveillance, and self-overcoming; (ix) consoles the herd animal by providing a reason to continue to live; and (x) augments the priest's power against the old masters.

Sections 23–25

After this critical analysis of Christianity, we might expect Nietzsche to welcome nineteenth-century scientists, scholars, and other intellectually rigorous free spirits as intellectual comrades.[3] Instead, he aims a blowtorch at them. They are, he thinks, one and all still unreflectively dedicated to an insidious facet of the ascetic ideal, that truth is valuable. The entire European intellectual menagerie is populated by allies to the ascetic ideal's valorization of truth, ersatz free spirits whose squawking about liberation from God only confirms their bondage to truth.

By the late nineteenth century, science and scholarship were already a threat to Christianity and other religions. Positivists and various intellectual boosters had for some years been busy announcing that science and scholarship represented a "counterpart," an "opposing ideal" that had fought and won the battle against the ascetic ideal, "master[ing] that ideal in all essentials" (GM III 23). Nietzsche thinks these boasts are just "noise and rabble-rousers' claptrap" that enthusiasts whose "voices do not come from the depths, the abyss of scientific conscience" (GM III 23) spew to camouflage their continued allegiance to the ideal they claim to have vanquished. He has fathomed this abyss and will describe it soon enough, but before he does so, he damns scientists and scholars with some faint praise. He admits that many scientists and scholars are "worthy and modest workers," busy academic bees who rightfully take pleasure in their craft and continuously remind others that there is always still "so much useful work to be done" (GM III 23). Still, as much as these intellectual wage earners may "like their little corner," science and scholarship remain a "hiding place for all kinds of ill-humor, unbelief, gnawing worms, despectio sui [contempt of self], bad conscience" (GM III 23).

[3] 'Science' is routinely used to translate *Wissenschaft*. As is often noted, 'science' is an inexact translation. *Wissenschaft* refers not only to natural sciences, such as mathematics, physics, chemistry, and biology, and social sciences, such as psychology, economics, sociology, and political science, but also to humanities disciplines such as history, literature, philosophy, and anthropology. The disciplines that Nietzsche targets as scientific thus form a larger set than the set of disciplines picked out by 'science.' To accommodate this difference, we refer to "science and scholarship" and to "scientists and scholars."

Sections 24 and 25 are flamboyant and agitated rants against self-serving depictions of science and scholarship and self-delusions of scientists and scholars. Stripped of their rhetorical excesses, these sections contain an audacious send-up of professional intellectual life and those who devote themselves to it. Despite thinking they are "as liberated as possible from the ascetic ideal," scientists and scholars are instead "very far from being *free* spirits: *because they still believe in truth*" (*GM* III 24). If that assertion does not get the reader's attention, what immediately follows it most certainly will. Nietzsche suggests that the members of the Order of Assassins, the medieval Muslim sect that thought targeted murder was a viable political tactic, were actual free spirits. The order's founder, Hassan-I Sabbāh (c. 1050–1124), gave to the Assassins their creed, when he apparently said as he lay dying, "Nothing is true, everything is permitted." Nietzsche quotes the Assassin's Creed with approval—"certainly *that* was *freedom* of the mind"—and he wonders whether any 'free spirit' anywhere in Europe has ever contemplated "the labyrinth of its *consequences*" (*GM* III 24).

Claiming that truth is an ascetic value that must be called into question and citing the Order of Assassins as support for the claim are incredible, even reckless, assertions. So consider the argument that leads to these shocking claims. Nietzsche is convinced that science/scholarship's laser focus on "the factual, the *factum brutum*" and its "renunciation of any interpretation" together express "the asceticism of virtue just as well as any denial of sensuality (it is basically just a *modus* of this denial)" (*GM* III 24). This sentence condenses an entire argument. Recall that Section 12 argued that there is only perspectival sensory experience, that there is only perspectival knowledge, and that there are only perspectival concepts of things. Since science and scholarship rely on and are warranted by observation and measurement, both of which are sensory experiences, both the concepts that science and scholarship use and the discoveries they make rely on and are warranted by perspectival perceptual experience. Hence, scientific and scholarly concepts and scientific and scholarly knowledge are perspectival and cannot deliver perspective-free facts. Since science's brute facts are supposed to be perspective-free, neither empirical science nor scholarship can discover brute facts. Assuming that 'perspective' can be substituted for 'interpretation,' we can infer that to the extent that science and scholarship think they discover brute facts rather than interpretations, to that extent do they mimic and reiterate asceticism's mistake of mistrusting sensory experience.

Science and scholarship's confidence that their findings are truths thus carry the vapors of religion, a point made in *GS*: "We see that science, too, rests on a faith; there is simply no 'presuppositionless' science. The question whether *truth* is necessary must get an answer in advance, the answer 'yes', and moreover this answer must be so firm that it takes the form of the statement, the belief, the conviction: '*Nothing* is *more* necessary than truth; and in relation to it, everything else has only secondary value'" (*GS* 344). Yet the scientific faith in truth is a necessary self-deception, or, as Nietzsche calls it, a "regulative fiction" (*GS* 344). Science must presuppose that truth is paramount in order to defend the knowledge it creates, but knowledge's perspectivity entails that truth's status is conditional and regional rather than unrestricted and universal.

Still, truth is a significant advance over other objects of faith, for its pursuit eventually leads both to questioning what it is and investigating whether it has the value it has heretofore been assumed to have. So it is important to qualify Nietzsche's criticism of science. He does not infer from science's perspectivity that it is no better than other perspectives and therefore no better than religion. For example, science is a better perspective than religion since its methods of knowledge acquisition produce a mental hygiene that fends off religious superstition and warrants confronting religion and philosophy directly: "We have science these days precisely to the extent that we have decided to accept the testimony of the senses, —to the extent that we have learned to sharpen them, arm them, and think them through to the end. Everything else is deformity and pre-science" (*TI* "'Reason' in Philosophy" 3). Close observation, hypothesis formation and testing, evidence support and disconfirmation, and rigorous analysis are, he thinks, "the essential thing, as well as the most difficult thing, as well as the thing that can be blocked by habit and laziness for a very long time" (*A* 59). Moreover, since it studies only the apparent world, science refrains from dividing the world into the "real" and apparent world, so that bit of nonsense and all that follows from it can be dismissed for the intellectual rot it is. As he sees things, scientific method was established in Greek and Roman culture, "sucked dry" by the "hidden need for revenge" (*A* 59), and won back recently only "with unspeakable self-overcoming" (*A* 59). Religious advocates and ascetic philosophers must attack science: "It is all over for priests and gods when people become scientific!—Moral: science is the taboo of all taboos—it is the only thing forbidden. Science is the first sin, the seed of all sins, the original sin" (*A* 48).

What characterizes science and scholarship as intellectual undertakings characterizes scientists and scholars as well. Their "unconditional will to truth" is nothing but "*faith in the ascetic ideal itself* . . . it is the faith in a *metaphysical* value, a *value as such of truth*" (*GM* III 24). Here we have another argument compressed into a sentence. We have just seen that since knowledge is perspectival, thinking that there is " 'presuppositionless' knowledge" will always fail; more than that, "[T]he thought of such a thing is unthinkable" (*GM* III 24). So, without presuppositionless knowledge to warrant the value of truth, scientists and scholars can only fall back on their belief that "truth can*not* be assessed or criticized" (*GM* III 24), that truth simply must be valuable. The faith in truth is thus bedrock not just for science and scholarship but for scientists and scholars as well. Like God, truth expects and demands fealty for the security of its categorical value. Not surprisingly, Nietzsche includes himself as one of the faithful. He candidly admits that "even we knowers of today, we godless antimetaphysicians, still take *our* fire from the blaze set alight by a faith thousands of years old, that faith of the Christians, which was also Plato's faith, that God is truth, that truth is *divine*" (*GM* III 24).

Godless antimetaphysicians such as Nietzsche understand that embodying the drive for truth has revealed that God is dead and can no longer backstop scientific and scholarly faith in truth. Recognizing that the value of truth may be regional rather than universal, conditional rather than unconditional, and qualified rather than categorical, free spirits must therefore acknowledge that "the will to truth needs a critique—let us define our own task with this—, the value of truth is tentatively to be *called into question*" (*GM* III 24). Unfortunately, having introduced the need for this critique, Nietzsche neither undertakes nor describes it here. Instead, he contrasts scholarship's faith in truth with art's sanctification of lying, where "the *will to deception* has good conscience on its side," thus exposing that art is more "fundamentally opposed to the ascetic ideal than science" (*GM* III 25). We return to these matters in Section 27, where he advances some brief additional reflections on what the critique of truth must confront and what it is likely to engender.

Nietzsche also offers up some psychological observations on the scientific/scholarly type. First, he calls attention to the similarity between "the confessional punctiliousness of Christian conscience" and the "scientific conscience" of valorizing "intellectual rigor at any price," and he disparages histories that are presented "as a constant testimonial to an ethical world order and ethical ultimate purpose" (*GM* III 27). Second, the ascetic ideal is embodied in the scientist's and the scholar's impoverished way of living, in which "emotions [are] cooled, the tempo slackened, dialectics replace instinct, *solemnity* [is] stamped on faces and gestures" (*GM* III 25). Third, scientists and scholars have contaminated what we think about ourselves. Science has been increasingly successful in convincing us that the self-respect we once enjoyed is "nothing but a bizarre piece of self-conceit" (*GM* III 25). Hence, Nietzsche concludes that " 'modern science' is . . . the *best* ally for the ascetic ideal" (*GM* III 25).

Again, Nietzsche's condemnation of scientists and scholars has to be qualified, for he also suggests that the scientific method can apply to his own kind, the free spirits who are, as he is, trying to understand and overcome our shared cultural heritage: "[W]e others, we reason-thirsty ones, want to face our experiences as sternly as we would a scientific experiment, hour by hour, day by day! We want to be our own experiments and guinea pigs" (*GS* 319). With the emergence of science comes the attendant promise of learning about the world and, more importantly, ourselves. As he puts it: "Let us introduce the subtlety and rigor of mathematics into all sciences to the extent to which that is at all possible; not in the belief that we will come to know things this way, but in order to *ascertain* our human relation to things. Mathematics is only the means to general and final knowledge of humanity" (*GS* 246). So by making sciences as rigorous and refined as mathematics, we better understand our perspectives on and our relations to things in the world, which in turn leads to a better understanding of ourselves. Of course, science is, as all knowledge is, perspectival. We shape our world and henceforth come to know it, but we also come to know ourselves as inhabitants of that world by experimenting with ourselves in the same manner as science experiments with the world.

Sections 26–28

Section 26 is a sideshow of scathing potshots aimed at scientists, contemplative intellectuals and scholars, and various other members of nineteenth-century intelligentsia. Nothing is so nauseating as the "'objective' armchair scholar . . . who reveals, by the mere falsetto of his approval, all that he lacks, *where* he lacks it, *where* the fates in his case have been . . . too surgical with their cruel scissors!" (*GM* III 26). Nietzsche goes on tirades against numerous types of intellectual castrati, all of whom are nothing but flimflam artists who like to dress up in "hero-outfits," pompously shake their "tinny rattles of great words," and sprinkle the spectacle of their scholarly seriousness and objectivity with "sugared, alcoholic sympathy" (*GM* III 26). Faced with the prospect of having to spend time with these ridiculous frauds or the self-important puff pastries found in universities, Nietzsche prefers "to wander through the somber, grey, cold mists with . . . historic nihilists" (*GM* III 26). They at least wear their hair shirts proudly and are, unlike academics and highbrows, honest. Their honesty explains Nietzsche's otherwise incongruous remark that he has "every respect for the ascetic ideal *in so far as it is honest*! so long as it believes in itself and does not tell us bad jokes!" (*GM* III 26).

Nietzsche assures us in Section 27 that he will expand on these matters in his upcoming revaluation of values, *Will to Power*, which we know he never finished. The immediate problem, to which he now returns, is the significance of the ascetic ideal. Exempting comedians who merely poke fun at it, Nietzsche suggests that the work of scientists and scholars now lacks any ideal other than the will to truth, which implacably samples every phantasm we have ever created for ourselves and spits them all out as indigestible. That same will to truth now confronts itself as one of the ascetic ideal's "last phases of development, one of its final forms and inherent logical conclusions," its "kernel" (*GM* III 27). The atheism spawned by the will to truth's ban against the "lie entailed in the belief in God" reveals that everything that follows from that lie—that nature is a providential expression of God's goodness, that history is the unfolding of an ethical "world order," and that our experiences, behaviors, and suffering have been for a reason, "sent for salvation of the soul"—is nonsense and "has conscience *against* it, . . . it is indecent, dishonest, a pack of lies" (*GM* III 27).

What is left of human ideals if all of them are indigestible? We now stare into an abyss that Nietzsche identified in Section 23. If the will to truth has already exposed the systemic falsity of "Christianity *as a dogma*," it now exposes that "Christianity *as a morality* must also be destroyed" (*GM* II 27). At best, ascetic values comprise a mindset for the suffering and a toolset for some free spirits. Having ruined Christian dogma and Christian morality, the will to truth finally confronts the only remaining value of the ascetic ideal: its core, truth itself. Turning truth against itself requires that we now ask, "'*What does all will to truth mean?*' . . . what meaning does *our* being have, if it were not that that will to truth has become conscious of itself *as a problem* in us?" (*GM* III 27). Nietzsche is the vanguard of a dreadful event now facing European culture, the collapse of all existing ideals, all moral values, and truth itself. He ends with the prediction that this "great drama in a hundred acts is reserved for Europe in the next two centuries, the most terrible, most questionable drama but perhaps also the one most rich in hope" (*GM* III 27).

Looking back over our own history, we can finally see that were it not for the ascetic ideal, humanity would have had "no meaning" and "no purpose" (*GM* III 28). The ascetic ideal reveals itself to be a response to our being unable to find any "justification or explanation or affirmation" for ourselves; we have "*suffered* from the problem of what [we] meant" (*GM* III 28) and have used the ascetic ideal to provide an answer to a question we fear has no other answer. Providing meaning for suffering is the great consoling function of the ascetic ideal. The human animal "does *not* deny suffering" at all and, as has been shown throughout *GM*, we even pursue and embrace it, so long as there is "a *meaning* for it, a *purpose* of suffering" (*GM* III 28). It is "the meaninglessness of suffering, *not* the suffering" itself that has been "the curse that has so far blanketed humanity" (*GM* III 28). Until now, the ascetic ideal has been the only interpretation and meaning of deep suffering, but it has been enough because any meaning is better than no meaning, and with its explanation and justification of suffering in hand, "[T]he door was shut on all suicidal nihilism" (*GM* III 28) for most of humanity.

Of course, the ascetic interpretation of life and its attendant herd morality and moral psychology—its concoctions of sin and guilt, its deceitful two-world metaphysics, and its perverse psychology of the soul and free will—have introduced additional kinds of suffering that are "deeper, more internal, more poisonous" and "gnaw away more intensely at life" (*GM* III 28) than other species of suffering. Still, humans tethered to the ascetic ideal are "no longer like a leaf in the breeze, the plaything of the absurd"; instead, we can "*will* something," even if what we will is "hatred of the human, and even more of the animalistic, even more of the material, this horror of the senses, of reason itself, this fear of happiness and beauty, this longing to get away from appearance, transience, growth, death, wishing, longing itself" (*GM* III 28). For more than two thousand years, we have been engaged in a "*will to nothingness*, an aversion to life, a rebellion against the most fundamental prerequisites of life" (*GM* III 28) because the alternative is to submit to absurdity and lifelessly play out the string or commit suicide. The ascetic ideal has saved many of us, and with it we have learned how to go on, confirming that even at the limit we would rather "*will nothingness* than *not* will" (*GM* III 28).

5.3 Discussion

Among many other things, Essay III addresses three issues of perennial philosophical interest: the value of scientific knowledge and knowledge in general, what truth is and whether it is valuable, and nihilism and meaninglessness. That it addresses some of these issues only obliquely and others only incompletely dictates what we take up here. We first investigate Nietzsche's perspectival understanding of experience and knowledge. Second, we lay out the relativist implications and paradoxical nature of truth perspectivism. Finally, we unpack his discussion of decadence, nihilism, and meaninglessness, using will to power as a normative fulcrum.

Perspectival Perception, Interoception, and Knowledge

At *GM* III 12, Nietzsche makes an extraordinary set of claims in an argument against the philosophical assumptions that "knowledge as such" and "pure reason" are epistemological standards that can be attained by a "pure, will-less, painless, timeless, subject of knowledge." Contrary to the philosophers and scientists who think like this, he claims that "there is *only* a perspectival seeing, *only* a perspectival 'knowing'; the *more* affects we are able to put into words about a thing, the *more* eyes, various eyes we are able to use for the same thing, the more complete will be our 'concept' of the thing, our 'objectivity'" (*GM* III 12). Since we have already analyzed how he uses these claims against the philosophers and even scientists, let us instead investigate the claims themselves, for their presuppositions are nowhere defended in *GM* and their implications are astonishing.

Each claim distills entire argumentative chains into simple slogans. Behind the claim that there is only a perspectival seeing lies a description of how interoception, perception, affect, and cognition work. Behind the claim that there is only a perspectival "knowing" lies a rejection of the traditional philosophical project of epistemology, according to which knowledge is neutral, not interested, and truth is objective and absolute rather than nonobjective and partial. Nietzsche's description of the formation of interoception, perception, affect, and cognition implies that all of them are perspectival. Likewise, his description of knowledge implies that all conscious perceptual and interoceptive psychological states, all beliefs and thoughts, and all propositions that are instances of knowledge are perspectivally warranted and perspectivally true. Hence, there are no givens in perception, interoception, affect, or cognition; there are no objectively warranted beliefs, thoughts, or propositions about anything; and there are no objectively or absolutely true beliefs or propositions about anything. In *GM*, Nietzsche assumes that these assertions are correct, and he uses them to argue that even scientific attempts to warrant beliefs by appealing to givens, to affirm objectivity as an epistemological standard, and to discover absolute truths are all empty vestiges of the ascetic ideal. Yet he does not seem to be aware that the very perspectivity of truth and knowledge that he assumes to reject the philosophers' and theologians' absolutist pretensions may induce a self-referential relativism that vitiates his rejection of their claims and so undermines his own alternatives to them.

Psychological Perspectivity

Nietzsche argues on behalf of three ways that knowledge is perspectival. First, he argues that the formation of conscious perceptual and interoceptive states, beliefs, thoughts, and propositions is perspectival. Second, he argues that their warrants are perspectival. Finally, he argues that truth is perspectival. He lays out a general argument for the psychological claim about the perspectival genesis of conscious perceptual states here:

> My eyes, however strong or weak they may be, can see only a certain distance, and it is within the space encompassed by this distance that I live and move, the line of this horizon constitutes my immediate fate, in great things and small, from which I cannot escape. Around every being there is described a similar concentric circle, which has a mid-point and is peculiar to him. Our ears enclose us within a comparable circle, and so does our sense of touch. . . . If our eyes were a hundredfold sharper, man would appear to us tremendously tall; it is possible, indeed, to imagine organs by virtue of which he would be felt as immeasurable. On the other hand, organs could be so constituted that whole solar systems were viewed contracted and packed together like a single cell: and to beings of an opposite constitution a cell of the human body could present itself, in motion, construction and harmony, as a solar system. The habits of our senses have woven us into lies and deception of sensation: these again are the basis of all our judgments and "knowledge"—there is absolutely no escape, no backway or bypath into the *real world*! We sit within our net, we spiders, and whatever we may catch in it, we can catch nothing at all except that which allows itself to be caught in precisely *our* net. (*D* 117)

Given that interoception is relevantly similar to perception, it follows immediately that both basic kinds of conscious experience are already perspectival. Let us unpack this argument, focusing first on perception.[4]

In the last hundred years science has discovered many details about perception. We now know that the eyes, ears, nose, mouth, and skin transduce environmental information and feed that information forward to cortical regions specific to sensory modality. In these cortical regions, preconscious processing sequentially builds up the content and qualitative character of conscious perceptual experience. Conscious perceptual experience is, thus, a product of preconscious cortical processing acting on transduced environmental information. To his considerable credit, Nietzsche recognizes that this must be so. He labels perception a kind of environmental "assimilation" (*GS* 354; see also *BGE* 36; *KSA* 11 40[15]) or "appropriation" (*BGE* 230; see also *KSA* 11 38[10]) that is informed by an organism's biological needs. A set of preconscious processes takes this assimilated environmental information and "interprets" (*BGE* 14; see also *GS* 374; *KSA* 11 34[55]) or, to use a term currently in vogue, scaffolds it to produce conscious perceptual experience. He puts this point as follows: "Sense-perception happens without our awareness: whatever we become conscious of is a perception that has already been processed" (*KSA* 11 34[30]; see also *BGE* 230).

We have already seen in Chapter 3 that biological drives induce salience hierarchies in perception and thereby structure sensory experience of the world. These biological and affective structures are legacies of genetically inherited evolutionary advantages at work in the preconscious processes that yield conscious perception. Every conscious perception already has significant evolutionarily affective and evaluative scaffolding built in: "[T]he *utility of preservation*—not some abstract-theoretical need not to be deceived—stands as the motive behind the development of the organs of knowledge—they develop in such a way that their observations suffice for our preservation" (*KSA* 13 14[122]). Thus our survival and preservation provide boundary conditions of these preconscious processes and set constraints on their functioning. One consequence is that perception is selective:

[4] See Leiter 2019; Riccardi 2021.

> Our perceptions, as we understand them: i.e., the sum of all those perceptions the becoming-conscious of which was useful and essential and to the entire organic process—therefore not all perceptions in general (e.g., not the electric); this means: we have senses for only a selection of perceptions—those with which we have to concern ourselves in order to preserve ourselves. (*KSA* 12 2[95])

Nietzsche immediately infers from the selectivity of perception that it is evaluatively saturated as well: "It cannot be doubted that *all sense perceptions are permeated with value judgments* (useful and harmful—consequently, pleasant or unpleasant)" (*KSA* 12 2[95]), a claim made even more vividly here: "There are no experiences other than moral ones, not even in the realm of sense perception" (*GS* 111; see also *KSA* 11 26[72]). We can evade the homuncularism present in these passages by restating the claim in a more deflationary way: the selective scaffolding of perception is the result of a lengthy process of evolutionary development that favors certain perceptual systems over others.

What holds for perception holds also for interoception. Experience of our intraorganismic status and of ourselves is also the result of significant preconscious scaffolding. As Nietzsche notes, "[T]he actual process of inner 'perception,' the causal connection between thoughts, feelings, desires, between subject and object, are absolutely hidden from us" (*KSA* 13 11[113]; see also *TI* "The Four Great Errors" 4). When experiencing interoceptive phenomena, we are little better than "the deaf-and-dumb, who divine the words they do not hear through movements of the lips" (*KSA* 13 14[144, 145]). Just as with perception, the conscious end-products of preconscious interoceptive processes are routinely assumed to be transparent first causes when they are instead nodes in more complicated and opaque causal networks of preconscious scaffolding. The tendency to misidentify causal sequences is, if anything, even more pronounced in the case of interoception than it is in sensory perception. In the case of sensory perception, we are familiar with the way that perceptual illusions and mirages underscore the epistemic distance between how things are and how they are sometimes perceptually experienced. However, the problems that warrant skepticism about perception have seemed to many philosophers to be absent from interoception. Interoception and introspective reports have long been thought to be transparent and indubitable, immediate and infallible, and certain and incorrigible. Nietzsche rejects these assumptions as naive speculation.

Basic conscious perception and interoception are routinely nodes in larger networks of psychological states, processes, and events, for basic conscious states are routinely the target of nonbasic psychological activity, such as thinking, reflection, monitoring, self-awareness and other higher-order states. What distinguishes basic conscious experience from nonbasic conscious experience is that the latter is structured with logical categories such as synchronic and diachronic identity, thingness, the philosophical subject, the categories of attribute, activity, object, substance, and form. And just as basic conscious experience is scaffolded preconsciously, so "[R]ational thought is interpretation according to a scheme that we cannot throw off" (*KSA* 12 5[22]). And from that it follows that reason is never unbiased: "[T] rust in reason and its categories, in dialectic, therefore the valuation of logic, proves only their usefulness for life, proved by experience" (*KSA* 12 9[38]).

Summarizing, psychological perspectivity is the conjunction of two descriptive genetic claims: first, the formation of all basic conscious experience (that is, perception and interoception) is indexed to the affective and evaluative dimensions of preconscious scaffolding, and second, the formation of all nonbasic conscious experience (thought, reflection, monitoring, and self-awareness) is indexed to the logical dimensions of preconscious scaffolding.

Epistemological Perspectivity

To this point, we have described a descriptive psychological claim about how basic perceptual and interoceptive states and nonbasic cognitive and propositional states are formed. And, as we saw in his criticism of science, Nietzsche also adopts the epistemological view that the warrants we develop for all basic and nonbasic conscious states are perspectival, as is the truth of any belief or proposition about basic or nonbasic conscious states.

Individual organisms lacking reliable scaffolding are less likely to have survived to reproduce or rear offspring than those outfitted with reliable scaffolding, so the relative frequency of those outfitted with reliable scaffolding has predictably increased. That reliability warrants basic conscious experience. Since basic conscious experiences are causal results of generally reliable preconscious scaffolding, we have good reason to depend on them. Of course, reliability is a comparative measure. Plenty of reliable beliefs turn out to be false. So we cannot infer from greater reliability that the more reliable is true while the less reliable is false. That is, reliability perspectivally warrants beliefs and propositions but does not objectively warrant them. Nietzsche finds this consequence not the least bit disturbing. He acknowledges that we cannot escape the spider's web of our own warranting perspectives, even if living inside that spider's web thwarts any epistemological ambition for something objectively warranted or objectively true:

> We do not consider the falsity of a judgment as itself an objection to a judgment; this is perhaps where our new language will sound most foreign. The question is how far the judgment promotes and preserves life, how well it preserves, and perhaps even cultivates, the type. And we are fundamentally inclined to claim that the falsest judgments (which include synthetic judgments *a priori*) are the most indispensable to us, and that without accepting the fictions of logic, without measuring reality against the wholly invented world of the unconditioned and self-dentical, without a constant falsification of the world through numbers, people could not live—that a renunciation of false judgments would be a renunciation of life, a negation of life. (*BGE* 4)

If life-preserving and species-preserving preconscious processing scaffolds basic conscious experience and can never be detached from it, then thinking that we can describe experience or the world without that scaffolding is a nonstarter. If so, then the contents of basic conscious experience and our descriptions of the world are not true outside of our phylogenetically fixed perspectives and are neither objectively true nor objectively false.

Here is one way of understanding Nietzsche's argument. First, basic conscious states and descriptions of the world do not and cannot occur without scaffolding. Second, the only epistemological assessment we can make of this scaffolding is that it is reliable. Third, we cannot know whether that reliability is a function of the way the world is or of the way our needs are. Fourth, if we cannot know whether reliability is a function of the way the world is or of the way our needs are, then it is not possible to determine the objective warrant for, or truth of, the content of any basic conscious state or any description of the world. So, it is not possible to determine that the content of any basic conscious state or a description of the world is objectively warranted or objectively true outside of the perspective fixed by scaffolding.

This conclusion likewise applies to nonbasic conscious states, such as logically categorized beliefs, thoughts, and propositions. Logical categorization regularizes, simplifies, orders, and equalizes by introducing "the 'thing,' the 'identical thing,' subject, attribute, activity, object, substance, form" (*KSA* 12 5[22]; see also *GS* 110, 111; *BGE* 4). As for perception and interoception, so also beliefs and thoughts with propositional content are logically categorized in the service of needs: "[B]ehind all logic and its autocratic posturings stand valuations, or stated more clearly, physiological requirements for the preservation of a particular type of life" (*BGE* 3). It is tempting to think that the logical categories are layered over basic conscious experience like a veneer that we could with effort peel away to reveal uncategorized kinds of thought. Nietzsche thinks this is not possible: "Our subjective compulsion to believe in logic only reveals that, long before logic itself entered our consciousness, we did nothing but introduce its postulates into events: now we discover them in events. . . . The world seems logical to us because we have made it logical" (*KSA* 12 5[22]; see also *GS* 110, 111; *BGE* 4). Again: "The most strongly believed a priori 'truths' are for me—provisional assumptions; e.g., the law of causality, a very well acquired habit of belief, so much a part of us that not to believe in it would destroy the race. But are they for that reason truths? What a conclusion! As if the preservation of man were a proof of truth!" (*KSA* 11 26[12]). Since even logical categories are evolutionary existence conditions, it follows that all of our categorized beliefs, thoughts, and propositions are perspectivally true and perspectivally warranted.

Expecting that neutral reason will generate knowledge "demand[s] that we should think of an eye . . . turned in no particular direction, in which the active and interpreting forces, through which alone seeing becomes seeing *something*, are supposed to be lacking" (*GM* III 12;

see also *BGE* 3). Nietzsche's alternative to traditional ways of thinking about knowledge acquisition and warrant recommends multiplying perspectives, refining them, cultivating them, comparing them one to another, discarding some while highlighting others depending on context, and being able to "control one's Pro and Con" (*GM* III 12). Nietzsche distills this claim argument neatly in a *Nachlass* note: "In so far as the word 'knowledge' has any meaning, the world is knowable; but it is *interpretable* otherwise, it has no meaning behind it, but countless meanings—'Perspectivism'" (*KSA* 12 7[60]). Thus, Nietzsche's claims are at odds with any view that stresses the role of disinterested reason in belief acquisition and knowledge justification, or any view that holds that beliefs infused by perspectival interests are for that reason degraded and cannot be knowledge.

Multiplying perspectives has limits. We have seen one of those limits already: thingness, subject, attribute, activity, object, substance, form, equality, and whatever else is logically unavoidable for us are elements of all categorized beliefs, thoughts, and propositions. A second limit is that since even basic conscious experience is scaffolded, we can never identify anything beyond it:

> In all perception, i.e., in the most original appropriation, what is essentially happening is an action, or more precisely: an imposition of shapes upon things. . . . It is in the nature of this activity not only to posit shapes, rhythms and successions of shapes, but also to appraise the formation it has created with an eye to incorporation or rejection. Thus arises our world, our whole world: and no supposed "true reality," no "in-themselves of things" corresponds to this whole world which we have created, belonging to us alone. Rather it is itself our only reality, and "knowledge" thus considered proves to be only a *means of feeding*. (*KSA* 11 38[10])

Again: "[T]he origin of our apparent 'knowledge' is . . . to be sought solely in older evaluations which have become so much part of us that they belong to our basic constitution" (*KSA* 12 7[2]). If so, then it is not possible to know anything about a world beyond or outside of the world provided to us by scaffolded perception and interoception. And if that is correct, then any philosophical claim to know anything about "true reality" or, as he puts it in *TI*, the "real world" is mythology.

A third limit exists. Even if we can imagine a world populated by beings whose basic conscious experience lacks our perceptual and interoceptive scaffolding and whose nonbasic conscious experience lacks our categorical scaffolding, we cannot occupy that world longer than the time it takes to come up the thought experiment:

> How far the perspectival character of existence extends, or indeed whether it has any other character; whether an existence without interpretation, without "sense," doesn't become "nonsense"; whether, on the other hand, all existence isn't essentially an *interpreting* existence—that cannot, as would be fair, be decided even by the most industrious and extremely conscientious analysis and self-examination of the intellect; for in the course of this analysis, the human intellect cannot avoid seeing itself under its perspectival forms, and *solely* in these. We cannot look around our corner: it is a hopeless curiosity to want to know what other kinds of intellects and perspectives there *might* be; e.g. whether other beings might be able to experience time backwards, or alternately forwards and backwards (which would involve another direction of life and a different conception of cause and effect). But I think that today we are at least far away from the ridiculous immodesty of decreeing from our angle that perspectives are *permitted* only from this angle. Rather, the world has once again become infinite to us: insofar as we cannot reject the possibility *that it includes infinite interpretations*. (*GS* 374)

Since we are warranted from within our own perspectives that there are other perspectives and since we cannot know what experience from perspectives that do not share our perceptual, interoceptive, and logical scaffolding might be like, we cannot know how the world might be like outside of our or any other perspective. Instead, precisely because we cannot look around our own perspectival corner, we must admit that it is overwhelmingly likely that there are many perspectives, indeed perhaps an infinite number of them. We cannot dismiss this probability, so we cannot know that our perspective is objectively true.

Summarizing, epistemological perspectivity is the conjunction of two philosophical claims: first, the warrants of basic and nonbasic conscious states are indexically formed and relative to a perspective, and second, the truth of basic perceptual and interoceptive states and nonbasic logically and conceptually structured thoughts and propositions are indexically formed and relative to a perspective.

Relativism and Paradox

If the perspectivity of truth is understood as a philosophical thesis, it would be the thesis that the truth of a belief or proposition is indexed, or relative, to a perspective. The relativistic implications of such a view are immediate: so long as a belief or proposition is affirmed by someone as true in a perspective, then that belief or proposition is true in that perspective. Truth perspectivism also appears to yield damaging consequences for Nietzsche's criticisms of others. He claims that many philosophical discoveries are myths or fictions, but if truth and falsity are indexed to a perspective, then any claim that some such discovery is instead a myth or a fiction is itself indexed to a perspective. For example, Nietzsche's claim that the faculty of free will is a metaphysical myth is itself indexed to a perspective, that is, it is true in his naturalist perspective. However, the metaphysical philosopher who claims that there is a free will faculty can reply that while Nietzsche's claim may be true in his naturalist perspective, it is false in their metaphysical perspective. Since there is no way to jump outside the two perspectives to settle the truth values of the contrary claims that comprise the disagreement, we reach a standoff.

These problems are not as debilitating as they appear. Even if truth indexes to a perspective, there are propositions that are true across multiple diverse perspectives, and since this is so Nietzsche may reject the pernicious relativist conclusion that every perspectival truth is as true as the next. Similarly, even if warrant indexes to a perspective, there are cross-perspectival warrants that can be submitted to cross-perspectival adjudication, thus undermining queasiness that warrant cannot escape particular perspectives. So, again, Nietzsche need not be saddled with the pernicious relativist conclusion that every reason for believing something is as good as the next. Nor need he try to avoid the standoff between naturalism and metaphysical perspectives by denying that the truth of his claims are indexed to a perspective. Indeed, he ought not try to avoid the standoff this way, for were he to do so, then the truth of at least some claims—his own claims—would, unlike the truth of other claims, not be indexed to a perspective after all, and in that case his truth perspectivism would not be consistent. Moreover, if psychological and warrant perspectivism are correct, then he would have no ground to stand on to assert that his claims are not perspectivally true.

A distinct problem for the thesis that truth is perspectival is that if truth is perspectival, then it appears that there can be no absolute truths of any kind. We might be inclined to argue that there are absolute truths about at least some things, so we might think that truth perspectivism gets things wrong. Here, just as he does with 'soul' and 'free will,' Nietzsche can reappropriate 'absolute truth' to defuse this kind of criticism. If 'absolute truth' refers to propositions that are true outside of any perspective, then he will insist that there are no absolute truths, for he denies that there are any extraperspectival truths. He may nevertheless claim that being true outside of all perspectives is different from being true across all perspectives. On this interpretation, propositions true across all perspectives are instances of absolute truths of a sort, viz., perspectivally true absolute truths, even if they are not instances of absolute truths of another sort, viz., extraperspectivally true absolute truths. So he can affirm the existence of absolute truths after all: absolute truths are propositions that are true across all perspectives. Whether there are any such truths is an open question.

An even more troubling problem emerges from allowing Nietzsche the claim that there are propositions that are true across all perspectives. The problem is that this claim may be paradoxical: even if it can be asserted, it cannot be true. Suppose we consider a version of perspectivism that asserts that for all propositions *p*, there is a perspective P in which *p* is true and a perspective P′ in which *p* is false. Call this thesis 'Perspectivism.' Now we can generate a dilemma for this thesis. First, let us assume that Perspectivism is true in all perspectives. If so, there are no perspectives in which Perspectivism is false. However, Perspectivism asserts that every proposition *p* is false in at least one perspective. Hence, Perspectivism is false on the assumption that it is true in all perspectives. Second, assume instead that Perspectivism is true in some but not all perspectives. If so, there are perspectives in which Perspectivism is false. In such a perspective, the negation of Perspectivism is true. This thesis—'Not-Perspectivism'—asserts that for at least one proposition *p*, it is not the case that there is a perspective P in which *p* is true and a perspective P′ in which *p* is false, which is equivalent to asserting that there is at least one proposition *p* that is true in all perspectives or false in all perspectives. However, if at least one proposition *p* is true in all perspectives or false in all perspectives, then Perspectivism is false. Hence, Perspectivism is false on the assumption that it is true in some but not all perspectives. So, on either assumption, Perspectivism turns out to be false. Hence, even if asserted, Perspectivism cannot be true, which implies that Perspectivism is a paradox.[5]

If sound, this dilemma poses a problem for truth perspectivism as a philosophical thesis about the behavior of truth. Whether the dilemma is sound is a matter of scholarly debate. We cannot settle that or the other debates that perspectivism prompts. "Further Reading" at the end of this chapter lists authors who discuss these matters. We may note that one implication of rejecting the perspectivism thesis is that Nietzsche would have to accept the existence of at least one proposition that is true or some propositions that are true across all perspectives. Perhaps perspectivism is the only proposition true across all perspectives; perhaps other propositions are also candidates. The perhaps surprising thing is that no great damage to Nietzsche's overall commitment to the perspectivity of truth results from admitting that some propositions are true across all perspectives. Even if there are such candidates, there are likely not to be many of them, and the propositions philosophers and theologians routinely offer up are much more than likely not to be among them.

[5] See Welshon 2009.

Asceticism, Decadence, and Nihilism

To this point, we have granted as much as is possible Nietzsche's conceit that *GM* is a preliminary study for the comprehensive revaluation-of-values project on which he was concurrently working. But the last six sections of Essay III accelerate into and then thunder through regions that, more than anywhere else in *GM*, reveal features of that revaluation project. Through clouds, we finally start to glimpse the contours of revaluing that Nietzsche has been using to guide himself through *GM*'s descriptive explorations into morality in the pejorative sense and its psychological presuppositions. He briskly argues in these sections that morality in this sense—Christian morality, European morality, herd/slave morality, the morality of compassion, in short, our morality—is unhealthy, decadent, nihilistic, "a sign of distress, of impoverishment, of the degeneration of life" that has "hindered human prosperity" (*GM* Preface 3). What justifies this scathing assessment? Nietzsche answers that our inherited morality fails when held against the standard of "the plenitude, force, and will of life, its courage, certainty, future" (*GM* Preface 3). Our task is to better understand these claims.

Readers will likely have divined already three evaluative principles that frame *GM*: power is good, will to power is good, and enhancing the feeling of power is good. A passage from *A* confirms the conjecture: "What is good?—Everything that enhances people's feeling of power, will to power, power itself. What is bad?—Everything stemming from weakness" (*A* 2). From these claims, we may infer that power, willing power, and enhancing the feeling of power are valuable, that is, that we actually do value them. Moreover, because they are all good, Nietzsche apparently thinks we may also infer that we should value them. This last claim is controversial. We may grant that power in Nietzsche's proprietary sense of the term is something we do value, that we do will power as his idiosyncratic descriptions portray, and that we do command ourselves and thereby enhance the feeling of power, and we may nevertheless doubt that we should value these states of affairs. Two questions can help us structure investigation into the issues raised by claiming that power, willing it, and enhancing its feeling are both accurate descriptive categories and evaluative principles. First, assuming that they are evaluative principles, how does Nietzsche use them to analyze the ascetic ideal, decadence, meaninglessness, and nihilism? Second, how does he defend the claim that these descriptive categories are also evaluative principles?

Power, Ascetic Values, Decadence, and Meaningless Suffering

Assume that power, will to power, and enhancing the feeling of power are evaluative principles. How does Nietzsche use them to analyze the ascetic ideal, decadence, meaninglessness, and nihilism? Recall that the ascetic ideal is a set of ascetic values, "compassion, self-denial, self-sacrifice" (*GM* Preface 5), "poverty, humility, chastity" (*GM* III 8), and "'selflessness' [and] 'self-renunciation'" (*EH* "Why I Am a Destiny" 8) chief among them. We are not here interested in strategic uses of these values by philosophers, artists, or other creators. Rather, our attention is here on their use by the kinds of life for which they are constitutive. Nietzsche argues that in these cases ascetic values are decadent values and therefore are not valuable.

The argument is straightforward. If power, will to power, and enhancing the feeling of power are what we should value, then their contraries—weakness, willing weakness, and enhancing the feeling of weakness—are what we should disvalue. However, herd valuing values the ascetic ideal, and the ascetic ideals' constitutive values are contrary to power, willing power, and enhancing the feeling of power. Hence, herd valuing of the ascetic ideal countermands and annuls what should be valued: what should be valued is not, and what should not be valued is.

One obvious counter to this argument is that herd values are valuable for the herd. Herd animals are, by hypothesis, not powerful, so perhaps they should not will it or enhance its feeling; perhaps they should instead will their weakness and enhance their feeling of weakness. Hence, perhaps they should value the ascetic ideal. After all, it gives them something to will, even if what they will confounds the conditions that make life possible. Nietzsche's response is twofold. We must first understand how utterly deviant weakness, willing weakness, and enhancing the feeling of weakness actually are. Second, it follows that only those who suffer the most can see willing weakness and enhancing feelings of weakness as solutions to their suffering.

We have seen in Chapter 4 that "the essence of life, its *will to power*, [is] spontaneous, aggressive, expansive, re-interpreting, re-directing and formative forces" (*GM* II 12) and that "the will to power . . . is simply the will to life" (*GS* 349). Willing weakness and enhancing the feeling of weakness are therefore not only contrary to willing power and enhancing the feeling of power; they are, by that equivalence, contrary to willing life and enhancing the feelings of life. Nietzsche presents a version of this argument in *TI*:

> [E]very *healthy* morality is governed by an instinct of life, —some rule of life is served by a determinate canon of "should" and "should not," some inhibition and hostility on the path of life is removed this way. But *anti-natural* morality, on the other hand, which is to say almost every morality that has been taught, revered, or preached so far, explicitly turns its back on the instincts of life, —it *condemns* these instincts. (*TI* "Morality as Anti-nature" 4)

He tightens the argument into an even more succinct formulation in *A*:

> I consider life itself to be an instinct for growth, for endurance, for the accumulation of force, *for power*: when there is no will to power, there is decline. . . . I call an animal, a species, an individual corrupt when it loses its instincts, when it chooses, when it *prefers* things that will harm it. . . . I understand corruption . . . in the sense of decadence. . . . My claim is that all the values in which humanity has collected its highest desiderata are *values of decadence*. (*A* 6)[6]

Note the equivalence of 'corruption' and 'decadence.' With that equivalence in tow, the second premise states that an animal or individual (or an entire species) is decadent when it loses its instincts or when it chooses or prefers things that harm it. Nietzsche uses this rephrased premise elsewhere in *TI*: "To *have* to fight the instincts—that is the formula for decadence: as long as life is *ascending*, happiness is equal to instinct" (*TI* "The Problem of Socrates" 11).

[6] The sentences as they appear here are reordered from their order in *A* so as to make the argument explicit.

Since "to choose instinctively what is harmful to yourself, to be tempted by 'disinterested' motives'" (*TI* "Skirmishes of an Untimely Man" 35), is the formula for decadence, and since herd morality encodes decadent values, the roles that the ascetic ideal plays in herd morality quickly become apparent. For herd animals to believe that the ascetic ideal is valuable and to will the ascetic ideal are symptoms of their prevailing stagnation and deterioration, expressions of their chronic fatigue, and protective devices against their further decay. Recall:

> [*T*]*he ascetic ideal springs from the protective and healing instincts of a degenerating life*, which uses every means to maintain itself and struggles for its existence; it indicates a partial physiological inhibition and exhaustion against which the deepest instincts of life, which have remained intact, continually struggle with new methods and inventions. The ascetic ideal is one such method: the situation is therefore the precise opposite of what the worshippers of this ideal imagine, —it and through it, life struggles with death and *against* death, the ascetic ideal is a trick for the *preservation* of life. (*GM* III 13)

Life struggles with and against death "in and through" the ascetic ideal because long-suffering individuals can will it for themselves to avoid confronting the alternative of willing nothing at all, that is, death. Willing the ascetic ideal provides those who suffer the most from life with something to will even in the dire circumstance where their only alternative is not to will at all and even if what they will is contrary to life itself. Willing the ascetic ideal may be willing "*nothingness*, an aversion to life, a rebellion against the most fundamental prerequisites of life, but it is and remains a *will*!" (*GM* III 28). This proves what Nietzsche claims at the start of Essay III: even when we are at our most desperate, we prefer "to will *nothingness* rather than *not* will" (*GM* III 1).

Those who are desperate value the ascetic ideal because their lives are characterized by a harsh, unremitting, and draining cycle of suffering against which even their ressentiment for those who live better lives proves inadequate. The ascetic ideal ascribes meaning to that deep suffering. Despite its decadence, and despite adding its own layers of "deeper, more internal, more poisonous" suffering . . . within the perspective of *guilt*" over original sin, the ascetic ideal shows "a *meaning* for it, a *purpose* for suffering" (*GM* III 28). The corrupted find purpose in the ascetic ideal and its regime of guilt, and that purpose infuses their otherwise meaningless suffering with the meaning needed to frustrate death: "Within [the ascetic ideal], suffering was interpreted; the enormous emptiness seemed filled; the door was shut on all suicidal nihilism" (*GM* III 28). Hence, even if to will the ascetic ideal is to "will to nothingness, nihilism" (*GM* III 14), it is an act of consolation for the miserable. By willing nothingness they find something to will, and by willing something rather than not willing at all they thwart their own suicidal nihilism and so defend themselves against death.

Nihilism

Despite the momentum that Sections 27 and 28 gather, determining what Nietzsche means by 'nihilism' and what has explanatory priority over what pose several challenges. It is worth pausing long enough to reflect on these matters. Nihilism is often understood as the denial that there are values or, equivalently, the affirmation that there are no values. Nietzsche ever so quickly hints at what can thus be called "rejection of values nihilism" in Section 27 but directly examines this kind of nihilism only elsewhere, notably in the planned but never completed *Will to Power*. It is apparent from the *Nachlass* notes for this part of *Will to Power* that he planned extensive analyses of nihilism and that he was aware that he would have to distinguish between different senses of the term 'nihilism.' Neither this disambiguation nor these analyses appear in *GM*.

The nihilism Nietzsche does address in *GM* is rooted not in the philosophical rejection of values but in the anguish that attends a failing life and responses to it. Since life and willing power are roughly equivalent and since willing power is expressed through drives and affects, the despair that fuels nihilism is that which accompanies an individual's failing at life, that is, the failure to will power in one's drives and affects. Such individuals have had too many episodes where acting on their drives and affects has resulted in exasperation or failure; or they cannot even hear their own drives or affects—the voices of their drives and affects have become silent to them or have been silenced for them; or they cannot organize their drives and affects into any cohesive unity because they are oppressed or ignored by others or are weak themselves; or they have listened too long to priests prattle on about sin and guilt and the virtues of self-sacrifice, purity, self-denial, humility, and compassion.

Caught in a destructive feedback loop of religious indoctrination, ressentiment, internal disorganization, and external ineffectiveness, life's failures become exhausted, worn out from flopping so predictably, no longer capable of expanding their impact, overcoming resistances, or forming themselves. They concede their stagnation and anticipate only further degeneration. In this degraded state, they succumb to willing nothingness and proclaim it to be wisdom: "The wisest men in every age have reached the same conclusion about life: it's no good. . . . Always and everywhere, you hear the same sound from their mouths, —a sound full of doubt, full of melancholy, full of exhaustion with life, full of resistance to life" (*TI* "The Problem of Socrates" 1). This complex psychological episode, in part affective, in part cognitive, is what can be called "no-to-life" nihilism or "the nihilism of despair."[7]

The nihilism of despair is as multifaceted and as productive as ressentiment. Its causes are, as just reviewed, diverse and cumulative, and its affective characters are likewise variable: sluggish apathy about the present and fretting dread of the future; wildly oscillating emotions and libertinism; raging against anyone's accomplishments as worthless; yielding to the futility of doing anything at all. And, as *GM* has demonstrated, the nihilism of despair is continuously productive, a bottomless well that ascetic religions and philosophies have drawn sustenance from over and over again. Christianity, in particular, "has been so especially subtle, so refined, so southerly refined in guessing which emotions to stimulate in order to conquer the deep depression, the leaden fatigue and the black melancholy of the physiologically obstructed, at least temporarily. For, to speak generally: with all great religions, the main concern is the fight against a certain weariness and heaviness that has become epidemic" (*GM* III 17). Christianity's great

[7] The term 'nihilism of despair' is Bernard Reginster's (2006). John Richardson (2020) uses 'no-to-life nihilism' to name a relevantly similar phenomenon. Ken Gemes (2008) describes what he calls 'affective nihilism.'

achievements were to marshal and redirect ressentiment and to create the ascetic ideal and its values as decadent formulas for treating the symptoms of those who suffer from the nihilism of despair.

The ascetic ideal also exacerbates the nihilism of despair it claims to combat. Consider Nietzsche's favorite target: compassion. While the priest presents compassion as valuable, a virtuous affect for acknowledging others' woe and aching along with them, it instead "negates life, it makes life worthy of negation, —compassion is the practice of nihilism. . . . by multiplying misery just as much as by conserving everything miserable, compassion is one of the main tools used to increase decadence—compassion wins people over to nothingness!" (*A* 7; see also *GM* Preface 5). Similar criticisms attach to the other ascetic values. Christianity takes those ascetic values and fastens them to the despairing herd's endemic ressentiment, thus giving the miserable permission to say "no to everything on earth that represent[s] the ascending movement of life" (*A* 24). With the ascetic ideal welded to the psychology of ressentiment, Christianity invites all who suffer the nihilism of despair to rename their misery as punishment, their failure as humility, their frustration as guilt, their weakness as strength, and their weariness as self-sacrifice. The devices cataloged in Sections 17–22 identify the mechanisms by which the ascetic ideal and ressentiment are operationalized in the herd animal's psyche. Sadly, the result of applying this system is predictable: it "makes the sick patient *more* sick in every case, even if it makes him 'better,'" and its success is measured by "a shattered nervous system added on to the sickness" (*GM* III 21).

The despairing nihilists' commitment to, and further debasement by, the ascetic ideal can thus be understood as giving them something to will even if what they will makes them worse off. Yet this explanation does not fully explain why priests and philosophers value the ascetic ideal or why they teach its values and advocate nihilism. One reason they value the ascetic ideal is that they themselves are decadent and value the ascetic ideal just as other despairing nihilists do, that is, as salve after too many dark nights of the soul. More than that, they also promulgate the ascetic ideal to others as a universal good and advocate on behalf of the judgment that life is no good: "Humanity . . . has been *taught* decadence values, and *only* decadence values, as the highest values . . . the fact 'I am in decline' [is] translated into the imperative 'thou *shalt* decline' . . . [This] *negates* life at the most basic level" (*EH* "Why I Am a Destiny" 7). Of course, the judgment that life is no good is one more reversal: "Instead of naively saying 'I am not worth anything anymore,' the moral lie in the decadent's mouth says 'nothing is worth anything, —life isn't worth anything' " (*TI* "Skirmishes of an Untimely Man" 35). This nihilistic judgment, that life is no good, "quickly grows in society's morbid soil into a tropical vegetation of concepts, now as religion (Christianity), now as philosophy (Schopenhauerianism)" (*TI* "Skirmishes of an Untimely Man" 35). Thus, the priests and ascetic philosophers have cultivated nihilism's conceptual jungle and taught humanity its decadent values.

Again, we must ask, why have they done it? Nietzsche's answer is blunt: for power. Priests are a "parasitical type of human . . . who, with their morality, have lied themselves into the position of determining values, —who see Christian morality as their means of wielding *power*" (*EH* "Why I Am a Destiny" 7). We might be tempted to think that the power priests wield is only against the aristocrats, the warriors, other noble types, or the flocks of herd animals over which they keep watch. As we have seen, priests and philosophers do will power in each of these ways. But they also have a deeper target: "[T]he teachers, the leaders of humanity, all of them theologians, were also all decadents: *this* explains why all values were revalued into ones hostile to life, *explains* morality. . . . *Definition of morality*: morality, the idiosyncrasy of decadents with the ulterior motive of taking revenge *on life*—and successfully" (*EH* "Why I Am a Destiny" 7). The revenge that ressentiment bids priests and philosophers to take against the cause of their suffering finds expression in the malignant judgment that life itself is to be condemned, a judgment expressed in Christianity's gloomy doctrines and the theoretical absurdities of its philosophical allies.

Some of Nietzsche's most scorching criticisms are reserved for priests and ascetic philosophers, whose nihilistic judgment that life is "no good" has played the leading role in diminishing humanity. The "priestly type . . . has a life interest in making humanity sick and twisting the concepts 'good' and 'evil,' 'true' and 'false' to the point where they endanger life and slander the world" (*A* 24). For them, "[D]ecadence is only a means" (*A* 24) to make all humans sick. Of course, they never admit that the ascetic ideal is a will to nothingness; instead, they talk about " 'the beyond'; or 'God'; or 'the true life'; or nirvana, salvation, blessedness" (*A* 7). These grandiose words only camouflage ingrained nihilism: "[I]nnocent rhetoric from the realm of religious-moral idiosyncrasy suddenly appears much less innocent when you see precisely which tendencies are wrapped up inside these sublime words: tendencies hostile to life" (*A* 7).[8] To counter the nihilism of despair built into Christian doctrine and its allied philosophical theorizing, only an "unconditional, honest atheism" suffices, one that "finally forbids itself the *lie entailed in the belief in God*" (*GM* III 27).

Defending Life against Antilife Morality

Having assumed that power and life, willing power and life, and enhancing the feelings of power and life are evaluative principles, and having shown how Nietzsche uses these principles to reveal the ascetic ideal's inherent nihilism, we must lastly ask, how does he defend these evaluative principles? His answer reveals how deep his commitments to naturalism and perspectivism are: since life is power, since willing life is willing power, since the feelings of life are the feelings of power, and since, as now argued, we cannot judge any evaluative principle outside of the perspective of life/power, these principles are the only evaluative principles consistent with life.

In *GM*, Nietzsche does not directly argue that the evaluative principles of power, willing it, and enhancing its feeling are ones by which

[8] Nietzsche exempts Jews from some of this criticism. As he notes, Jews posed as decadents as a strategy to conquer the world, and, as a consequence, are not decadents:

> Jews are the people with the toughest life force; when transplanted into impossible conditions they took sides with all the instincts of decadence, and they did this freely and out of the most profoundly shrewd sense of self-preservation—not because they were dominated by these instincts, but rather because they sensed that these instincts had a power that could be used to prevail against "the world." The Jews are the opposite of decadents: they had to act like decadents to the point of illusion, they knew, with a *non plus ultra* of theatrical genius, how to put themselves at the forefront of all movements of decadence (—like the Christianity of Paul—) so they could make these movements into something stronger than any yes-saying defenders of life. (*A* 7)

we should be guided. This omission is partially remedied by arguments that he was working on while he was writing *GM* that were to be included in his unfinished work on the revaluation of values. One of those arguments found expression in *TI*:

> If you have understood how sacrilegious it is to rebel against life (and this sort of rebellion is practically sacrosanct for Christian morality), then, fortunately, you have understood something else as well: the futility, fallacy, absurdity, *deceitfulness* of a rebellion like this. A condemnation of life on the part of the living is, in the end, only the symptom of a certain type of life, and has no bearing on the question of whether or not the condemnation is justified. Even to raise the problem of the *value* of life, you would need to be both *outside* life and as familiar with life as someone, anyone, everyone who has ever lived: this is enough to tell us that the problem is inaccessible to us. When we talk about values we are under the inspiration, under the optic, of life: life itself forces us to posit values, life itself evaluates through us, *when* we posit values. (*TI* "Morality as Anti-nature" 5)

Here Nietzsche claims that all evaluative principles—whether, as he has it, they be those regarding power, willing it, and enhancing its feelings or, as others have it, those regarding asceticism, willing it, and enhancing its feelings—are expressions of and valued by natural living organisms. This argument raises problems, two for priests and ascetic philosophers and two others for Nietzsche. We conclude discussion of Essay III by describing and assessing these problems.

Priests, Ascetic Philosophers, and Antilife Morality

Priests and ascetic philosophers claim that God's word warrants condemning life even if doing so entails valuing states of affairs that are inconsistent with life and inconsistent with what we actually value. Nietzsche challenges these claims by uncovering the priest's and ascetic philosopher's presumption to have access to a perspective that is outside life but still exhaustively familiar with it. Unfortunately, they cannot access this perspective because they too are living beings and accordingly are perspectivally, but not exhaustively, familiar with life. Hence, despite what they claim, priests and ascetic philosophers cannot escape the reaches of life's perspectival implications. Hence, their appeal to God's word and its condemnation of life fails.

Moreover, as Nietzsche also notes, one of life's implications is that we cannot but posit values. As long as we are alive, our drives, instincts, and affects continuously value certain states of affairs. Asserting that the states of affairs implied by condemning life are valued must therefore be consistent with or implied by the demands made for the lives that value them. As has already been argued, these lives are characterized by frustrated affects, drives, and instincts, by ressentiment and envy, and subsumed by suffering and exhaustion. So the judgment that life is no good "is the judgment of a declining, weakened, exhausted, condemned life" (*TI* "Morality as Anti-nature" 5).

In short, to be in a position to condemn life, priests and ascetic philosophers must either access an inaccessible perspective or acquiesce to their own decadence. They have to admit either that they cannot exist outside the judgments of life or that life has made a judgment against them. If the former, then life is not condemned after all, and if the latter, then their own lives are condemned. Either way, priests and ascetic philosophers incriminate themselves, and their condemnation of life collapses in on itself.

Since herd moral values flow directly from the ascetic condemnation of life, they too are "anti-natural . . . the converse of life" (*TI* "Morality as Anti-nature" 5). Hence, herd morality is "the *instinct of decadence* making an imperative of itself: it says: '*be destroyed!*'—it is the judgment of the condemned" (*TI* "Morality as Anti-nature" 5). If so, then the warrants for herd morality's evaluative principles also collapse, and for the same reasons as those just canvassed. After all, if herd morality cannot access the perspective necessary for justifying its evaluative principles as universally binding, then it does not command at all, and if it backpedals enough to access the only perspective it can, then it commands only other decadents. So until the advocates of herd morality show that Nietzsche's arguments for this collapse fail, they are in no position to assert that their evaluative principles are superior to his or others.

We thus reach a standoff. Nietzsche argues for naturalism and perspectivism and uses them against the priests' and ascetic philosophers' claims about the content and scope of herd morality, while priests and ascetic philosophers assume antinaturalism and absolutism to warrant their claims about herd morality's content and scope. The standoff is not, however, a stalemate: the amassed weight of *GM*'s arguments implies that the burden of proof shifts to priests and ascetic philosophers to show that those arguments on behalf of naturalism and perspectivism fail. Until that burden is discharged, both herd morality's presumption to command all of us from outside life's perspectives and its presumption to command any of us not condemned by life are indefensible.

Nietzsche, Life, and Power

Nietzsche's recurrent appeals to nature and life and his equation of life with power can raise suspicions that he is either playing a sleight-of-hand trick or that he is stacking the deck in his favor. One version of the former concern is that he is guilty of a naturalistic fallacy. That is, he appears to argue we should value power, willing it, and feeling it simply because we do value it. A version of the latter concern is that he mistakenly reduces all valuing to valuing power, willing it, and feeling it. That is, he appears to argue not only that we do and should value power, willing power, and the feeling of power, but also that we do and should value only them.

The accusation that Nietzsche's arguments for power, willing it, and feeling it commit a naturalistic fallacy can be defused in a number of ways. Here are two. First, he is aware that describing herd values and the evaluative principles that support them does not suffice for criticizing those values or principles. We can then charitably suggest that he is also aware that describing life's values and the evaluative principles that support them does not suffice for commending those values or principles to us and that other considerations must be introduced in order to commend them. Those considerations are not discussed in *GM* except indirectly and cryptically. However, his equation of life with power and his arguments regarding power, life, and decadence show one direction his thinking was taking for closing this argumentative gap. Whether this maneuver works depends largely on whether his equation of life and power is defensible. We investigate this matter presently.

Nietzsche has a second response to the accusation that his arguments for power, willing it, and feeling it commit a naturalistic fallacy. This response is simply to deny that the naturalistic fallacy is a fallacy. After all, if naturalism is correct, then the only candidates for what should be come from the domain of what is. Of course, even if a state of affairs that should be cannot but be a state of affairs that is, there are some states of affairs that should not be. The states of affairs that should not be comprise the set of bad states of affairs. Grant that there are bad states of affairs. Still, the existence of states of affairs that should not be is consistent with the existence of states of affairs that should be. That is, in addition to bad states of affairs, there are also good states of affairs. And a candidate for a good state of affairs is one where humans flourish while they live.

If we are prepared to grant that flourishing is a good state of affairs, Nietzsche can argue as follows. First, having power, willing power, and feeling power can be described only naturalistically. Second, having power, willing power, and feeling power together comprise flourishing for those who are not decadent, while nothing else comprises flourishing for those who are not decadent. Third, flourishing is a good state of affairs. Fourth, other things being equal, we should pursue what is good. Hence, other things being equal, those who are not decadent should pursue power, willing power, and feeling power.

Either of these arguments, if sound, provides Nietzsche with what is needed to defuse the charge that he illegitimately tries to derive evaluative principles from descriptive claims. Unfortunately, both arguments rely on claims that fuel the suspicion that he unjustifiably stacks the deck in his favor. The suspicion can be stated thusly: even if we accept naturalism and perspectivism, his inference from them to values and evaluative principles of power, willing power, and the feeling of power may be too hasty. That is, it may be that naturalism and perspectivism do not together imply that all values and evaluative principles revolve around power, willing it, and feeling it. That would be so if life and power were not equivalent or if flourishing could be pursued by doing something other than pursuing power, willing it, and feeling it. If so, then naturalism and perspectivism would be consistent with some values and evaluative principles distinct from those advocated by Nietzsche.

Here is one way to develop this thought. Perhaps our naturalized psychology is more multifaceted than Nietzsche allows. That is, perhaps we have drives for states of affairs other than power, willing it, and feeling it, and, hence, value some states of affairs in addition to power, willing it, and feeling it. If that is so, then our naturalized psychology might be consistent with valuing states of affairs such as cooperatively helping others for mutual benefit or even altruistically helping others at our own expense. Evolutionary game theory suggests that we do value such states of affairs, for it shows that and how cooperative and even altruistic behavior emerges in kinship and nonkinship groups. If this scientific work is sound and not infected with decadence, then even where psychological egoism governs behavior, cooperation and altruism can and do develop. If so, then perhaps even some nondecadents do and should behave cooperatively or altruistically, and Nietzsche's insistence that altruistic actions and values are only for the weak—"An 'altruistic' morality . . . is always a bad sign" (*TI* "Skirmishes of an Untimely Man" 35)—would turn out to be mistaken.

Unsurprisingly, Nietzsche thought about these issues, albeit not in *GM*. It appears from what he says elsewhere (at, for example, *TI* "Skirmishes of an Untimely Man" 33, 35; *A* 2, 7; *BGE* 225) that he rejects cooperation and altruism when premised on compassion for others' decadent suffering from life. After all, cooperation and altruism then do no more than compound already existing decadent suffering by valuing it and assisting others to continue to experience and value it. Even if Nietzsche must reject this kind of suffering and these cases of helping others, he need not reject other kinds of suffering and other cases of helping others, for not all suffering occurs as a result of unhealthiness, weakness, and a declining life. Some suffering occurs in the service of power, willing power, and feeling it. This vital suffering is not merely tolerated as a necessary byproduct of valuing power, willing it, and feeling it, but at least on occasion it is and should be cultivated as an expression of life, growth, and power. So our responses to suffering must vary as a function of the kind of suffering at hand. When we respond to decadent suffering with compassion and to vital suffering with resentment, we acquiesce to the hostility to life. When, to the contrary, we respond to decadent suffering with firmness, clarity, and contempt and respond to vital suffering with encouragement and assistance, we celebrate life, growth, and power. In such cases, we help from a position of power, harming neither ourselves nor those vitally suffering.

Cooperating with and assisting vital suffering may not be altruistic co-operation in the strict sense of the term, but nor is it apathy, hostility, or resentment. It is, instead, a response licensed by Nietzsche's nuanced view that distinguishes between kinds of suffering and distinguishes between kinds of responses to those dissimilar kinds.

Further Reading

For more on the role of the priests in the slave revolt, see Anderson 2011; Hatab 2011; Loeb 2018; Migotti 1998; Morrison 2014.

For more on perception, knowledge, and perspectivism, see Anderson 2002; Clark 1990; Clark and Dudrick 2009b, 2012; Gemes 2001a, 2013; Hales and Welshon 2000; Janaway 2007; Nehamas 1985; Poellner 2001; Welshon 2004, 2009; Wilcox 1974; Williams 2006b.

For more on ascetic values, decadence, and nihilism, see Forster 2017; Gemes 2008; Havas 1995; Katsfanas 2015a; May 2011b; Müller-Lauter 2006; Reginster 2006, 2013, 2021.

For more on normativity, power, and life, see Doyle 2018; Hussain 2011, 2013; Janaway 2007; Katsfanas 2019; Leiter 2002; Miyasaki 2015; Poellner 1995, 2013; Richardson 1996, 2004, 2020; Schacht 1983.

Bibliography

Acampora, C. (ed.) 2006a. *Critical Essays on the Classics: Nietzsche's "On the Genealogy of Morals"*. Lanham, MD: Rowman and Littlefield.

Acampora, C. 2006b. "Naturalism and Nietzsche's Moral Psychology." In Ansell Pearson 2006: 314–333.

Acampora, C. 2006c. "On Sovereignty and Overhumanity: Why It Matters How We Read Nietzsche's *Genealogy* II, 2." In Acampora 2006a: 25–53.

Alfano, M. 2019. *Nietzsche's Moral Psychology*. New York: Cambridge University Press.

Anderson, R. L. 2002. "Sensualism and Unconscious Representations in Nietzsche's Account of Knowledge." *International Studies in Philosophy* 34(3): 95–117.

Anderson, R. L. 2011. "On the Nobility of Nietzsche's Priests." In May 2011a: 24–55.

Anderson, R. L. 2012. "What Is a Nietzschean Self?." In Janaway and Robertson 2012: 202–233.

Anderson, R. L. 2013. "Nietzsche on Autonomy." In Gemes and Richardson 2013: 432–460.

Anderson, R. L. 2022. "Nietzschean Autonomy and the Meaning of the 'Sovereign Individual.'" *Philosophy and Phenomenological Research* 105(2): 362–384.

Ansell Pearson, K. (ed.) 2006. *A Companion to Nietzsche*. Oxford: Basil Blackwell.

Aschheim, S. 1992. *The Nietzsche Legacy in Germany, 1890–1990*. Berkeley: University of California Press.

Bittner, R. 1994. "*Ressentiment*." In Schacht 1994: 127–138.

Blondel, E. 1994. "The Question of Genealogy." In Schacht 1994: 306–317.

Bloom, A. 1987. *The Closing of the American Mind*. New York: Simon and Schuster.

Bloom, H. 1997. *The Anxiety of Influence: A Theory of Poetry*. 2nd ed. New York: Oxford University Press.

Brobjer, T. 2004. "Nietzsche's Reading and Knowledge of Natural Science: An Overview." In Moore and Brobjer 2004: 21–50.

Brobjer, T. 2008. *Nietzsche's Philosophical Context: An Intellectual Biography*. Urbana: University of Illinois Press.

Burnyeat, M. (ed.) 2006. *The Sense of the Past: Essays in the History of Philosophy*. Princeton, NJ: Princeton University Press.

Clark, M. 1990. *Nietzsche on Truth and Philosophy*. New York: Cambridge University Press.

Clark, M. 2000. "Nietzsche's Doctrine of Will to Power: Neither Ontological nor Biological." *International Studies in Philosophy* 32(3): 119–135.

Clark, M. 2013. "Nietzsche Was No Lamarckian." *Journal of Nietzsche Studies* 44(2): 282–296.

Clark, M. and Dudrick, D. 2006. "The Naturalisms of *Beyond Good and Evil*." In Ansell Pearson 2006: 148–167.

Clark, M. and Dudrick, D. 2009a. "Nietzsche on the Will: An Analysis of *BGE* 19." In Gemes and May 2009: 247–268.

Clark, M. and Dudrick, D. 2009b. "Nietzsche's Post-positivism." *European Journal of Philosophy* 12(3): 369–385.

Clark, M. and Dudrick, D. 2012. *The Soul of Nietzsche's "Beyond Good and Evil"*. New York: Cambridge University Press.

Conway, D. 2008. *Nietzsche's "On the Genealogy of Morals": A Reader's Guide*. New York: Continuum.

Cox, C. 1999. *Nietzsche: Naturalism and Interpretation*. Berkeley: University of California Press.

Danto, A. 1965. *Nietzsche as Philosopher: An Original Study*. New York: Columbia University Press.

Darwin, C. 1859/1993. *On the Origin of Species*. New York: Modern Library.

Davey, N. 1987. "Nietzsche and Hume on Self and Identity." *Journal of the British Society for Phenomenology* 18(1): 14–29.

Deleuze, G. 1983. *Nietzsche and Philosophy*. Trans. H. Tomlinson. New York: Columbia University Press.

Doyle. T. 2011. "Nietzsche, Consciousness, and Human Agency." *Idealistic Studies* 41: 11–30.

Doyle, T. 2018. *Nietzsche's Metaphysics of the Will to Power*. New York: Cambridge University Press.

Doyle, T. 2019. "Nietzsche's Philosophical Naturalism." In Loeb and Meyer 2019: 146–164.

Dries, M. (ed.) 2017. *Nietzsche on Consciousness and the Embodied Mind*. Berlin: de Gruyter.

Dries, M. and Kail, P. (eds.) 2015. *Nietzsche on Mind and Nature*. New York: Oxford University Press.

Elgat, G. 2017. *Nietzsche's Psychology of* Ressentiment: *Revenge and Justice in "On the Genealogy of Morality"*. New York: Routledge.

Emden, C. 2014. *Nietzsche's Naturalism: Philosophy and the Life Sciences in the Nineteenth Century*. New York: Cambridge University Press.

Foot, P. 1994. "Nietzsche's Immoralism." In Schacht 1994: 1–14.

Foot, P. 2001. "Nietzsche: The Revaluation of All Values." In Richardson and Leiter 2001: 210–220.

Forber, P. 2013. "Biological Inheritance and Cultural Evolution in Nietzsche's *Genealogy*." *Journal of Nietzsche Studies* 44(2): 329–341.
Forster, M. 2017. "Nietzsche on Morality as a 'Sign Language of the Affects.'" *Inquiry* 60(1): 165–188.
Foucault, M. 1977/2001. "Nietzsche, Genealogy, and History." In Richardson and Leiter: 341–359.
Fowles, C. 2019. "Nietzsche on Conscious and Unconscious Thought." *Inquiry* 62(1): 1–22.
Fowles, C. 2020. "The Heart of the Flesh: Nietzsche on Affects and the Interpretation of the Body." *Journal of the History of Philosophy* 58(1): 113–139.
Gemes, K. 2001a. "Nietzsche's Critique of Truth." In Richardson and Leiter 2001: 40–58.
Gemes, K. 2001b. "Post-modernism's Use and Abuse of Nietzsche." *Philosophy and Phenomenological Research* 52: 337–360.
Gemes, K. 2008. "Nihilism and the Affirmation of Life: A Review of and Dialogue with Bernard Reginster." *European Journal of Philosophy* 16(3): 459–466.
Gemes, K. 2009a. "Freud and Nietzsche on Sublimation." *Journal of Nietzsche Studies* 38(1): 38–59.
Gemes, K. 2009b. "Nietzsche on Free Will, Autonomy and the Sovereign Individual." In Gemes and May 2009: 33–50.
Gemes, K. 2013. "Life's Perspectives." In Gemes and Richardson 2013: 553–575.
Gemes, K. and Janaway, C. 2005. "Naturalism and Value in Nietzsche." *Philosophy and Phenomenological Research* 71(3): 729–740.
Gemes, K. and May, S. (eds.) 2009. *Nietzsche on Freedom and Autonomy*. New York: Oxford University Press.
Gemes, K. and Richardson, J. (eds.) 2013. *The Oxford Handbook of Nietzsche*. New York: Oxford University Press.
Golomb, J. (ed.) 1997. *Nietzsche and Jewish Culture*. New York: Routledge.
Golomb, J. and Wistrich, R. (eds.) 2002. *Nietzsche, Godfather of Fascism? On the Uses and Abuses of a Philosophy*. Princeton, NJ: Princeton University Press.
Green, M. 2002. *Nietzsche and the Transcendental Tradition*. Urbana: University of Illinois Press.
Grimm, R. 1977. *Nietzsche's Theory of Knowledge*. Berlin: Walter de Gruyter.
Guay, R. 2006. "The Philosophical Function of Genealogy." In Ansell Pearson 2006: 353–370.
Guay, R. 2013. "Order of Rank." In Gemes and Richardson 2013: 485–508.
Hales, S. and Welshon, R. 2000. *Nietzsche's Perspectivism*. Urbana: University of Illinois Press.
Harcourt, E. (ed.) 2000. *Morality, Reflection, and Ideology*. New York: Oxford University Press.
Hatab, L. 2008. *Nietzsche's "On the Genealogy of Morality": An Introduction*. New York: Cambridge University Press.

Hatab, L. 2011. "Why Would Master Morality Surrender Its Power?" In May 2011a: 193–213.
Havas, R. 1995. *Nietzsche's "Genealogy": Nihilism and the Will to Knowledge*. Ithaca, NY: Cornell University Press.
Hayman, R. 1980. *Nietzsche: A Critical Life*. New York: Oxford University Press.
Hill, R. 2003. *Nietzsche's Critiques: The Kantian Foundations of His Thought*. New York: Oxford University Press.
Hollingdale, R. 1999. *Nietzsche: The Man and His Philosophy*. 2nd ed. New York: Cambridge University Press.
Holub, R. 2015. *Nietzsche's Jewish Problem: Between Anti-Semitism and Anti-Judaism*. Princeton, NJ: Princeton University Press.
Huddleston, A. 2021. "*Ressentiment*." *Ethics* 131: 670–696.
Huenemann, C. 2013. "Nietzsche's Illness." In Gemes and Richardson 2013: 63–80.
Hussain, N. 2007. "Honest Illusion: Valuing for Nietzsche's Free Spirits." In Leiter and Sinhababu 2007: 157–191.
Hussain, N. 2011. "The Role of Life in the *Genealogy*." In May 2011a: 142–169.
Hussain, N. 2013. "Nietzsche's Meta-ethical Stance." In Gemes and Richardson 2013: 389–414.
Janaway, C. 1998. *Willing and Nothingness: Schopenhauer as Nietzsche's Educator*. New York: Oxford University Press.
Janaway, C. 2006. "Naturalism and Genealogy." In Ansell Pearson 2006: 337–352.
Janaway, C. 2007. *Beyond Selflessness: Reading Nietzsche's "Genealogy"*. New York: Oxford University Press.
Janaway, C. 2009. "Autonomy, Affect, and the Self in Nietzsche's Project of Genealogy." In Gemes and May 2009: 51–68.
Janaway, C. 2012. "Nietzsche on Morality, Drives, and Human Greatness." In Janaway and Robertson 2012: 183–201.
Janaway, C. and Robertson, S. (eds.) 2012. *Nietzsche, Naturalism, and Normativity*. New York: Oxford University Press.
Jenkins, S. 2018. "*Ressentiment*, Imaginary Revenge, and the Slave Revolt." *Philosophy and Phenomenological Research* 96(1): 192–213.
Jensen, A. 2013. *Nietzsche's Philosophy of History*. New York: Cambridge University Press.
Johnson, D. 2010. *Nietzsche's Anti-Darwinism*. New York: Cambridge University Press.
Johnson, D. 2013. "Reassessing the Nietzsche-Darwin Relationship." *Journal of Nietzsche Studies* 44(2): 342–353.
Kail, P. 2009. "Nietzsche and Hume: Naturalism and Explanation." *Journal of Nietzsche Studies* 37: 5–22.
Kail. P. 2011. "'Genealogy' and the *Genealogy*." In May 2011a: 214–233.
Kail, P. 2015. "Nietzsche and Naturalism." In Dries and Kail 2015: 212–227.

Kail, P. 2017. "Value and Nature in Nietzsche." In Katsfanas, P. (ed.) *The Nietzschean Mind*. New York: Routledge, 233–246.

Katsafanas, P. 2005. "Nietzsche's Theory of Mind: Consciousness and Conceptualization." *European Journal of Philosophy* 13(1): 1–31.

Katsafanas, P. 2011. "The Relevance of History for Moral Philosophy: A Study of Nietzsche's *Genealogy*." In May 2011a: 170–192.

Katsafanas, P. 2013a. *Agency and the Foundations of Ethics: Nietzschean Constitutivism*. New York: Oxford University Press.

Katsfanas, P. 2013b. "Nietzsche's Philosophical Psychology." In Gemes and Richardson 2013: 727–755.

Katsafanas, P. 2015a. "Fugitive Pleasure and the Meaningful Life: Nietzsche on Nihilism and Higher Values." *Journal of the American Philosophical Association* 1(3): 396–416.

Katsafanas, P. 2015b. "Value, Affect, Drive." In Dries and Kail 2015: 163–188.

Katsafanas, P. 2016. *The Nietzschean Self: Moral Psychology, Agency, and the Unconscious*. New York: Oxford University Press.

Katsafanas, P. (ed.) 2017. *The Nietzschean Mind*. New York: Routledge.

Katsafanas. P. 2019. "Nietzsche's Moral Methodology." In Loeb and Meyer 2019: 165–184.

Kaufmann, W. 1974. *Nietzsche: Philosopher, Psychologist, Anti-Christ*. 4th ed. Princeton, NJ: Princeton University Press.

Knobe, J., and Leiter, B. 2007. "The Case for Nietzschean Moral Psychology." In Leiter and Sinhababu: 83–109.

Leach. S. (ed.) 2016. *Consciousness and the Great Philosophers*. New York: Routledge.

Leiter, B. 1994. "Perspectivism in Nietzsche's *Genealogy of Morals*." In Schacht 1994: 334–357.

Leiter, B. 2002. *Nietzsche on Morality*. New York: Routledge.

Leiter, B. 2009. "Nietzsche's Theory of the Will." In Gemes and May 2009: 107–126.

Leiter, B. 2011. "Who Is the Sovereign Individual? Nietzsche on Freedom." In May 2011a: 101–119.

Leiter, B. 2013. "Nietzsche's Naturalism Reconsidered." In Gemes and Richardson 2013: 576–598.

Leiter, B. 2015. "Nietzsche's Hatred of 'Jew Hatred.'" *New Rambler: An Online Review of Books*, December 21. https://newramblerreview.com/book-reviews/philosophy/nietzsche-s-hatred-of-jew-hatred.

Leiter, B. 2019. *Moral Psychology with Nietzsche*. New York: Oxford University Press.

Leiter, B. 2022. "Nietzsche's Naturalistic Moral Psychology: Anti-realism, Sentimentalism, Hard Incompatibilism." In Vargas and Doris 2022: 121–135.

Leiter, B. and Sinhababu, N. (eds.) 2007. *Nietzsche and Morality*. New York: Oxford University Press.

Loeb, P. 1995. "Is There a Genetic Fallacy in Nietzsche's *Genealogy of Morals*?" *International Studies in Philosophy* 27(3): 125–141.

Loeb, P. 2015. "Will to Power and Panpsychism: A New Exegesis of *Beyond Good and Evil* 36." In Dries and Kail 2015: 57–88.

Loeb, P. 2018. "The Priestly Slave Revolt in Morality." *Nietzsche-Studien* 47(1): 100–139.

Loeb, P. and Meyer, M. (eds.) 2019. *Nietzsche's Metaphilosophy: The Nature, Method, and Aims of Philosophy*. New York: Cambridge University Press.

Magnus, B. and Higgins, K. (eds.) 1996. *The Cambridge Companion to Nietzsche*. New York: Cambridge University Press.

May, S. 1999. *Nietzsche's Ethics and His War on "Morality"*. New York: Oxford University Press.

May, S. (ed.) 2011a. *Nietzsche's "On the Genealogy of Morality": A Critical Guide*. New York: Cambridge University Press.

May, S. 2011b. "Why Nietzsche Is Still in the Morality Game." In May 2011a: 78–100.

Migotti, M. 1998. "Slave Morality, Socrates, and the Bushmen: A Reading of the First Essay of *On the Genealogy of Morals*." *Philosophy and Phenomenological Research* 58(4): 745–779.

Migotti, M. 2013. "'A Promise Made Is a Debt Unpaid': Nietzsche on the Morality of Commitment and the Commitments of Morality." In Gemes and Richardson 2013: 509–524.

Miyasaki, D. 2015. "The Equivocal Use of Power in Nietzsche's Failed Anti-egalitarianism." *Journal of Moral Philosophy* 12(1): 1–32.

Moore, G. 2002. *Nietzsche, Biology and Metaphor*. New York: Cambridge University Press.

Moore, G. 2006. "Nietzsche and Evolutionary Theory." In Ansell Pearson 2006: 517–531.

Moore G. and Brobjer, T. (eds.) 2004. *Nietzsche and Science*. Aldershot: Ashgate.

Morrisson, I. 2014. "Ascetic Slaves: Rereading Nietzsche's *On the Genealogy of Morals*." *Journal of Nietzsche Studies* 45(3): 230–257.

Mulhall, S. 2011. "The Promising Animal." In May 2011a: 234–264.

Müller, M. 1888/2004. *Biographies of Words and the Home of the Aryas*. Kessinger Publishing reprint.

Müller-Lauter, W. 1971/1999. *Nietzsche: His Philosophy of Contradictions and the Contradictions of His Philosophy*. Trans. D. J. Parent. Urbana: University of Illinois Press.

Müller-Lauter, W. 2006. "Nihilism and Will to Nothingness." In Acampora 2006a: 209–219.

Nehamas, A. 1985. *Nietzsche: Life as Literature*. Cambridge: Harvard University Press.

Owen, D. 2000. "Is There a Doctrine of Will to Power?" *International Studies in Philosophy* 32(3): 95–106.

Owen, D. 2007. *Nietzsche's "Genealogy of Morality"*. Montreal: McGill University Press.

Parkes, G. 2013. "Nietzsche and the Family." In Gemes and Richardson 2013: 19–45.

Pippin, R. 2006. "Lightning and Flash, Agent and Deed." In Acampora 2006a: 131–146.

Poellner, P. 1995. *Nietzsche and Metaphysics*. New York: Oxford University Press.

Poellner, P. 2001. "Perspectival Truth." In Richardson and Leiter 2001: 85–117.

Poellner, P. 2007. "Affect, Value and Objectivity." In Leiter and Sinhababu 2007: 227–261.

Poellner, P. 2009. "Nietzschean Freedom." In Gemes and May 2009: 151–180.

Poellner, P. 2011. "*Ressentiment* and Morality." In May 2011a: 120–141.

Poellner, P. 2013. "Nietzsche's Metaphysical Sketches: Causality and Will to Power." In Gemes and Richardson 2013: 675–700.

Poellner, P. 2015. "*Ressentiment* and the Possibility of Self-Deception." In Dries and Kail 2015: 189–211.

Prescott-Crouch, A. 2015. "Nietzsche, Genealogy, and Historical Individuals." *Journal of Nietzsche Studies* 46(1): 99–109.

Ratner-Rosenhagen, J. 2012. *American Nietzsche: A History of an Icon and His Ideas*. Chicago: University of Chicago Press.

Rée, P. 2003. *Basic Writings*. Trans. and ed. R. Small. Urbana: University of Illinois Press.

Reginster, B. 1997. "Nietzsche on *Ressentiment* and Valuation." *Philosophy and Phenomenological Research* 57(2): 281–305.

Reginster, B. 2006. *The Affirmation of Life: Nietzsche on Overcoming Nihilism*. Cambridge: Harvard University Press.

Reginster, B. 2011. "The Genealogy of Guilt." In May 2011a: 56–77.

Reginster, B. 2013. "The Psychology of Christian Morality: Will to Power as Will to Nothingness." In Gemes and Richardson 2013: 701–725.

Reginster, B. 2021. *The Will to Nothingness: An Essay on Nietzsche's "On the Genealogy of Morality"*. New York: Oxford University Press.

Riccardi, M. 2015. "Inner Opacity: Nietzsche on Introspection and Agency." *Inquiry* 58(3): 221–243.

Riccardi, M. 2021. *Nietzsche's Philosophical Psychology*. New York: Oxford University Press.

Richardson, J. 1996. *Nietzsche's System*. New York: Oxford University Press.

Richardson, J. 2004. *Nietzsche's New Darwinism*. New York: Oxford University Press.

Richardson, J. 2020. *Nietzsche's Values*. New York: Oxford University Press.

Richardson, J. and Leiter, B. (eds.) 2001. *Nietzsche*. New York: Oxford University Press.

Ridley, A. 1998. *Nietzsche's Conscience: Six Character Studies from the "Genealogy"*. Ithaca, NY: Cornell University Press.

Ridley, A. 2006. "Nietzsche and the Re-evaluation of Values." In Acampora 2006a: 77–92.

Ridley, A. 2009. "Nietzsche's Intentions: What the Sovereign Individual Promises." In Gemes and May 2009: 181–196.

Ridley, A. 2018. *The Deed Is Everything: Nietzsche on Will and Action*. New York: Oxford University Press.

Risse, M. 2001. "The Second Treatise in *On the Genealogy of Morality*: Nietzsche on the Origin of Bad Conscience." *European Journal of Philosophy* 9(1): 55–81.

Risse, M. 2007. "Nietzschean 'Animal Psychology' versus Kantian Ethics." In Leiter and Sinhababu 2007: 57–82.

Robertson, S. 2020. *Nietzsche and Contemporary Ethics*. New York: Oxford University Press.

Robertson, S. and Owen, D. 2013. "Influence on Analytic Philosophy." In Gemes and Richardson 2013: 185–206.

Salomé, L. 1894/2001. *Nietzsche*. Trans. S. Mandel. Urbana: University of Illinois Press.

Schacht, R. 1983. *Nietzsche: The Arguments of the Philosophers*. New York: Routledge.

Schacht, R. (ed.) 1994. *Nietzsche, Genealogy, Morality: Essays on Nietzsche's "On the Genealogy of Morals"*. Berkeley: University of California Press.

Schacht, R. 2000. "Nietzsche's 'Will to Power.'" *International Studies in Philosophy* 32(3): 83–94.

Schacht, R. 2012a. "Nietzsche's Naturalism." *Journal of Nietzsche Studies* 43(2): 185–212.

Schacht, R. 2012b. "Nietzsche's Naturalism and Normativity." In Janaway and Robertson 2012: 236–257.

Schacht, R. 2013a. "Nietzsche and Lamarckism." *Journal of Nietzsche Studies* 44(2): 264–281.

Schacht, R. 2013b. "Nietzsche's *Genealogy*." In Gemes and Richardson 2013: 323–343.

Scheler, M. 1961. *Ressentiment*. Trans. W. Holdheim. New York: Free Press of Glencoe.

Schopenhauer, A. 1819/2010. *The World as Will and Representation*. Vol. 1. Trans. J. Norman, A. Welchman, and C. Janaway. Cambridge: Cambridge University Press.

Schrift, A. 1995. *Nietzsche's French Legacy: A Genealogy of Poststructuralism*. New York: Routledge.

Silk, A. 2017. "Nietzsche and Contemporary Metaethics." In Katsfanas 2017: 247–263.

Simmel, G. 1907/1991. *Schopenhauer and Nietzsche*. Trans. H. Loiskandl, D. Weinstein, and M. Weinstein. Urbana: University of Illinois Press.

Snelson, A. 2017. "The History, Origin, and Meaning of Nietzsche's Slave Revolt in Morality." *Inquiry* 60(1): 1–30.

Soll, I. 2012. "Nietzsche's Will to Power as a Psychological Thesis: Reactions to Bernard Reginster." *Journal of Nietzsche Studies* 43(1): 118–129.

Soll, I. 2013. "Schopenhauer as Nietzsche's 'Great Teacher' and 'Antipode.'" In Gemes and Richardson 2013: 160–184.

Stack, G. 1983. *Lange and Nietzsche*. Berlin: de Gruyter.

Stack, G. 1992. *Nietzsche and Emerson: An Elective Affinity*. Athens: Ohio University Press.

Strawson, G. 2015. "Nietzsche's Metaphysics?" In Dries and Kail 2015: 10–36.

Vargas, M. and Doris, J. (eds.) 2022. *The Oxford Handbook of Moral Psychology*. New York: Oxford University Press.

Wallace, R. J. 2007. "Ressentiment, Value, and Self-Understanding: Making Sense of Nietzsche's Slave Revolt." In Leiter and Sinhababu 2007: 110–137.

Welshon, R. 2004. *The Philosophy of Nietzsche*. Montreal: McGill University Press.

Welshon, R. 2009. "Saying Yes to Reality: Skepticism, Antirealism, and Perspectivism in Nietzsche's Epistemology." *Journal of Nietzsche Studies* 37: 23–43.

Welshon, R. 2014. *Nietzsche's Dynamic Metapsychology: This Uncanny Animal*. New York: Palgrave Macmillan.

Welshon, R. 2015. "Nietzsche, Neuroscience, and the Self." In Kail and Dries 2015: 120–141.

Welshon, R. 2016. "Nietzsche and the Problem of Consciousness." In Leach 2016: 162–171.

Wilcox, J. 1974. *Truth and Value in Nietzsche: A Study of His Metaethics and Epistemology*. Ann Arbor: University of Michigan Press.

Williams, B. 2000. "Naturalism and Genealogy." In Harcourt 2000: 148–161.

Williams, B. 2006a. "Nietzsche's Minimalist Moral Psychology." In Burnyeat 2006: 299–310.

Williams, B. 2006b. "There Are Many Kinds of Eyes." In Burnyeat 2006: 325–330.

Young, J. 2010. *Friedrich Nietzsche: A Philosophical Biography*. New York: Cambridge University Press.

Yovel, Y. 1998. *Dark Riddle: Hegel, Nietzsche, and the Jews*. University Park: Penn State University Press.

Yovel, Y. 2006. "Nietzsche and the Jews: The Structure of an Ambivalence." In Acampora 2006a: 277–289.

Zavatta, B. 2019. *Individuality and Beyond: Nietzsche Reads Emerson*. Trans. A. Reynolds. New York: Oxford University Press.

Index

For the benefit of digital users, indexed terms that span two pages (e.g., 52–53) may, on occasion, appear on only one of those pages.

Printed in the USA/Agawam, MA
October 26, 2023

853758.001